PAUL SELIGSON
CAROL LETHABY
LUIZ OTÁVIO BARROS

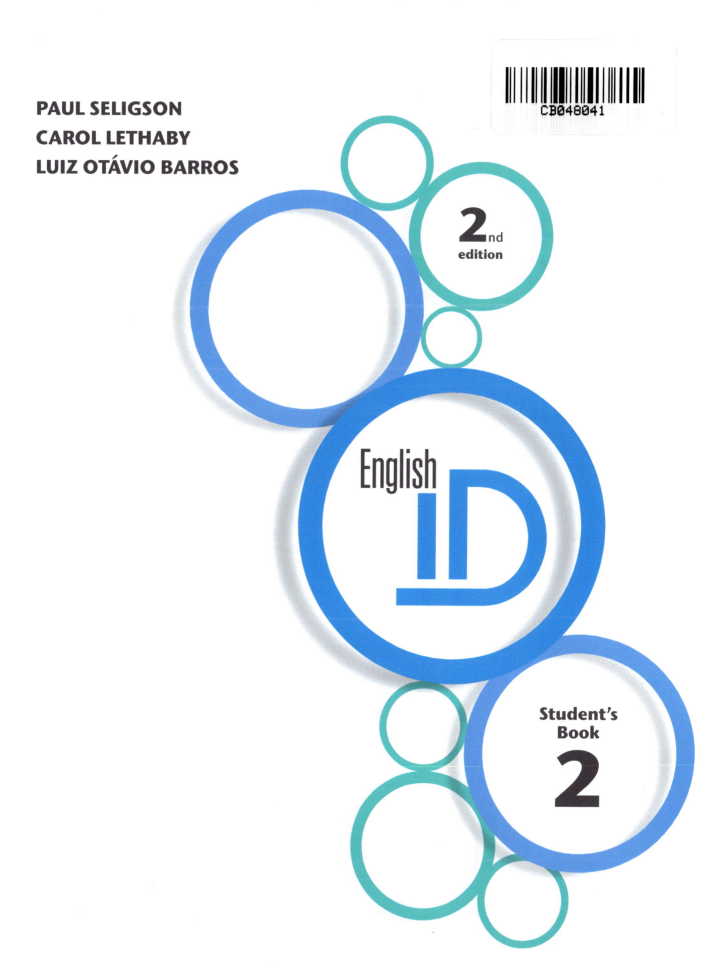

2nd edition

English ID

Student's Book 2

ID Language map

Question syllabus		Vocabulary	Grammar	Speaking & Skills
1	**1.1** What's really important in life?	Life priorities	Review of present tenses & simple past	Talk about life priorities Create a personal profile Talk about working / studying from home
	1.2 Which sense do you use the most?	The senses + sense verbs & adjectives		Talk about sensations & experiences Talk about favorite things
	1.3 Do you read, hear, or watch a lot of ads?		*Will / won't* for predictions / unplanned decisions	Make predictions Write and act out an ad
	1.4 What shouldn't you do to stay healthy?	Common illnesses	*Should / shouldn't* for advice	Talk about and identify common illnesses Give advice
	1.5 Will people live on the moon by 2050?			Make predictions
	When do you ask for help?	Expressions for offering, accepting & refusing help		Offer and accept / refuse help
Writing 1: A personal email		**ID Café 1: Old school**		
2	**2.1** Do you ever read newspapers?	News media Genres of news stories		Talk about how you get your news Do a news survey
	2.2 What were you doing at 8 o'clock last night?		Past continuous	Talk about family communication Describe photos
	2.3 What's the world's most serious problem?	Global problems Natural phenomena		Talk about global / local problems Describe TV shows Talk about natural phenomena
	2.4 Was your mom living here when you were born?		Past continuous vs. simple past	Invent / test an alibi Read about a total solar eclipse Talk about dramatic interruptions
	2.5 What do you carry in your pockets?			Understand and retell a story
	Are you a good listener?	Listening & reacting phrases		Be a good listener
Writing 2: A survey report		**ID Café 2: Nature boy and natural woman**		**Review 1** *p.30*
3	**3.1** How often do you travel?	Traveling		Compare feelings about traveling Do a travel quiz Share travel experiences
	3.2 Have you ever been to another country?		Present perfect 1: past experiences	Talk about solutions Talk about past experiences
	3.3 Have you sung a song in English yet?	Bucket list items	Present perfect 2: completed actions (*already, just, yet*)	Talk about what you have already done List 10 life ambitions
	3.4 How long have you lived here?	Gap years	Present perfect 3: unfinished past (*for, since*)	Talk about advantages / disadvantages of taking a gap year Talk about unfinished experiences
	3.5 Do you write reviews?	Hotel descriptions		Talk about hotel reviews
	Are you a logical person?	Suffixes *-ic, -ment, -al, -ion*		React to unexpected information
Writing 3: An internship application		**ID Café 3: Under the moon**		
4	**4.1** Were you spoiled as a child?	Childhood Personality adjectives *Do & make*		Talk about the kind of child you were
	4.2 What did you use to do as a child?		*Used to* and simple past	Talk about childhood habits & memories
	4.3 Has your taste in music changed?	Ways of listening to music	Past simple vs. *Used to*	Talk about how you listen to music Write a tweet giving an opinion about music
	4.4 Do you speak English as often as possible?	Adjectives	Comparatives / superlatives / *as... as...*	Make comparisons Talk about first experiences
	4.5 How many pets have you had?		*So / but*	Talk about pets
	Have you thought about moving abroad?		Prepositions + *-ing*	Make recommendations
Writing 4: A social media post		**ID Café 4: Animal instincts**		**Review 2** *p.56*
5	**5.1** What would you like to study?	School subjects & facilities		Talk about choosing a college and career plans
	5.2 What do you have to do tonight?	Class activities	Obligation & prohibition	Talk about class activities Talk about rules in your life
	5.3 Are you a good student?	Good study habits	*Too / enough / too much / too many*	Give tips about school Talk about reasons for quitting school / a job
	5.4 What will you do when you pass this course?		Zero & first conditional	Talk about how to make friends Make suggestions for changes
	5.5 How do you usually get in touch?	Ways of communicating Family generations	Pronouns & referencing	Compare generations Understand references
	Do you often take risks?	Warnings & promises phrases		Give warnings & make promises
Writing 5: A personal statement		**ID Café 5: Man and cyberman!**		**Mid-term review** *p.70*

Welcome

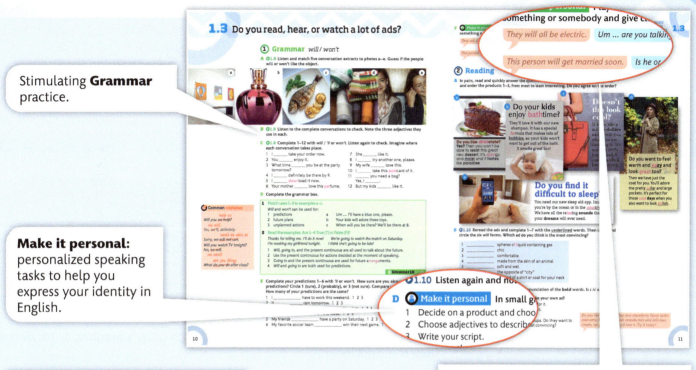

Stimulating **Grammar** practice.

Make it personal: personalized speaking tasks to help you express your identity in English.

Speech bubbles: models for speaking.

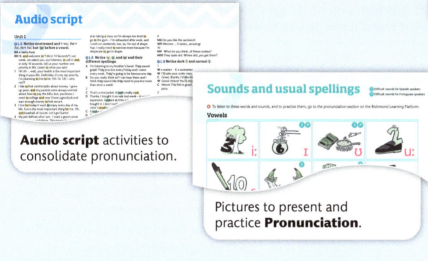

Audio script activities to consolidate pronunciation.

Pictures to present and practice **Pronunciation**.

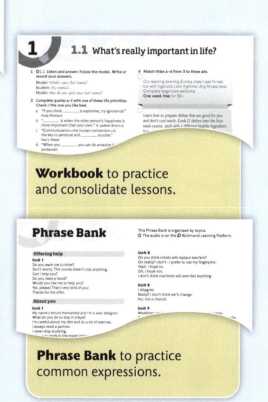

Workbook to practice and consolidate lessons.

Phrase Bank to practice common expressions.

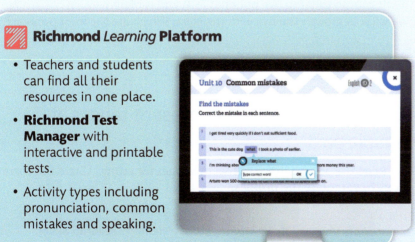

Richmond Learning Platform

- Teachers and students can find all their resources in one place.
- **Richmond Test Manager** with interactive and printable tests.
- Activity types including pronunciation, common mistakes and speaking.

Learn to express your identity in English!

1

1.1 What's really important in life?

1 Vocabulary Life priorities

A ▶1.1 Match priorities a–e to photos 1–5. Then listen to 10 questions and, after the beep, say which priority a–j each refers to. Notice the word stress.

a ca**reer** ____	f cul**ture** ____
b fi**nan**cial se**cu**rity ____	g edu**ca**tion ____
c **fit**ness ____	h **free** time ____
d **ha**ving fun ____	i **friends** and **fa**mily ____
e **health** ____	j **love** ____

> **Common mistakes**
> ~~career~~ **major**
> My career is philosophy.
> ~~I'm not~~ **I don't**
> I'm not agree with that.
> ~~to work out~~ **working out**
> I enjoy to work out.

B Get to know a partner. Ask and answer questions about the life priorities in **A**. Report two discoveries to the class.

> *What do you do to stay in shape?*   *I'm careful about my diet and do a lot of exercise.*

C ▶1.2 Listen to the radio show and write each caller's number, 1–10, next to their top priority in **A**.

D ▶1.2 Which caller 1–10 gave the answers below? Listen again to check. What else did you pick up this time?

Life in 10 Seconds ... your priorities

a I never stop studying. ☐
b I always need to have a partner. ☐
c I'm planning to live to be 100. ☐
d I don't want to live in a world without art and music. ☐
e I like to feel comfortable about money. ☐
f People are more important than things. ☐
g Time to enjoy things is more important than money. ☐
h I want to stay in shape. ☐
i I live for today! ☐
j My job de**fines** who I am. ☐

E 👤 **Make it personal** In small groups, work out your top five priorities.
1 Which statements in **D** do / don't you agree with? Why (not)?
2 Each choose your top five priorities in **A** and explain why.
3 Share your group's top five with the class. Which are the most popular?

> *For me, financial security is the top priority. If you don't have enough money, you can't have a comfortable life.*

2 Grammar Review of present tenses and simple past

A ▶1.3 Read the ad and listen to two messages for Jenny. Circle the correct options to complete the profiles.

Are you ready for a life or career change?
Talk to Jenny Gonzalez, life coach. Jenny really can improve your life. Call her on 1-800-help-me-JG and leave your profile.

Profile 1
Name: Casey **Murray** / **Hurry**
Age: **22** / **23**
Education: **high school** / **college**
Job: security **guard** / **assistant**
Goal: to be a **dancer** / **singer**

Profile 2
Name: **Richard** / **Ricardo** Sutton
Age: **28** / **38**
Education: **grad school** / **college**
Job: **attorney** / **travel agent**
Goal: to **get in shape** / **go on vacation**

B ▶ 1.3 Listen again. True (T) or False (F)? Correct the false ones.
1 Casey's job is interesting.
2 She enjoys video games and shopping.
3 She has enough money to do what she wants.
4 Ricardo likes his job a lot.
5 He speaks three foreign languages well.
6 He's going to night school at the moment.

♪ *Girls like you, Love fun, yeah me too
What I want when I come through
I need a girl like you*

1.1

Common mistakes

He like to play football. → *s*
She studying for an an exam in this moment. → *'s* / *at the*
He don't have enough money. → *doesn't*
Did he went to college? → *go*
I'm an university student. → *a*

C Complete the grammar box. Go to AS 1.3 on p. 162 and find one example of each tense in ➕ and ➖ forms.

Match statements 1–3 to uses a–c. Which one is most true for you?
1 I use English in my life. ☐   a a finished action
2 I'm taking English classes. ☐   b regular action, a habit
3 I studied hard last year. ☐   c happening now, or around now   ➡ **Grammar 1A** p. 138

D ▶ 1.4 Listen and complete Jenny's notes. Suggest two ways Yazmin can improve her life.

Yazmin Stanford is 29 years old and she studied _____ at college. She's a hairstylist. She _____ work at 7 a.m. and she _____ get her children from school at 3 p.m. She _____ make more money.

E 🎤 **Make it personal** Complete then record your own profile. Listen to a partner's profile and suggest two ways they can achieve their goals. Who has the best ideas?

Name: _____
Age: _____
Education: _____
Job: _____
Goal: _____

My name's Arturo Hernandez, I'm 22, and I finished college two years ago. At the moment, I'm a web designer. I'd love to work in the movie industry.

③ Reading

A Would you like to work from home? Why (not)? Then read the article. Are 1–10 advantages (A) or disadvantages (D)?

So … you're thinking of working from home?

The Internet means you don't have to leave home to work anymore and many companies and schools allow you to work or study remote**ly from your own home. But, is it a good idea for you? Here are some of the pros and cons you need to con**si**der:**

1 It's quieter at home than in an office.
2 You have to find a space in your home.
3 You can start and finish when you want to.
4 There are a lot of dis**trac**tions at home.
5 You can get help from your family or the people you live with.
6 You save money on clothes – you can work in your pajamas, if you want to!
7 You don't have to spend time and money on travel.
8 You need to se**p**arate your home and work – it can be hard to do this.
9 It can be lone**ly without classmates or work colleagues.
10 You have to m**o**tivate yourself – it's easy to spend the day doing other things.

B ▶ 1.5 Quickly reread the text then cover it. Listen and try to complete 1–10 before the audio.

C 🎤 **Make it personal** List two advantages and two disadvantages of your work / study life right now. Compare answers in small groups. Any similarities / big differences?

One big advantage is I love my job. I also have good friends at work. Two disadvantages are that I live 15 km from my office, and I can't afford a car.

7

1.2 Which sense do you use the most?

1 Listening

A ▶1.6 Listen to five conversations and number the photos 1–5.

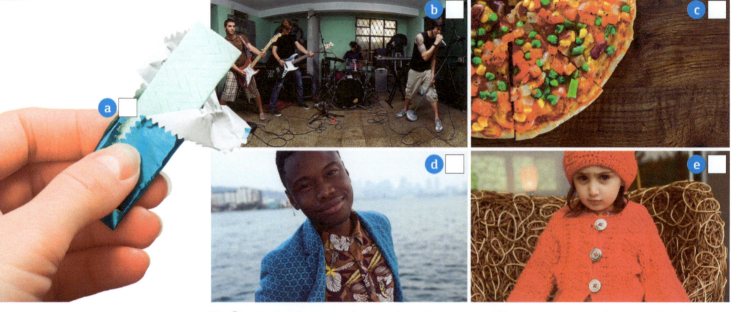

B ▶1.6 Match expressions 1–5 to photos a–e. Then answer 1–7. Listen to check.

1 It feels rough. /rʌf/ ☐   3 It tastes awesome. ☐   5 They smell awful. ☐
2 They sound great. ☐   4 It looks cool. ☐

1 How often do the band practice?
2 Does the boy think the band are going to be famous?
3 Did the man make a quick decision to buy the jacket?
4 Is the jacket his favorite color?
5 What flavor is the gum?
6 Do the couple plan to stay at the restaurant?
7 Why doesn't the girl like wearing the sweater? Why does she need to wear it?

Common mistakes

remind me of
Those pizzas remember me to my dad's cooking!

C 🔵 **Make it personal** Do the photos in **A** remind you of anything or anyone?

Number 1 reminds me of a band my brother was in. They were awful!

The girl in photo 5 looks a bit like my cousin.

2 Vocabulary and pronunciation   The senses

8

Welcome to English ID!

Finally, an English course you can understand!

Famous **song lines** illustrate language from lessons.

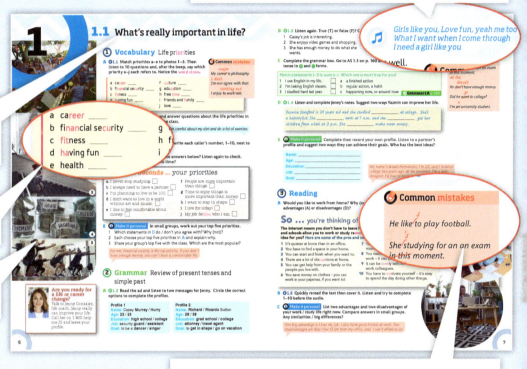

Lesson titles are questions to help you engage with the content.

Word stress in pink on new words.

Contextualized Picture Dictionary to present and review vocabulary.

Focus on **Common mistakes** accelerates accuracy.

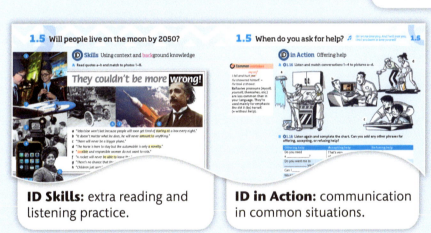

ID Skills: extra reading and listening practice.

ID in Action: communication in common situations.

Authentic videos present topics in real contexts.

ID Café: sitcom videos to consolidate language.

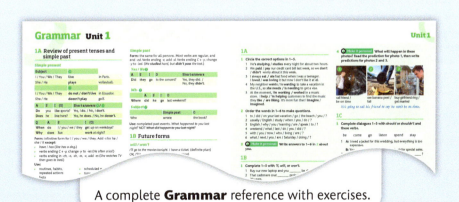

A complete **Grammar** reference with exercises.

Reviews systematically recycle language.

		Question syllabus	Vocabulary	Grammar	Speaking & Skills
6	6.1	Have you ever been to Florida?	Leisure time activities	*Go gerund (verb + -ing)*	Talk about leisure time activities Talk about a vacation in Florida
	6.2	Would you like to try hang gliding?	Verbs of movement	Prepositions & adverbs Compound nouns	Talk about how you feel about adventurous sports
	6.3	Do you feel like going out tonight?	Prepositions of movement		Retell a story about an extreme race Complete a humorous postcard about a vacation
	6.4	What do you enjoy doing on your birthday?	Sports equipment Phrasal verbs	Verb + infinitive / gerund	Describe how to play a sport Reply to an invitation
	6.5	What's the highest place you've been to?			Guess meaning Talk about phobias
		Would you rather stay in or go out?	Phrases to express preferences	*Would rather / prefer*	Make difficult decisions
	Writing 6: An adventure vacation blog		**ID Café 6:** Brain vs. brawn		**Review 3** *p.84*
7	7.1	How often do you go to the movies?	Movies		Talk about movies Analyze favorite movies
	7.2	Are you crazy about music?	Passionate interests	Pronouns *some-, any-, every-, no-*	Talk about what you feel passionate about Find a relevant song line
	7.3	What do you have a lot of at home?		*So & such*	Talk about unusual collections
	7.4	Who was Instagram created by?	Numbers & fractions	Passive voice: present & past	Talk about online piracy Write a trivia quiz
	7.5	What do you think about reality TV?	Reality shows Devices to improve fluency		Talk about reality TV
		Are you a good singer?	Agreeing / disagreeing		Give opinions
	Writing 7: A TV series review		**ID Café 7:** Sound tracks		
8	8.1	Are you into science fiction?	Technology		Talk about the technology you use Give opinions about technology
	8.2	Do you ever switch off from technology?	Pronouns in phrasal verbs Intonation in questions	Phrasal verbs	Share experiences of technology
	8.3	Will space vacations be popular soon?		Future forms 1	Compare predictions about life in the future
	8.4	Is technology making us more, or less, social?	False cognates	Future forms 2	Talk about conversation habits Role-play replying to invitations
	8.5	Who do you talk to when you need help?	Coaching services		Understand ads Talk about coaching professionals
		Will you ever get married?	Expressions for certainty & doubt		Make fortune-telling predictions
	Writing 8: A formal enquiry email		**ID Café 8:** Back to your future		**Review 4** *p.110*
9	9.1	What do you think of marriage?	Weddings		Compare weddings Talk about marriage & weddings
	9.2	Do you think romantic movies are entertaining?	Romance Intensifiers	*-ed & -ing* adjectives	Give advice about romantic problems Compare intense feelings
	9.3	If you had three wishes, what would they be?		Second conditional	Talk about unreal situations
	9.4	Have you ever performed for an audience?	Performers	*May, might, could, must, can't + be*	Talk about performers Make conclusions Share stories about wrong conclusions
	9.5	How do you get on with your siblings?	Birth order		Talk about the effect of birth order
		Is there something I can help with?			Give advice
	Writing 9: Giving advice		**ID Café 9:** Green-eyed monsters		
10	10.1	Do you often feel stressed?	Causes & symptoms of stress *over- / under- / a lack of*		Talk about the biggest causes of stress Talk about ways to cope with stress
	10.2	Would you like to change anything in your life?	Lifestyle changes	Relative pronouns: *that & who*	Talk about lifestyle changes Describe photos
	10.3	What's your attitude to money?	Money Alternative lifestyles		Talk about a documentary movie Compare attitudes to money / recycling
	10.4	How often do you post on social media?		Asking questions: review *How* + adj / adv question stress	Talk about reunions Compare attitudes to language learning Create a social media chat using emojis
	10.5	Do you enjoy reading in English?			Read faster
		How would you describe your best friend?		*one / ones*	Describe people & things
	Writing 10: A narrative		**ID Café 10:** The dog days of August		**Review 5** *p.136*

Grammar p. 138   Irregular verbs p. 158   Sounds and usual spellings p. 160   Audioscript p. 162

A **Look at the ad and …**

♪ *I feel alone in your arms, I feel you breaking my heart, Say my name, say my name, If you love me, let me hear you*   **1.2**

1 match the senses to photos 1–5.

> hearing   sight   smell   taste   touch

2 match these verbs to the senses. Which is your favorite verb?

> eat   feel   hear   listen (to)   look (at)   see
> smell   sound   stink   taste   touch   watch

> *You eat with your mouth so that goes with taste.*

3 order the senses from the most to the least important for you.

> *The one I use the least is …*

B ▶1.7 **Listen to 10 conversations and notice the connections between consonant and vowel sounds in the answers. Listen again while reading AS 1.7 on p. 162.**

C ▶1.7 **Test your memory! Listen and try to answer the questions before the audio. How many did you get right?**

D **In pairs. Take turns asking and answering questions using these verbs and adjectives. Remember to use linking.**

> sound   look   smell
> feel   taste   think

> amazing   awesome   awful
> cheap   expensive   old

> *What do you think about chocolate?*
> *It tastes awesome!*

E **Match the senses to the adjective groups. In pairs, define or give an example for each. The underlined pairs are opposites. Which group can be used with any sense?**

It feels   delicious sweet smoky fresh / rotten
It smells   awful / great bad / good awesome / terrible
It sounds   bland / spicy sweet / sour salty delicious
It tastes   soft / rough
It looks   loud / quiet

> *Bland means "without taste." For example, soup without salt or pepper.*   *A kitten feels soft.*

F **Study Common mistakes and choose the best sense verb from A to complete 1–5.**

1 It's very noisy here. We can't _____ you very well.
2 Where are we? It's too dark to _____ anything.
3 Hey! _____ that poster over there! It's really funny!
4 Do you want to _____ the radio? There's a good show coming on now.
5 Why don't you _____ the match with me? It's really exciting!

G 🔘 **Make it personal** **Complete the chart. Compare with a partner and ask about their chart.**

My favorite	The best thing I
sound *is children laughing.*	heard yesterday
taste	ate yesterday
smell	smelled yesterday
item of clothing	saw yesterday

> *My favorite sound is my mom singing.*   *Really! Does she have a good voice?*

> *The best thing I heard yesterday was a new song by Cardi B.*   *Oh yeah? What's the name of the song?*

🔘 Common mistakes

What are you doing?
I'm looking at TV.
  watching

Look at
Watch that plane. Can you see it?
See refers to ability and is unintentional, *look (at)* is intentional, and *watch* is intensive.

9

1.3 Do you read, hear, or watch a lot of ads?

1 Grammar will / won't

A ▶1.8 Listen and match five conversation extracts to photos a–e. Guess if the people will or won't like the object.

B ▶1.9 Listen to the complete conversations to check. Note the three adjectives they use in each.

C ▶1.9 Complete 1–12 with *will* / *'ll* or *won't*. Listen again to check. Imagine where each conversation takes place.

1. I _____ take your order now.
2. You _____ enjoy it.
3. What time _____ you be at the party tomorrow?
4. I _____ definitely be there by 9.
5. I _____ download it now.
6. Your mother _____ love this perfume.
7. She _____ like it.
8. I _____ try another one, please.
9. My wife _____ love this.
10. I _____ take this postcard of it.
11. _____ you need a bag? Yes, I _____.
12. But my kids _____ like it.

D Complete the grammar box.

> **1** Match uses 1–3 to examples a–c.
> *Will* and *won't* can be used for:
> 1 predictions   a Um ... I'll have a blue one, please.
> 2 future plans   b Your kids will adore these toys.
> 3 unplanned actions   c When will you be there? We'll be there at 8.
>
> **2** Read the examples. Are 1–4 True (T) or False (F)?
> *Thanks for telling me. I'll do it now!   We're going to watch the match on Saturday.*
> *I'm meeting my girlfriend tonight.   I think she's going to be late!*
> 1 *Will*, *going to*, and the present continuous are all used to talk about the future.
> 2 Use the present continuous for actions decided at the moment of speaking.
> 3 *Going to* and the present continuous are used for future arrangements.
> 4 *Will* and *going to* are both used for predictions.
>
> → Grammar 1B p. 138

▶ **Common mistakes**

Will you ~~we help~~ *help us*?
Yes, ~~we'll~~, *we will* definitely.
Sorry, we ~~will not can~~ *won't be able to*.
Will you watch TV tonight?
No, ~~no will~~ *we won't*.
What ~~do you do~~ *are you doing* after class?

E Complete your predictions 1–6 with *'ll* or *won't*. How sure are you about your predictions? Circle 1 (sure), 2 (probably), or 3 (not sure). Compare with a partner. How many of your predictions are the same?

1. I _____ have to work this weekend. 1 2 3
2. It _____ rain tomorrow. 1 2 3
3. There _____ be homework for this class. 1 2 3
4. I _____ eat chicken this week. 1 2 3
5. My friends _____ have a party on Saturday. 1 2 3
6. My favorite soccer team _____ win their next game. 1 2 3

F 🎤 **Make it personal** Play *Crystal ball!* **A:** Predict the future of something or somebody and give clues. **B:** Guess what or who it is.

🎵 *When the night has come, And the land is dark, And the moon is the only light we'll see, No I won't be afraid, no I won't be afraid, Just as long as you stand, stand by me.*

1.3

They will all be electric.　Um … are you talking about stoves?　No. There won't be any more gas stations.　Oh, OK. Cars?　Yes!

This person will get married soon.　Is he or she in this class?

2 Reading

A In pairs, read and quickly answer the questions in the product ads. Then read the ads and order the products 1–5, from most to least interesting. Do you agree on the order?

a

Do you like chocolate?
Yes? Then you won't be able to **resist** this great new **dessert**. It's **spon**gy and **moist** and it **tastes** like **paradise**.

b **Do your kids enjoy bathtime?**
They'll love it with our new shampoo. It has a special **for**mula that makes lots of **bubbles**, so your kids won't want to get out of the bath. It **smells** great too!

c **Doesn't this look cool?**
It looks like a million **dollars** and so will you when you are carrying it. It's made of 100% **leather** and it comes in black, brown, or red.

d **Do you want to feel warm and cozy and look great too?**
Then we have just the coat for you. You'll adore the pretty collar and large pockets. It's perfect for those cold days when you also want to look stylish.

e

Do you find it difficult to sleep?
You need our new sleep aid app. Imagine you're by the ocean or in the countryside. We have all the re**lax**ing **sounds** that your **dreams** will ever need.

B ▶1.10 Reread the ads and complete 1–7 with the underlined words. Then listen and circle the six *will* forms. Which ad do you think is the most convincing?

1	_____	spheres of liquid containing gas
2	_____	chic
3	_____	comfortable
4	_____	made from the skin of an animal
5	_____	soft and wet
6	_____	the opposite of "city"
7	_____	the part of a shirt or coat for your neck

C ▶1.10 Listen again and notice the pronunciation of the **bold** words. Is *s* /s/ or /z/?

D 🎤 **Make it personal** In small groups, make your own ad!
1 Decide on a product and choose a photo for it.
2 Choose adjectives to describe your product.
3 Write your script.
4 Rehearse, then read your ad to other groups. Do they want to buy your product? Which ad is the most convincing?

Do you like ice cream? Our new strawberry flavor tastes awesome. Made with fresh strawberries and delicious cream, we guarantee you'll love it. Try it today!

11

1.4 What shouldn't you do to stay healthy?

1 Vocabulary Common illnesses

A ▶1.11 Listen and say why there's nobody at the party.

B ▶1.11 Match illnesses a–g to photos 1–7. Listen again to check pronunciation.

a a cold ☐ c a fever ☐ e a headache ☐
   /oʊ/   /iː/   /ɛ/ /eɪ/
b a cough ☐ d the flu ☐ f a stomach ache ☐ g a toothache ☐
   /ɔ/   /u/   /ʌ/ /ə/ /eɪ/   /u/ /eɪ/

> **Common mistakes**
> My head hurts ~~me~~.
> I have ~~headaitch~~ (a headache) (hɛdeɪk).

C ▶1.11 Try to match the people to illnesses a–g in **B**. Listen again to check.
Fran ____ Lenny ____ Gaby ____ Helen ____ Marcos ____ Jenny ____ Brad ____

D Match the expressions with a similar meaning.
1 My stomach hurts.   a His back hurts.
2 He has backache.   b Her tooth hurts.
3 She has a toothache.   c He has a headache.
4 His head hurts.   d I have a stomach ache.

E 🔊 **Make it personal** In pairs, play **Ouch!**
A: Mime a health problem and say, "Ouch!"
B: Say what the problem is.

> Your ears hurt and you're very tired? I know, you have earache!

2 Grammar should / shouldn't

A ▶1.12 Listen to four conversations and write what the problems are.
1 _____ 3 _____
2 _____ 4 _____

B ▶1.12 Complete the suggestions with *should* or *shouldn't*. Listen again to check. Notice the *o* and *l* are silent.
1 You _____ take a painkiller. You _____ go to the party.
2 You _____ stay in bed and rest. You _____ eat anything.
3 You _____ see a dentist as soon as possible. You _____ eat or drink anything hot or cold.
4 You _____ go out. You _____ drink a lot of warm fluids and you _____ stay warm.

C Complete the grammar box with *should* or *shouldn't*.

> Use *should* / *shouldn't* to give and ask for advice.
> ➕ They _____ be more careful.
> ➖ Your son _____ watch so much TV. What should I do to stop him?
> ❓ Short answers
>   _____ I eat anything?
>   Yes, you _____.
>   No, you _____.
>
> ➡ Grammar 1C p. 138

D What's a good idea and a bad idea for each problem in photos 1–7? Take turns making suggestions to a partner, using the ideas below, plus your own. Who has the best suggestions?

drink cold fluids / lots of fluids   eat chicken soup / chocolate / spicy food   talk to a teacher
go to bed / class / work / a party / the beach / the movies   visit friends   work out
stay in bed / relax / rest   see a dentist / a doctor   take a painkiller / some medicine

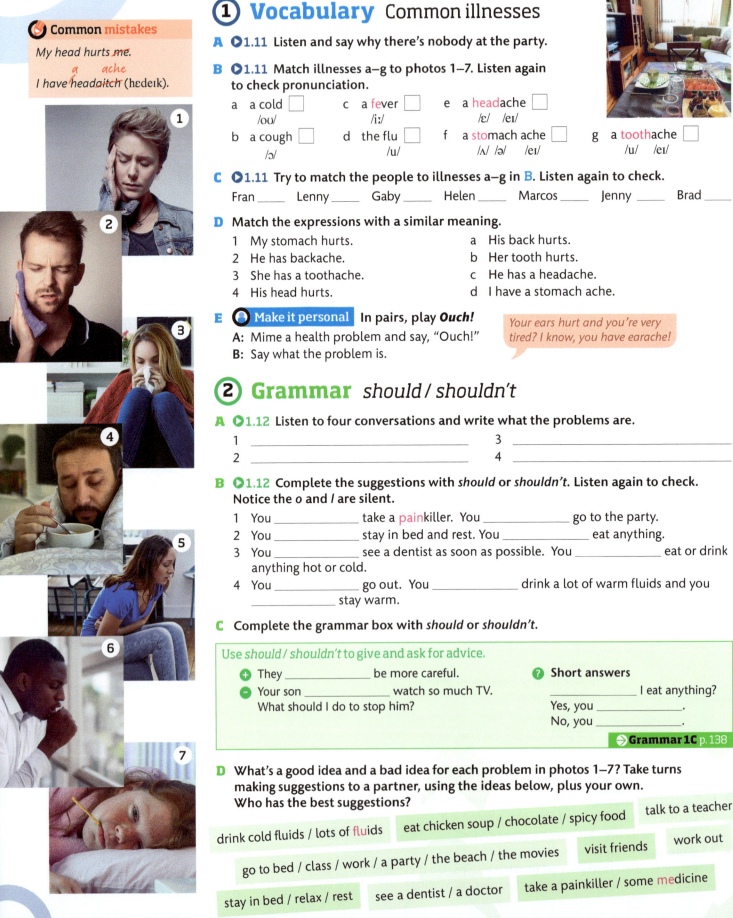

12

E 🟢 **Make it personal** In pairs, role-play these situations.

1. **A:** You need to learn English but work 12 hours a day and often miss classes.
   B: You're A's teacher. Make some suggestions.
2. **B:** You're a hypochondriac and often see the doctor with imaginary illnesses. Tell the doctor how you feel.
   A: You're the doctor. Give your patient some advice.

I missed class last week and I have a test tomorrow. I'm really worried.

 Should I stay or should I go now? If I go, there will be trouble, And if I stay it will be double, So you gotta let me know, Should I stay or should I go?

1.4

Common mistakes

~~an~~ some
I have ~~an~~ advice for you.
You should ~~to~~ stay in bed.

When you ~~will~~ take an aspirin, you'll feel better.

I'll
Good idea. ~~I'm going to~~ do that.

③ Reading

A Read these "Letters to Lori". Match her replies 1–3 to letters a–d. One letter has no reply.

Letters to Lori

a *Dear Lori,*
I'm 22 years old and I'm in my second year of college. My problem is that I want to leave. I don't want to be a student. I'm a very inde**pen**dent person and I love to travel. I need to be free and see the world. What should I do?
Free Spirit ☐

b *Dear Lori,*
My son is 19 and he has a great girlfriend and a baby son who is a year old. He works hard and is a good father to my grandchild, but he doesn't spend enough time with him and his girlfriend. I'm w**o**rried that his girlfriend will leave him and she'll take the child and then I won't see them again. How can I make my son spend more time with his family?
Worried Grandma ☐

c *Dear Lori,*
My father-in-law lives next door to us. He comes in and out of our house as he likes and borrows things when we're not here. We have no pr**i**vacy. I always fight with my husband about my father-in-law. My husband won't talk to his father about this problem. How can I make him understand that this is not his house?
Unhappy Wife ☐

d *Dear Lori,*
I have a se**r**ious problem. I can't find a girlfriend. I am very pick**y** and I have a long list of things that I want. No one is good enough for me. What can I do? Where can I find a partner?
Lonely Boy ☐

1 You shouldn't try to find a girlfriend by using a che**ck**list. You should date different people and get to know them. At the moment, you're re**jec**ting people before you know anything about them.

2 You can't force your son to spend more time with his family. He has to decide that for himself. You should continue to visit and sup**port** his girlfriend and your grandchild. That way, if your son and his girlfriend decide to separate, you will still see your grandchild.

3 You should try to find a career that will give you the oppor**tu**nity to travel. For example, if you are a teacher of English, you can live in other places. You shouldn't leave college right now, but you should choose a pro**fes**sion that is right for you and your independent spirit.

B ▶ 1.13 Listen and reread. In pairs, after each letter and answer, say if you agree with Lori's advice. Think of one more piece of advice for each person.

C 🟢 **Make it personal** Now be Lori!

1. In groups, brainstorm advice for the problem in **A** with no reply. Then, in pairs, write a short reply. Present your reply to the group and decide which is the best one.

Why don't you tell him you'll move house if he doesn't stop?   *He shouldn't have a key to your house.*

2. ▶ 1.14 Listen to Lori's reply to the problem. Is the advice similar to or different than yours? What do you agree or disagree with?

Her answer isn't as good as ours.

1.5 Will people live on the moon by 2050?

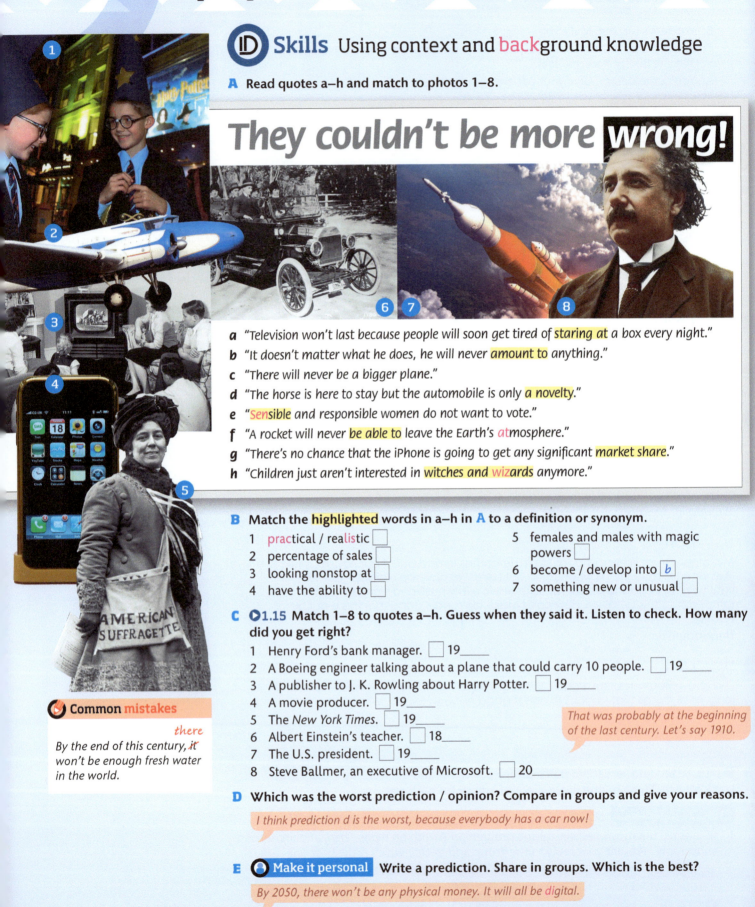

Skills Using context and background knowledge

A Read quotes a–h and match to photos 1–8.

They couldn't be more wrong!

a "Television won't last because people will soon get tired of staring at a box every night."
b "It doesn't matter what he does, he will never amount to anything."
c "There will never be a bigger plane."
d "The horse is here to stay but the automobile is only a novelty."
e "Sensible and responsible women do not want to vote."
f "A rocket will never be able to leave the Earth's atmosphere."
g "There's no chance that the iPhone is going to get any significant market share."
h "Children just aren't interested in witches and wizards anymore."

B Match the highlighted words in a–h in A to a definition or synonym.

1 practical / realistic ☐
2 percentage of sales ☐
3 looking nonstop at ☐
4 have the ability to ☐
5 females and males with magic powers ☐
6 become / develop into [b]
7 something new or unusual ☐

C ▶1.15 Match 1–8 to quotes a–h. Guess when they said it. Listen to check. How many did you get right?

1 Henry Ford's bank manager. ☐ 19___
2 A Boeing engineer talking about a plane that could carry 10 people. ☐ 19___
3 A publisher to J. K. Rowling about Harry Potter. ☐ 19___
4 A movie producer. ☐ 19___
5 The New York Times. ☐ 19___
6 Albert Einstein's teacher. ☐ 18___
7 The U.S. president. ☐ 19___
8 Steve Ballmer, an executive of Microsoft. ☐ 20___

> That was probably at the beginning of the last century. Let's say 1910.

Common mistakes

By the end of this century, ~~it~~ *there* won't be enough fresh water in the world.

D Which was the worst prediction / opinion? Compare in groups and give your reasons.

> I think prediction d is the worst, because everybody has a car now!

E 👤 **Make it personal** Write a prediction. Share in groups. Which is the best?

> By 2050, there won't be any physical money. It will all be digital.

14

1.5 When do you ask for help?

🎵 *Girl let me love you, And I will love you, Until you learn to love yourself*

ID in Action Offering help

> **Common mistakes**
> I fell and hurt ~~me~~ *myself*.
> He showered himself. = He took a shower.
> Reflexive pronouns (*myself, yourself, themselves*, etc.) are less common than in your language. They're used mainly for emphasis: *She did it (by) herself.* (= without help).

A ▶ 1.16 Listen and match conversations 1–4 to pictures a–d.

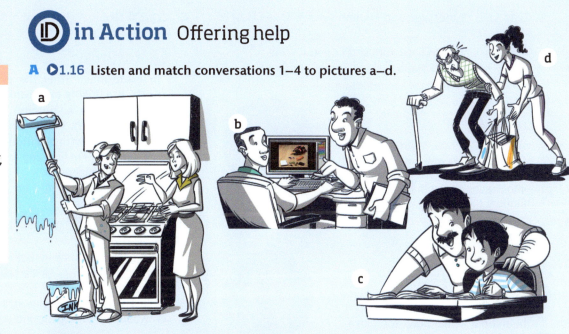

B ▶ 1.16 Listen again and complete the chart. Can you add any other phrases for offering, accepting, or refusing help?

Offering help	Accepting help	Refusing help
Do you need a _____?	That's very _____ of you.	Thanks for the _____.
Do you want me to _____ you?	Yes, _____!	Thanks, but I have to do it _____.
Can I _____ you?		
Would you _____ me to help?		

C Role-play pictures 1–3. In pairs, take turns offering help and accepting / refusing.

> Do you need a hand?   Yes, please. I don't know what to do!

D **Make it personal** Offer help to your classmates. How many accept / refuse your offer? Use these ideas to help you:

turn on / off	the fan / the A/C
open / close	the window / door
borrow / lend (me / you)	a pen / some money / my phone
carry	your bag / shopping
buy	a sandwich / a cookie
get	a coffee / some water
do	your homework / your chores

> Do you want me to do your homework?
> Thanks for the offer, but I can do it myself!

> **Common mistakes**
> Can you ~~borrow~~ *lend* me some money?
> Do you want to ~~lend~~ *borrow* my coat? You look cold!
> Do you need ~~of~~ a ride to the party?

Writing 1 A personal email

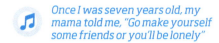
Once I was seven years old, my mama told me, "Go make yourself some friends or you'll be lonely"

A Read Laura's message and Nathan's reply. True (T) or False (F)?
1. Laura's been to New York and knows it well.
2. Nathan spends too much time partying.
3. Nathan's answer is full and friendly.

Hi Nathan,

I'm from Córdoba in Argentina and I'm coming to New York to study in September. Can you give me some information about the city and being a student there?

Thanks, Laura

Hi Laura,

a I was a stranger here too – I come from a small town 200 km away. I've been here a year now, and I love it.

b New York is an amazing place. **Per**sonally, **I think** it's one of the most interesting, exciting cities in the world. The problem is, I'm so busy with college work that I don't get much time to enjoy it. **I mean**, I have classes every day and lots of homework. I really enjoy my course, though.

c **Anyway**, this weekend I plan to do some sightseeing. There are great museums, beautiful parks, and famous landmarks everywhere you look. **To be hon**est, this is one of the best things about the city. **Ba**sically, it's full of history and culture.

d **Speaking of** culture, if you like music, there are live music venues everywhere. **It seems to me** that you can find just about any kind of music here any night of the week – from clas**sic**al to Latin to hip-hop. **In fact**, I'm going to a concert tonight with some friends.

e **By the way,** there are lots of Argentinian students at the university. I met two cool guys from your city at a soccer game last week. Small world, huh?

f OK, I need to go and start planning my next essay. Take care,
Nathan

B Match paragraphs a–f to questions 1–6.
1. What can you do in New York?
2. Have you ever met anyone from Argentina?
3. Have you lived in New York for a long time?
4. What kind of live music can you listen to?
5. Are you enjoying your course?
6. Do you have any plans for the weekend?

C Read **Write it right!** Match the six other **bold** linking expressions in the email to ca**t**egories a–c.

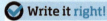 **Write it right!**

In less formal writing, like emails and social media posts, use linking expressions to:
a introduce an opinion
   Personally, I think Billie Ellish is great.
b support with additional information
   In fact, I'm listening to her right now.
c change topic
   Anyway, hope to hear your news soon.

D Complete the message with linking expressions.

I'm a student in Beijing, but I don't always enjoy the city. _____¹ it's a really difficult place to live and study. _____², it's one of the most polluted cities on the planet, it's noisy, and it's really crowded, so getting around takes a long time.

_____³, if you come here, you should take language classes in Mandarin. It's a difficult language to learn, but I think you'll enjoy it. _____⁴ if you're going to spend time in another country, you should try to learn the language. _____⁵, it can help you communicate more easily, make new friends, and understand the culture better.

_____⁶ making friends, I recently met some Canadian students who are here on an exchange program. _____⁷, they are some of the nicest people I've ever met!

E Imagine Laura has emailed you about coming to your city. Make notes about:
• three aspects of your city you could tell her about
• three aspects of being a student there.

F **Make it personal** Write your reply to Laura in 150–200 words.

Before	Use your notes in **E**. Look back at Nathan's post in **A** and underline any words or phrases you want to use in your own email.
While	Follow the structure of the email in **A**. Include six paragraphs and use linking expressions to introduce an opinion, add information or support an opinion, and change the topic.
After	Exchange replies with another student. Are your suggestions / opinions similar?

16

1 Old school

1 Before watching

A Check the items you prefer.

Old school	Modern
printed books	downloaded books
newspapers and magazines	news websites
text messages	tweets, WhatsApp
letters	emails
birthday cards	ecards
LPs or CDs & MP3s or MP4s	streaming, downloads

B 🗣 **Make it personal** In pairs, compare and explain your lists. Who's more "old school"?

I don't really see the point of ecards.

C Watch the ⓘD Café intro once. In pairs, remember and describe each person and what they were doing. If you studied English ⓘD 1, what do you know about them?

Rory	Daniel	Paolo	Andrea	Lucy
August	Genevieve	Zoey		

First up was Rory. He's sporty, for sure, and he was …

D Use the photo and exercises above to guess what the people are saying, thinking, and planning.

Maybe Genevieve is trying to interrupt Lucy and Daniel's date for some reason?

2 While watching

A Watch up to 0:56. Check the words each time you hear them. Compare in pairs. Listen again to check. What else did you pick up?

birthday	cousins	hang out	partied	party
perfect	place	together	twins	

B Watch up to 1:58 and check the correct name in the chart. Which of them do you think will be "old school"?

Lucy	Daniel	
		has made invitations
		is critical of them
		suggests a better alternative
		is defensive because they were hard to make
		apologizes for not looking closely
		justifies evites in many ways
		enjoys traditional books and mailing
		likes to get cards at special times

C Watch again. What five advantages does Daniel give for evites? What does he decide to do?

D Watch from 2:00–2:44. Which of the characters in 1C …
1. does martial arts?
2. really likes Zoey?
3. requested Lucy on Facebook?
4. is from Quebec?
5. should meet Genevieve?
6. remembers to invite Rory?
7. adds more names to the list?
8. takes the invitations home?

E How do you think the episode ends? Watch again to check. What justification does Daniel give?

3 After watching

A Complete 1–5 with *will / won't* or *be + going to*.
1. Where _____ we _____ have this party for August and Andrea's birthday?
2. Auggie and Andrea _____ love it!
3. If you guys need any help, my boss _____ let you rent the place out.
4. They're better and faster. We _____ send evites.
5. … evites are faster, cheaper, and we can easily see how many people _____ attend. And plus, we're not using paper, so we _____ make an impact on the planet.

B In pairs, check the things that are important for a party. Then order the actions logically, 1–8. What else is important?

- [ ] choose a date
- [ ] choose food and drinks
- [ ] create a party playlist
- [ ] decide on a theme
- [ ] decorate the party room
- [ ] make a guest list
- [ ] rent a place / venue
- [ ] send out invitations

First, I guess you need to … *Maybe we should decide how much money we have for the party!*

C What does "old school" mean to you? In pairs, plan an "old school" party, then compare with another pair. Which party sounds better?

OK, where should we have the party?

2.1 Do you ever read newspapers?

1 Vocabulary   News media

A Match the phrases to photos 1–6. How many digital screens can you see?
- in a **news**paper ☐
- on a **mo**bile de**vice** ☐
- on a news **web**site or app ☐
- on **so**cial **me**dia ☐
- on the **ra**dio ☐
- on TV ☐

B ▶2.1 Listen and match the interviewees' answers 1–6 to the photos.

C ▶2.1 Listen again and match their answers to reasons a–f. Do you know anyone like these people?
- a can discuss the news at family mealtimes ☐
- b it's better for the environment ☐
- c it's the easiest ☐
- d prefers this experience of reading ☐
- e is on the Internet all the time ☐
- f gets the news and exercises at the same time ☐

> A friend of mine refuses to read newspapers. He doesn't believe anything in them.

D 🧑 **Make it personal** In groups. How do you get your news? How often? Explain your answers. Do you think newspapers have a future? Then summarize the most common trends in your group.

> I'm like the man in number 1. I look quickly at the headlines until I see something interesting.

> I hardly ever read the news, it's always so depressing. But I always check the sports results on my phone.

> Most of us get our news online now.

⚠️ **Common mistakes**

That's an important new~~.~~ → *piece of* ~~s~~
You ~~lose~~ time reading. → *waste*
I saw it ~~in~~ a news app. → *on*

Use *on* with electronic devices / digital media, but *in* with traditional paper items.

18

♪ Tell me why are we wasting time, on all your wasted crying, when you should be with me instead?

2.1

2 Listening

A ▶2.2 Listen and match news stories 1–7 to the genres. There's one extra genre.

- [ ] entertainment / celebrity gossip
- [ ] local news
- [ ] national news
- [ ] sports
- [ ] traffic
- [ ] weather
- [ ] world news
- [ ] business news

B ▶2.2 Listen again and circle the correct answers. What else did you hear?
1. It will be **a lot** / **a little** colder **today** / **tomorrow**.
2. *Miracle* / *Medical* Men stars **Ben** / **Bill** Gardner.
3. There's a lot of **traffic** / **pollution on the highways** / **downtown**.
4. **Texas** / **Arizona** is in the final of the **National** / **World** Series.
5. There were **only 8** / **more than 50** leaders at the **summit** / **meeting**.
6. **People** / **Students** are protesting about **taxes** / **high prices**.
7. Maria **Braun** / **Brown chased** / **spoke to** reporters.

C In groups, write sentences for seven different news genres. Take turns reading them to another group. They identify the genre and say if the story is real or invented.

> A cat walked onto the court during the Brazil–Spain volleyball match yesterday.

> OK, that's a sports story and it isn't real!

D 🎤 **Make it personal** In groups, do the Class News Survey. Who follows day-to-day news most closely?

> For me, the most important story was when Mexico beat Argentina 3–1 at soccer.

> Yeah, it was an exciting game, but I think the President's visit to China was more important.

🔊 Common mistakes

I never pay attention to celebrity gossip*s*.

Last night's news w~~ere~~ *was* shocking.

News and gossip are uncountable.

Class News Survey
1. What were the two most important news stories this week?
2. Which two ways do you usually get your news?
3. How often do you check the news headlines?
4. Do you pay more attention to local, national, or international news?
5. What news genres are you most / least interested in?
6. Do you ever post comments about news stories?
7. Do you ever check news is true before you share it? How?
8. Have you heard a fake news story recently? What was it?
9. Did you ever appear on TV or in the papers? If so, why?

2.2 What were you doing at 8 o'clock last night?

1 Listening

A ▶2.3 Listen to Allie and her dad. How many calls did he make last night? Did he sound happy or unhappy? Why?

B ▶2.3 True (T) or False (F)? Listen to check.
1. Allie couldn't hear the phone when her dad called because she was watching TV.
2. Her dad also called Mike on the phone.
3. Mike often makes burgers.
4. The best way to contact the twins is to call them on the phone.
5. Allie's dad had some important news for the family.

C 🔵 Make it personal How is your family similar to or different than the family in **A**?

> My mom's like that, she calls me at least three times a week!

2 Grammar Past continuous

A ▶2.3 Listen again and circle the correct options.
1. What **did you do** / **were you doing** when I called last night?
2. I **watched** / **was watching** a fantastic nature show about the jungle.
3. He **made** / **was making** dinner at 8 o'clock.
4. They **played** / **were playing** video games.

B Look at 1–4 in **A**. Then complete the grammar box.

1. Circle the correct options.
   Past continuous is formed with was / were + **infinitive** / **-ing**.
   Word order and short answers are **the same as** / **different than** the present continuous.
2. Match 1–3 to a–c. Use:
   1. past continuous for   a an event that started and finished in the past
   2. present continuous for b an event in progress at a specific time in the past
   3. simple past for   c an event that is happening right now or a future arrangement.

➡ Grammar 2A p.140

Common mistakes

working
I was ~~work~~ when the Internet went down and I ~~was losing~~
all my work.   *lost*

Were
~~Was~~ you sleeping when she called?

taking
No, I wasn't. I was ~~take~~ a shower. / Yes, I ~~were~~.
                                        was

C Put 1–3 in order to make questions. In pairs, ask and answer.
1 doing / were / what / you / night / at / 7 p.m. / last / ?
2 about / night / at / 9 p.m. / last / you / eating / were / dinner / ?
3 Sunday / 11 p.m. / you / were / sleeping / night / at / on / ?

 Thought we were going strong, Thought we were holding on, Aren't we? You and me got a whole lot of history, We could be the greatest team that the world has ever seen

2.2

D Read and circle the best options. Give a reason for your answer.
1 **I was really enjoying / really enjoyed / really liked** the movie last night when my dad changed the TV channel.
2 Yesterday at 5 p.m. her parents **texted / was texting** her.
3 **Were you having / Did you have / Were you going to have** a car when you were a student?
4 **Did you have / Were you having / Didn't you have** dinner when I called yesterday?
5 Now, **I'm thinking / I thought / I was thinking** this is a good idea.
6 How **did that soup tasting / did that soup taste / was that soup tasting**?

E Who's the best eye witness? Study this picture for 45 seconds, then close your book. Remember and note as much as you can about what the eight people were doing.

In groups, compare what you wrote. Who had the most accurate information?

Ken was driving the red car.   *I thought he was driving the blue car.*

No, he wasn't. He was driving the red one and he was texting at the same time.

F **Make it personal** In pairs. Show and describe a photo for one minute, explaining what you / the people in it were doing, where you were, why, when, etc. Then hide it. Your partner remembers and describes the photo.

You were having dinner with your girlfriend and you were wearing a new shirt that she gave you.

Correct! What color was the shirt?

2.3 What's the world's most serious problem?

1 Vocabulary Global problems

A ▶2.4 Match the words in column 1 to photos a–d. Try to pronounce all eight words. Listen to the radio show, check, and number them 1–8 in the order you hear them.

a

b

c

d

Common mistakes

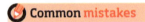
pollution
Air contamination is a big problem for cities.

☐ disease /dɪziːz/
☐ pollution
☐ poverty
☐ unemployment
☐ animal extinction
☐ climate /klaɪmət/ change
☐ crime /kraɪm/
☐ corruption /kərʌpʃn/

B How do the problems in **A** affect these things?

oceans   lakes and rivers   wildlife   cities
rainforests   deserts   jungles   people

I think pollution affects oceans, lakes, rivers, and cities.

I agree. It can kill fish and contaminate the food we eat.

C **Make it personal** What do you think are the most serious problems in your country? Order the problems in **A** from 1 (most serious) to 8 (least serious). In groups, compare your lists. How similar are they?

I think crime is the most serious problem here.   *For me, it's unemployment. Unemployment leads to poverty and crime.*

2 Reading

A ▶2.5 Read the TV guide and match the shows to channels 1–6. Listen to check.

1 Animal Planet

2 OUR WORLD

3 ACTION!

4 Glorious food!

5 CRIME SCENE

6 Home and Family

CHANNEL	8 p.m.–9 p.m.	EID TV GUIDE
	The Wilsons Carrie is upset because her grandmother Betty won't give her her secret chocolate cake recipe. Penelope shows Brendon that it's possible to have fun even when you don't have much money.	
	Jungle Stories Jungles are rich habitats that support amazingly diverse plants and animals. This episode looks at the inhabitants of the tropical rainforests of Indonesia.	
	What on Earth Is Happening? Most scientists agree: Earth's temperature is increasing. This show investigates climate change and asks if human activity is accelerating the process. Are we responsible for the extreme weather events happening around the world?	
	Kitchen Stars Four young chefs compete to create the best plate of food using surprise ingredients. The two best chefs advance to the semi-finals. And is romance in the air too?	
	Alvarez and Novak: Washed Away The cool Californian surfing detectives investigate some missing jewelry, but soon discover a fraud involving millions of missing dollars.	
	MOVIE: *Captain Marvel* Carol Danvers becomes Captain Marvel, a galactic superhero who uses her powers to end a war between two extraterrestrial civilizations.	

B ▶2.6 Listen and match conversations 1–6 to the show in **A** they were watching.

C In pairs, choose and compare the shows you would most and least like to watch. Explain why.

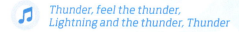
Thunder, feel the thunder, Lightning and the thunder, Thunder

2.3

I'd go for the movie because I love action movies!

Ugh, really?! A movie about superheroes?! No, I prefer real life so I'd watch the show about the jungle.

D **Make it personal** In groups, take turns describing what was happening in a show or movie you watched recently. The rest of the group guess its name.

A family was visiting Disneyworld. *Were you watching Modern Family?* *No, I wasn't.*

Were you watching Fresh off the Boat? *Yes, I was!*

③ Listening

A ▶2.7 Match the first three weather words plus any others you recognize to photos 1–9. Use the pink stress and vowel phonetics to guess their pronunciation. Then listen to the TV show to check. Were your guesses close?

- [ ] an e**cl**ipse /ɪklɪps/
- [ ] a hur**ri**cane /hərəkeɪn/
- [ ] a tsu**na**mi /tsunɑmiː/
- [ ] a **drou**ght /draʊt/
- [ ] an **ear**thquake /ɜrθkweɪk/
- [ ] a **fl**ood /flʌd/
- [ ] a **wild**fire
- [ ] a rainbow
- [ ] a thunderstorm

B ▶2.7 Listen again and match places 1–9 to what's happening a–i.

1	Bangladesh	a	high waves
2	London	b	**day**time **dark**ness
3	Argentina	c	sun and rain together
4	Florida	d	power **out**ages
5	South Africa	e	no rain
6	Chile	f	strong winds
7	Indonesia	g	de**struc**tion of buildings
8	Mexico	h	too much rain
9	Greece	i	an uncon**trolled** fire

Common mistakes

afraid / scared / terrified
I was ~~having fear~~.

frightening / scary / terrifying
That was ~~scaring~~.

C **Make it personal** In pairs. Which phenomenon in A is the scariest? Why? Compare with other pairs. Can the class agree on the scariest phenomenon?

For me, a hurricane is the scariest.

Me too. I was in a hurricane in Cuba and it was terrifying.

23

2.4 Was your mom living here when you were born?

1 Grammar Past continuous vs. simple past

A ▶2.8 Listen to a conversation about a thunderstorm. Why does the woman say she has to go?
1. Because the lights went out and she couldn't see.
2. Because her phone had no battery charge left.
3. Because she needed to help her son with his homework.

B ▶2.8 Listen again and circle the words you hear.
1. What **were you doing** / **did you do** when the outage **happened** / **was happening**?
2. I **was cooking** / **cooked** dinner when suddenly the lights **went out** / **were going out**!
3. The lights **went out** / **were going out** while he **was watching** / **watched** TV.
4. So what **were you doing** / **did you do** when the lights **went out** / **were going out**?
5. I **was finding** / **found** a flashlight and some candles.

C Answer a–e in the grammar box about the sentences in **B**. Then complete f with the correct tenses.

> ⏱ **Common mistakes**
>
> ~~When I was a kid I was eating~~ ate
> a lot of candy.
>
> ~~Jay ran in the park when he~~ was running
> slipped on a banana skin.

a In 2 and 3, which two actions were in progress? What verb form do they use?
b What action interrupted them? What verb form is used for that action?
c Which two words in 1–4 connect the two clauses?
d In 4, does *when* mean "after" or "at the same time"?
e Is 5 an action in progress or a result?
f So, for actions in progress use _____, and for actions that interrupt use _____. For resulting actions use _____.

➡ **Grammar 2B** p. 140

D ▶2.9 Use these words to summarize the story in **A** in two sentences. Listen to check.

| call | cook | go out | find | flashlight | happen |
| husband | lights | outage | she | then | |

E ▶2.10 Check the best options to complete the picture story. Listen to check.

☐ Jane was chatting online when her phone rang.

☐ Jane's phone was ringing when she chatted online.

☐ Her mom was coming in when she talked on the phone.

☐ Her mom came in when she was talking on the phone.

☐ When she was hanging up, her mom read her emails.

☐ When she hung up, her mom was reading her emails.

☐ Her parents were talking when Jane went downstairs.

☐ Her parents talked when Jane was going downstairs.

F In pairs, cover the story and take turns retelling it. Do you think Jane's mom was wrong to read Jane's emails? Why (not)?

> *I think she was right to read her daughter's emails. Jane is young and her mother needs to protect her.*

24

G 🎧 **Make it personal** Play **Alibi!**

🎵 *I was blind, now I can see, You made a believer out of me, I'm movin' on up now, Getting out of the darkness, My light shines on*

2.4

1 In pairs, make an alibi for last night between 8 and 10 p.m.
What / doing / eating / drinking / watching / listening to / playing?
Who / with? / talking to?
/ go out? Where? How long? What time / leave / arrive home?

2 Test the alibi. Another pair ask you questions individually to check that your stories are exactly the same.

What were you doing last night between 8 and 10 p.m.? | *We were watching a movie.*

What time did the movie start? | *8.15 p.m.* | *What time did it end?*

② Reading

A ▶ **2.11 Cover the article and listen. After each web post 1–8, say if the person had a positive or negative experience.**

What were you doing when the world went dark?

Solar eclipses are not uncommon – they occur every two years or so somewhere on the planet – but everyone who sees one remembers the experience. Here are some of our favorite posts about the 2017 total eclipse in the U.S.

1 I was standing in a sports field when suddenly I screamed, "It got dark!" I knew this was going to happen, but I don't know why it still surprised me. **Louise**, *Oregon*

2 I was watching quietly with my family when it went dark. I felt small and I felt connected to the universe. I understand what all those scientists were trying to say now. I saw totality for only about one second, because of the cloud, but it was enough. **Jason**, *Illinois*

3 We drove 10 hours to a place that was in the path of totality, but we couldn't buy any eclipse glasses because they were sold out. We had nothing to eat and nothing to drink and it was over very quickly. One of the most overrated experiences of my life! **Martha**, *California*

4 We walked two blocks from home to a public park. People were sitting in chairs on the grass. They were wearing eclipse glasses and looking up at the sky. Everyone was outside and everyone was waiting. **Brooke**, *Wyoming*

5 As it started to get darker, I was feeling weird and uneasy. When totality happened those feelings left me and I was filled with joy. Some people were shouting but the only noise that came out of me was the word "Wow!" The event wasn't shocking, it was calming and inspiring. **Taylor**, *Idaho*

6 As the time for totality was getting nearer, the clouds got thicker and the rain came down. It was dark and raining – what a disappointment after all the expectation! **Tariq**, *Nebraska*

7 Darkness fell over Nashville and cicadas started screeching, while birds everywhere returned to their nests all at the same time. **Marina**, *Tennessee*

8 My boyfriend and I climbed to the top of Table Rock Mountain and we were watching eagles when the eclipse began. Everyone was silent and lost in thought, and then Venus suddenly appeared like a jewel. It was sublime. **Rosie**, *South Carolina*

B Read the article and and say who:

1 had different feelings during the eclipse. ☐
2 talks about insects. ☐
3 saw a planet during the eclipse. ☐
4 saw the eclipse from near their home. ☐
5 was surprised at the darkness. ☐
6 didn't see the eclipse because of the weather. ☐
7 understood why people talk about eclipses so much. ☐
8 had a long journey to watch the eclipse. ☐

C In pairs, take turns describing or miming a highlighted or pink-stressed word for your partner to say.

D 👤 **Make it personal**

1 Which posts in **A** remind you of experiences you have had?
2 What were you doing when something dramatic or interesting happened? How did you react? Who had the most interesting reaction?

⚡ **Common mistakes**

knew
I ~~was knowing~~ this was going to happen.

saw
I ~~was seeing~~ totality for a second.

had
We ~~were having~~ nothing to eat or drink.
State verbs aren't usually used in the continuous. See Grammar 2A p.140.

It's like the world but bigger. | *It's the opposite of easy.*

Universe. | *Uneasy.*

Number 3 reminds me of one New Year's Eve. We waited hours for the fireworks, but then it started raining really heavily at 11.30!

25

2.5 What do you carry in your pockets?

🆔 Skills Understanding and retelling a story

A Read the story on the "Strange Things Happen" website and choose the best title.

Cooking can be dangerous   Woman hurt by beach rocks   Kids find phosphorous at home

Strange Things Happen!

UNBELIEVABLE! Did you read this story about the woman who had rocks in her cargo shorts when suddenly something weird happened?

So, the woman was carrying the orange stones in her shorts, because her children found them on the beach and gave them to her. (What nice kids! 😃) The poor woman was standing in the kitchen about an hour after they got home when her shorts caught fire! Yes!! Her shorts CAUGHT FIRE!! Imagine her husband's surprise too – the poor guy was reading the paper or something and suddenly he saw that his wife was on fire!! Well, he thought fast and he took her outside and started hosing her down with water from the garden hose. And that's when the firefighters and paramedics arrived – as he was spraying his wife with water. So, of course, the surprised paramedics treated her and took her off to the hospital. They said it was the first time they ever saw something like that. The rocks were still smoking when they arrived at the hospital! Those were very flammable rocks!

Anyway … so what on earth happened? Well, the authorities are investigating, but they think that there was phosphorous on the rocks (if you look at the photo you can see that they're orange – that's phosphorous). Apparently, when phosphorus is exposed to air, it burns at extremely high temperatures. And the woman? Well, she got severe burns on her right leg and her right arm and her husband got burns on his arm too, but they survived.

The moral of the story? Don't put things your kids give you in your pockets! 😂

B ▶ 2.12 Listen, reread, and, in pairs, whenever the teacher pauses the audio, imitate the last five words you heard.

C True (T) or False (F)?
1 The rocks were in the woman's pocket. ☐
2 She found the rocks on the beach. ☐
3 The woman was sitting down when the rocks caught fire. ☐
4 Her husband put water on the fire. ☐
5 The paramedics often see burning rocks. ☐
6 Phosphorous caused the fire. ☐
7 Both of them got badly burned arms and legs. ☐

D 👤 **Make it personal** Imagine you are a character from the story. Write a blog about what happened from your perspective. Then, in groups, read each other's stories and choose the best one.

> *You're not going to believe this! Yesterday, we were relaxing at the fire station when someone called to say there was a woman on fire!*

2.5 Are you a good listener?

You can't start a fire, You can't start a fire without a spark, This gun's for hire, even if we're just dancing in the dark

ID in Action Being a good listener

A ▶ 2.13 Listen to the conversation and order the pictures 1–4.

B ▶ 2.13 Listen again and check the expressions you hear. Can you think of any more?

Show you're listening	React to something positive	React to something negative
Uh-huh?	Wow! Really?	Oh no!
Yes?	How interesting!	No way!
And then what happened?	That's good.	That's awful!
	That's great!	That's terrible!

How about "Is that right?"

Common mistakes

What happened ~~with~~ *to* you?
He ~~let fall~~ *dropped* the food.
He ~~fall~~ *fell* down.

C In pairs, take turns telling the story in your own words. Your partner reacts using the expressions in **B**.

So the boy was riding his bike to school. *Yes?* *And he got a flat tire.* *Oh no!*

D Role-play. In pairs, take turns telling the picture story, choosing different characters. What's the same and what's different in your versions?

Last night I was having dinner with my boyfriend in a restaurant in town. *Yeah? Then what happened?*

E **Make it personal** Think of a story that happened to you recently. In groups of three, take turns:

A: telling your story.
B: listening carefully and reacting to the story.
C: observing and noting the expressions B uses to react to A's story. Does B sound interested? Give them feedback.

So, I was going to work on the bus on Tuesday when suddenly the bus stopped. *Really? What happened?*

Well, we got off the bus and I waited for another bus. *Uh-huh.*

OK, you said "Really?" and "Uh-huh" but you didn't make eye contact. You didn't look very interested!

Writing 2 A survey report

Everybody's changing and I don't feel right,
Everybody's changing and I still feel the same,
Everybody's changing and I don't feel the same

A Read the report and match it to graph 1 or 2.

Survey Report — by Marc Hernandez

a We conducted an online survey of people in four Latin American countries to find out where they usually get their news. Here is a summary of the results for Chile.

b Most people said they get their news online or on television. Just under 90 percent get news online, and three-quarters get news from TV. Approximately 70% get their news from social media – the most popular platforms are Facebook, WhatsApp, and YouTube. Some people still get their news from print newspapers and magazines, but this is only around 40% (or two-fifths). A small number of people, 9%, said they pay for online news.

c The results show that most people get their news from four main sources, and that traditional sources such as newspapers and magazines are now much less popular than TV or online. I found it surprising that just over half of all interviewees said they trust the news, which means that around 50% of people don't believe what they read or hear!

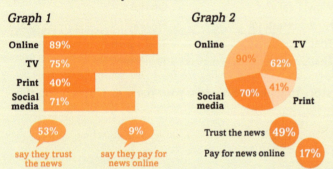

Graph 1
Online 89%
TV 75%
Print 40%
Social media 71%
53% say they trust the news
9% say they pay for news online

Graph 2
Online 90%
TV 62%
Print 41%
Social media 70%
Trust the news 49%
Pay for news online 17%

B Match paragraphs a–c to 1–3.
a introduction ☐   b results ☐   c conclusion ☐
1 The writer's reaction to the results.
2 The topic of the survey and information about where it refers to.
3 Survey details, starting with the largest number.

C Read **Write it right!**, then find and underline the 10 number expressions in the report. Express them another way.

✓ Write it right!

- In formal text, write numbers one to nine as words. Write larger numbers in figures.
- Write fractions in words or figures, but be consistent.
  10% = one tenth (1/10); 50% = a half (½);
  25% = a quarter (¼); ⅓ = a third; ⅔ = two-thirds.
- To talk about approximate numbers, use *approximately, around, just over / under*, or these expressions:

0 ——————————————————— 100%
no one | some people | most people | everyone
a small number of people | many people

D Complete this report about the other graph in **A** with numbers or expressions from **Write it right!**

We interviewed people in Mexico to find out where they usually get their news. Here is a summary of the results.

We found that _____¹ people get their news online and from social media. _____² of people said they get their news online, and _____³ 75% get their news from social media – the most popular platforms are Facebook, WhatsApp, and YouTube. Just _____⁴ 60% of people get their news from TV. _____⁵ still get their news from print newspapers and magazines, but this is only _____⁶. A small number of people, _____⁷, said they pay for online news.

The results show that _____⁸ get their news from four main sources. I found it surprising that just under _____⁹ of all interviewees said they trust the news, which suggests that just _____¹⁰ half don't believe what they read or hear!

E Choose a question, 1–5. Think of five possible categories to form a more detailed survey question.
1 What kind of news is the most interesting for you?
   sports, international, local, celebrity gossip, business
2 What do you do most online?
3 Which social media platforms do you use most often? What for?
4 What do you like to read most in your first language?
5 What do you read most in English?

F Conduct the survey with your class and record the results. Look at the example.

What kind of news is the most interesting for you?
sports ———— ●●●●
international news ———— ●●●●●
local news ———— ●●●
celebrity gossip ———— ●●●●●●
business ———— ●●

G 🎤 **Make it personal** Write a report of your survey in 100–120 words. Include a graph to show the results.

Before	Look back at the reports in **A** and **D**. Decide how to display your results in a graph. What are your main conclusions?
While	Write a report on your survey in three paragraphs, following the structure in **B**. Include: 1) an introduction describing what your survey was about; 2) the results of your survey; 3) a personal conclusion from your survey.
After	Share your report with someone who chose the same question. Are your results and conclusions similar?

2 Nature boy and natural woman

 Café

1 Before watching

A Match words 1–5 to meanings a–e.

1 an audition
2 coverage
3 a host
4 a nightmare
5 to wonder

a the presenter of a (TV) show
b a bad dream
c a short test performance
d ask yourself
e the media reporting of an event

B 🔵 Make it personal What's Daniel doing in the photo? In pairs, answer 1–3.

1 Are you good with a camera?
2 How good are you on camera? Would you make a good host?
3 How many (online) interviews have you done? Do you interview well? Have you ever done an audition?

> I love taking photos and videos. I think the result is normally pretty good!

> I had an audition for a part in a play once, but I was terrible!

2 While watching

A Watch until 0:53. Complete Daniel's mistakes with these words. Do you often make mistakes when recording yourself?

| coverage | my | news shows | the | we |

1 He says _____ instead of _____.
2 He pauses in the middle of the phrase _____ and _____.
3 He gives up after saying, "Here _____."

> Yes, I get very nervous. I hate hearing myself, especially in English!

B Watch until 2:20. True (T) or False (F)? Guess how the episode ends.

1 Lucy and Genevieve are planning a party.
2 Genevieve called Daniel "natural boy" because of his eco-obsessions.
3 The girls were discussing party invitations when Daniel called.
4 Genevieve leaves to give Lucy some privacy.
5 Lucy was thinking about travel-themed decorations.
6 Daniel's audition video is going well.
7 Lucy was waiting for him to ask for help.
8 Lucy's a film director.

C Watch the rest of the episode. Did you guess correctly? Then order what Daniel says his show will be about, 1–6. There are two extra.

☐ a animals
☐ b birds
☐ c close-ups of green celebrities
☐ d down inside the Earth
☐ e Earth's daily activities
☐ f marine life
☐ g nature news
☐ h news from around the globe

3 After watching

A In pairs, explain the lesson title.

> It's called this because …

B Correct three mistakes in each sentence.

  Daniel
1 ~~Lucy~~ was making mistakes when she was recording herself.
2 Daniel was thinking he could edit it himself and make it look really cool.
3 Lucy was very nervous until Daniel helped her through it.

C Order Daniel and Lucy's dialogue, 1–6, and complete with ⊕ or ⊖ of simple past or past continuous, according to the video.

☐ I _____ (try) to record myself and it _____ (be) a nightmare. I _____ (wonder) … _____ (can) you help me out?
☐ Hey, you got a minute?
☐ And I _____ (wonder) when you were gonna ask me. Don't worry, it'll be great!
☐ Maybe.
☐ Can I ask you something?
☐ Sure.

D Put the words in order to make sentences from the video. Who said them?

1 he / they / I / me / wanted / green / out / paper / convinced / to / ones / send / but / weren't / that
  I wanted _____
2 that / I / thinking / be / a / too / much / might / little / to / ask / was
  I was _____
3 ever / wonder / slept / while / what / you / doing / was / our / planet
  Ever wonder _____

E 🔵 Make it personal Role-play! Use the dialogue in 3C to help you. **A:** You're Daniel. Ask B for help. Then role-play introducing your own TV show. **B:** Agree to help A. Then film and direct A's TV show.

29

R1 Grammar and vocabulary

A **Picture dictionary.** Cover the words on these pages and use the pictures to remember:

page	
6	5 life priorities
8	5 senses and 2 adjectives for each one
12	7 common illnesses
18	6 ways to get news
21	5 actions that were happening in the picture
22	4 global problems
23	9 natural phenomena
24	Jane's story
158	11 pairs of picture words for the 11 vowel sounds

B 🎧 **Make it personal** Choose two of photos 1–6. In pairs, take turns using sense verbs to describe each of them, until your partner guesses which it is. Use *X* instead of the pronoun.

> *X smell bad but taste amazing!*

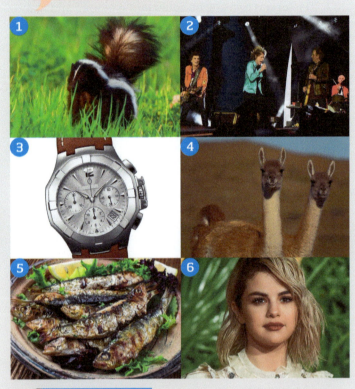

C 🎧 **Make it personal** Use prompts 1–6 to make questions. In pairs, ask and answer, and ask at least two follow-up questions. What's the most interesting thing you found out about your partner?

1 have / get up early?
2 want / be famous?
3 where / last vacation?
4 what / after work or school?
5 how / feeling today?
6 need / study before a test?

> *Do you have to get up early?*
>
> *It depends on the day. I get up …*

D You're Lori. Read 1–6 and write a piece of advice using *should* for each. In pairs, compare and choose the best advice in each situation.

1 I have a test tomorrow morning, and I'm really worried about it!
2 My house is full of water from the flood!
3 I have a toothache, but I'm terrified of dentists!
4 My 4-year-old son has a fever and can't sleep.
5 My kids are 13 and 17. They want to go to a party, but they have school tomorrow.
6 We don't have any money and we have to pay for our electricity, our car, and our vacation. Help!

E 🎧 **Make it personal** Record five things you think your partner will / won't do before next class. Then check.

> *OK. My first prediction was "He'll eat pizza." Did you eat pizza?*
>
> *Yes, in fact I did! I had an awesome pizza last night.*

F ▶ R1.1 🎧 **Make it personal** Put the words in 1–4 in order and add an auxiliary verb to make questions. Listen, check, and repeat. Then, in pairs, ask and answer.

1 doing / what / you / last night / 6 p.m. / at / / ?
2 evening / yesterday / you / do / what / / ?
3 work / in / who / you / the / last activity / with / / ?
4 you / doing / what / class / before / the / started / / ?

G In pairs, compare the two problems in 1–5. Which is more serious and why? Any disagreements?

1 animal extinction or pollution?
2 unemployment or crime?
3 climate change or poverty?
4 corruption or diseases?
5 droughts or earthquakes?

> *I think animal extinction is more serious than pollution because …*

H Correct the mistakes. Check your answers in units 1 and 2.

⏱ **Common mistakes**

1 We enjoy play the video games. (2 mistakes)
2 I go to the movies yesterday. (1 mistake)
3 When you will start working, you'll get up more early. (2 mistakes)
4 Will you to help we with our homework? (2 mistakes)
5 I will writing that on my notebook. (2 mistakes)
6 Here is an advice and a news for you. (2 mistakes)
7 What was you doing at 8 p.m. the last night? (2 mistakes)
8 Was you scared during the thunderstorm? (1 mistake)
9 When he was young he was crying all the time! (1 mistake)
10 I played soccer when I fell and broke the leg. (2 mistakes)

30

Skills practice

Blackbird singing in the dead of night, Take these broken wings and learn to fly, All your life, You were only waiting for this moment to arise

R1

A 🎤 **Make it personal** In pairs, play *Crystal Ball!*
A: Predict the future of something or somebody.
B: Guess what or who A is talking about.

Everyone will have them.   *Are you talking about cars?*

No, they will do chores in the house.

Children! Only joking. Robots!   *You got it! Your turn.*

B Read the email. Are 1–7 True (T) or False (F)? Correct the false ones.
1 His head was aching before he went to the store.
2 It was raining all day.
3 He took his bike into the mall.
4 He was wet when he went into the store.
5 His bike was there when he left the mall.
6 He knows where his keys are.
7 He opened a window to get into his apartment.

Hi!
What a terrible day! First, I had a really bad headache, but I had to go to the store to get some food. So, I was riding to the mall when the rain started. There was a huge thunderstorm and I was on my bike, so I got really wet! Then I left my bike outside the mall and went in. When I came out of the mall my bike wasn't there! Gone! Can you believe it??? After that I had to walk home, wet and cold. Then when I got home I couldn't find my keys! Guess what I did. I climbed in an open window at the back! But a neighbor saw me, thought I was a thief, and called the police. Now I have to take my ID to the police station, I have no keys, no bike, and a terrible cold from the rain! What should I do?
Larry :-(

C In pairs, imagine Larry is your friend. Think of three pieces of advice you could give him.

You should get a car!   *Yeah, and take care of your keys!*

D ▶ R1.2 Listen to a message from Larry's sister. What five pieces of advice does she give him? Listen again to check. Is any of her advice the same as yours?

E In pairs. A: You're Larry. Tell B your story. Can you remember all the details? B: Listen and react to A's story.

You won't believe what happened yesterday!   *What?*

F In groups, take turns miming a problem. The others race to offer advice. Use these ideas to help.

| heavy bags | hot | hungry | no money |
| really tired | sick | too much work | |

You shouldn't go clubbing this week!

H ▶ R1.3 🎤 **Make it personal**   **Question time!**
1 Listen to the 12 lesson titles in units 1 and 2.
2 In pairs, practice asking and answering. Use the book map on p. 2–3. Ask at least two follow-up questions. Try to answer in different ways. Can you have a short conversation about the questions?

What's really important in life?

For me, it's having fun! You have to enjoy life.

What do you do to have fun?

31

3.1 How often do you travel?

1 Vocabulary Traveling

A ▶3.1 Listen to Vic talking about his vacation and number pictures a–g in the order you hear them, 1–7.

B In pairs, use the phrases and expressions below to compare your feelings about traveling. Any big differences?

I	love / like / hate	to travel / traveling	alone.
	enjoy / don't mind / can't stand	traveling	with family / friends.

- traveling long distances by car / plane / train / bus / boat
- going to exotic places
- taking short day trips
- doing nothing / rushing around
- hitchhiking

I don't mind traveling long distances by car. I find it relaxing.

That's because you don't drive! I hate driving.

C Cover the second column of the quiz. Match the **bold** words to the photos in **A**. Check in pairs and predict how sentences 1–8 end.

♪ *I'm on my way, Driving at ninety down those country lanes, Singing to "Tiny Dancer", And I miss the way you make me feel, and it's real*

3.1

What kind of traveler are you? Take our quiz and find out.

BEFORE THE JOURNEY

1 You've saved a lot of money and **booked** an expensive hotel online. The kind you've always dreamed of. When you get there ...

... you discover the place is not what you saw on the site. It's not even finished! What do you do?

2 It's 4 p.m. You've tried all you could, but you couldn't get to the station on time and **missed** your train. Now you have to ...

... wait five hours for the next one. All the stores at the train station are closed. What do you do?

3 It's December 23rd . You're at a **crowd**ed and cold bus station, **stand**ing in line. The ticket agent says ...

... there are no more tickets available. You won't be home on December 24th. What do you do?

4 It's time to go to the airport. You've **packed** all your bags, turned off the lights, and called a taxi. On the way to the airport ...

... the taxi breaks down and stops in the middle of the street. What do you do?

DURING THE JOURNEY

5 You've **board**ed an old and crowded plane. All you want to do is get some sleep. You hope there's no one sitting next to you, but ...

... you see a mother and a very young kid. What do you say?

6 You're on the plane. The flight attendant has dropped a cup of coffee on your laptop. You turn it on ...

... but it isn't working. You don't know if the problem is permanent. What do you do?

AFTER THE JOURNEY

7 You've arrived at the hotel and checked in. You're exhausted after your journey. The three elevators ...

... are out of order and your room is on the 10th floor. What do you do?

8 You've just come back from a shopping trip to Miami. You're stopped at **customs**. In your suitcase ...

... there are a lot of things you forgot to declare. What do you do?

D 🔲 **Make it personal** In pairs, uncover the second column and check your predictions. How many endings were similar to yours? Then answer the questions.

> *In a situation like this, I stay calm and don't shout. I ask for my money back.*

② Listening

A ▶ 3.2 Listen to the complete quiz and choose a, b, or c for each question.

B Calculate your score, then read what it means. Do you agree?

⚠ Common mistakes

pack
I have to ~~make~~ my bags.

missed
I got up late and ~~lost~~ my plane.

We need to ~~do the~~ check in before dropping our bags.

What kind of traveler are you? Score **a** = 3, **b** = 2, **c** = 1

8–11 Calm and in control	**12–19** Balanced	**20–24** Stressed and impatient
Your friends probably think you're a great travel companion. You don't get stressed when things go wrong and you always see the positive side of any bad situation.	You know how to have a good time and don't usually let small incidents interfere with your vacation, but, depending on the situation, you can get angry or impatient.	It's probably hard to travel with you. You get really annoyed if things go wrong and don't enjoy your vacation as much as you could.

> *Well, it says I'm stressed, which is true, but I don't think I'm impatient.*

C 🔲 **Make it personal** In pairs, use the pictures in **1A** to remember and tell your own funny / stressful / surprising travel experiences. Are they "good traveler" or "bad traveler" stories?

> *Photo b reminds me of my grandma's birthday party. I missed the bus and then the train was canceled. I had to take a cab. It was really expensive!*

> *OK, that's a "bad traveler" story!*

33

3.2 Have you ever been to another country?

1 Listening

A ▶3.3 Which city does the photo show? What do you know about it? Listen to part one of Paula and Harry's conversation and complete 1–4.
1 Paula has seen the photos of _____.
2 Cathy lives in _____.
3 She wants Harry to _____.
4 Paula went there on _____.

B ▶3.4 Why do you think Harry is hesitant to go? Listen to part two to check. Were you right?

> Well, maybe's he's nervous about meeting her face to face.

C ▶3.5 Listen to part three. True (T) or False (F)?
1 Cathy makes a lot of money.
2 She knows about Harry's phobia.
3 Harry goes to therapy twice a week.

D 👤 **Make it personal** In pairs, answer 1–3. Any similar opinions / stories?
1 What do you think is the best solution to their problem?
2 Do you think long-distance relationships can be successful in the long term?
3 Do you know anyone who has a phobia? What is it?

> I think he should be honest with Cathy.

> Some friends of mine have been together for three years, and they live in different countries!

> My son is afraid of spiders.

Common mistakes

Avicii ~~has~~ died in 2018.
　　　has
Ed Sheeran ~~sold~~ five million albums this year so far.
　　　did
When ~~has~~ Ariana Grande last ~~played~~ in Asia?

2 Grammar Present perfect 1: past experiences

A ▶3.6 Match 1–5 to Paula and Harry's responses a–e. Listen to check.

1 I've **been** to Australia twice.
2 Have you **seen** photos of her?
3 Have you ever **traveled** by plane?
4 Have you ever **tried** therapy?
5 She's **seen** photos of me too.

a Once. My mom took me to Disneyland when I was five.
b Yep, you showed them to me last week.
c And she still liked you after you showed them to her?
d Oh yeah? Did you go on business?
e Twice. It didn't work.

B Complete the grammar box.

1 Study the sentences in **A**. Read and circle Yes (Y) or No (N).
  • Sentences 1–5 in **A** are about past experiences. Y / N
  • We don't know / care when the things happened. Y / N
  • The **bold** verbs are in the simple past. Y / N
  • The present perfect = *have / has* + past participle. Y / N
  • Some past participles end *-ed* and have the same form as the simple past. Y / N
  • Some past participles are irregular and have a different form. Y / N

2 In the responses, which tense is used to ask for / give more details?
3 Is a similar tense used for the sentences in **A** in your language?

➡ **Grammar 3A** p.142

34

C Read **Common mistakes**. In pairs, how many true sentences about Harry's story can you make in two minutes? Pronounce the s in 's and hasn't /z/ not /s/.

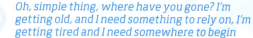
Oh, simple thing, where have you gone? I'm getting old, and I need something to rely on, I'm getting tired and I need somewhere to begin

3.2

Paula
Harry
Cathy

be
see
travel
try

Australia
plane
Disneyland
therapy
–'s photos

before
once
twice

Common mistakes

'*ve   been to*
I never ~~was~~ in Moscow.
      been
I've ~~gone~~ to a U2 show.
Use *been* for completed visits (there and back), *gone* if someone hasn't returned.

Harry's been to Disneyland once. That's one.

D Make questions to ask Paula about her trip. Each / means a missing word. Stress the **bold** words.
1 when / you **go** there?   *When did you go there?*
2 how long / / **stay** there?
3 what **places** / / visit?
4 how / / **weather**?
5 / you stay / / **hotel**?
6 / your **partner** / with you?
7 how much **work** / / do?
8 / / like / **go again**?

E Match 1–6 in the survey report to photos a–f. Complete with these verbs in the present perfect.

be (x 2)   meet   see   travel   try

Class Survey Report

1 Two or more people *have been* to the United States.

2 Four or more students _____ by plane.

3 No one _____ an A-list celebrity face to face.

4 At least two students _____ all the *Avengers* movies.

5 Everyone in the group _____ Japanese food.

6 Most of the students _____ to a live, professional soccer game.

F **Make it personal**   **Class survey!** In pairs, use the verbs in E to ask and answer *Have you …?* questions about different subjects. Ask at least one follow-up question each time. Report your answers to the class.

Let's see … Have you ever seen the Amazon River?   Yeah, once.

Really? When did you see it?   I flew over it in 2018.   Wow! Where were you flying to?

3.3 Have you sung a song in English yet?

1 Reading

A In groups, look at the title of the article. Decide which tip, 1–4, is the most important when traveling with a friend. If you disagree, try to convince your group.
1 Be pre**pa**red to com**pro**mise.
2 Dis**cuss** money.
3 Do things se**pa**rately sometimes.
4 Plan carefully.

I think it's really important to compromise.   *Of course, but for me that's not …*

B ▶3.7 Read the article and match tips 1–4 in **A** to paragraphs a–c. There's one extra tip. Then listen, reread and, after each paragraph, repeat the pink-stressed words. What's your reaction to the text?

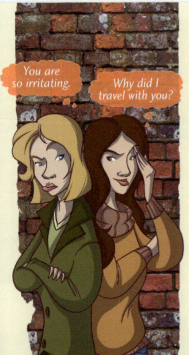

How to travel together without killing each other!

Traveling with people you don't know in**ti**mately can be fun … or a nightmare. Your perso**na**lity differences can get mul**ti**plied by 10. So here are three things to con**si**der before you go:

a **Be honest about your bu**dget. If you can only spend $60 a night for accommo**da**tion, say it before you go. Also, plan how you intend to share all the other ex**pen**ses: transpor**ta**tion, food, and enter**tain**ment. And think about this: is it OK for you to travel with someone who has more money than you? Would you mind paying a bit extra to help a friend who has less?

b **Sometimes you'll need to make quick decisions on the road** and maybe disa**gree** on what you want to do. If your perso**na**lities and in**te**rests are different, you'll have to plan a bit and be fle**xi**ble with each other. If one of you is a heavy s**mo**ker and the other hates smoke, it's important to find a so**lu**tion that sa**tis**fies both sides. So, consider this: can you make con**ces**sions when you travel with others? Would you ever travel with someone who has a few i**rri**tating habits?

c **Spending too much time with each other can be very irritating.** Plan to take some breaks from each other from time to time, espe**cia**lly on a longer trip. Then you can meet for dinner and share fun s**to**ries. So, before traveling ask your**self**: are you comfortable spending the en**ti**re day with a friend when you travel? Do you need to spend some time a**lo**ne when traveling?

Common mistakes

~~of~~ **on**
It depends ~~of~~ your budget.
Traveling   having
~~To travel~~ without ~~have~~ money is difficult.
leaving   anticipating
Before ~~leave~~, ~~anticipate~~ problems is essential.
Use -ing forms when the subject is a verb + preposition.

C 🗣 **Make it personal** In pairs, ask and answer the last two questions in each paragraph. Are you compatible travelers?

Is it OK for you to travel with someone who has more money than you?
I guess so, but it depends on how much, I think.

2 Listening

A ▶3.8 Lisa and Meg are spending a few days in London. What problems are they having? Listen and match days 1–3 to the travel tips in **1A**.
Day 1 ☐   Day 2 ☐   Day 3 ☐

B ▶3.8 Listen again and write Lisa (L) or Meg (M) for 1–4. Who …
1 really dislikes the hotel?
2 went shopping yesterday?
3 probably likes art?
4 's reading *101 Things To Do Before You Die*?

C 🗣 **Make it personal** Who would be worse to travel with – Lisa or Meg? Why?

Lisa wants to stay in expensive rooms so that ruins the holiday.

③ Grammar Present perfect 2: completed actions

♪ *It's been a long time since I came around*
Been a long time, but I'm back in town
This time I'm not leaving without you

3.3

A Match 1–5 to their present result.

1 This place has changed.
2 Have you stayed here before?
3 We've only just arrived!
4 We haven't paid yet.
5 I've already told you.

	They don't have our money.
	We haven't checked in yet.
	You know that.
1	It's different now.
	It's my second visit.

B Study sentences 1–5 in **A** and **Common mistakes**. Then complete the grammar box.

> Cross out the incorrect options in rules a–d.
>
> a The experience and / or present result of the action is **more / less** important than the time it happened.
> b *Just* (very recently) and *already* (before now) are used in **positive / negative** sentences.
> c *Yet* (up to now) can be used in questions and **positive / negative** sentences.
> d **Use / Don't use** the present perfect for specific past times (*a week ago, when I arrived*).
>
> ➤ **Grammar 3B** p. 142

C ▶3.9 Complete 1–7 with the verbs in the correct tense. Listen to check. In pairs, say which rule a–d each sentence illustrates.

1 Julie _____ (**be**) there and she says it's fantastic.
2 I _____ (**not be**) to the West End yet.
3 You _____ (**spend**) a lot of money yesterday.
4 The weather _____ (**change**). It's really cloudy now.
5 I'm reading *101 Things To Do Before You Die*. _____ (**you / read**) it?
6 I _____ (**start**) it when we got on the plane.
7 I _____ (**already / read**) the first 20 ideas.

D Test a partner. Take turns choosing a photo on p. 32 and describing what's just happened. Your partner identifies it.

He's just booked the hotel.   *Picture g, right?*

E ▶3.10 Read the list. Guess which seven activities Lisa and / or Meg have done. Listen to check, and notice the irregular past participles of the **bold** verbs. Describe what Lisa and Meg have / haven't done using *already*, *just*, and *yet*. Listen again to check.

Well, they're visiting London, so they've already done that.

Yeah, of course. And …

101 things to do before you die

☐ **be** a DJ at a party	☐ **make** a birthday cake
☐ **do** volunteer work	☐ plant a tree
☐ **do**nate blood	☐ **ride** an animal
☐ **fall** in love	☐ **swim** with dolphins
☐ **go** abroad	☐ try an extreme sport
☐ **have** a child	☐ visit London
☐ learn to dance	☐ **write** a story

F 🔵 **Make it personal** List 10 things you really want to do. In groups, compare lists, ask, and answer. Who wants to do the most unusual thing? Who has done the most things? Have you made any plans to achieve your ambitions?

I really want to go to Europe.   *I've been abroad, but only once.*   *Oh really? Where did you go?*

⟳ Common mistakes

hasn't called
She ~~haven't call~~ me yet.
have already
We ~~already have~~ worked together.
I ~~have~~ studied a lot yesterday evening.

37

3.4 How long have you lived here?

① Reading

A Would you like to spend a year somewhere different before you start college or work? Where would you go and what would you do? Consider these ideas.

a learn a new language
b work as a volunteer
c work in a restaurant / store / hospital
d work with children
e travel to different places
f learn new skills

I'd go to Italy and learn Italian.

Would you work there or travel around?

B Read the article. Was each person's experience Positive (P) or Negative (N)?

Taking a Gap Year

A waste of time or the time of your life?

Parents, teens, and educators all talk about the benefits of taking a gap year before college. It's become so popular that even the British royal family have done it! Prince William, for example, volunteered in Chile, and Prince Harry worked on a ranch in Australia and helped to build a clinic in Lesotho, Africa. We spoke to six people and asked, "Is a gap year a good idea?" Read their stories and get some inspiration but also some warnings.

Derek I'm very shy. Really, you have no idea how shy I am. So guess how I'm spending my gap year? Teaching English as a foreign language in Cambodia. Yep – to groups of 30 students. And you know what? I love my students and I think they love me back. I've only known them since June[1], but it feels like we've always been friends[2]. I don't get paid, but I get free board and accommodation and that's really all I need.

Sandra My gap year has been amazing so far! I'm traveling alone around South America practicing my Spanish and meeting incredible people. So far I've been to Chile, Argentina, Uruguay, Paraguay, and Bolivia[3] and I plan to go to Peru, Ecuador, and Colombia before I go home. I've learned so much! I've met a lot of people and I've had some great experiences as well as a couple of bad bad ones.[4] By the time I get home, I'll be ready to start college next fall.

Ross Well, I lived in Cairo for a year with my aunt and uncle[5] and the experience taught me more valuable lessons than my last 10 years at school. I learned to be much more open to other cultures, values, and religions – things you don't learn in class. And I learned to be fluent in Arabic which was my goal![6]

Rita In 2015 I lived and worked as an au pair in Barcelona for nine months[7]. All I wanted was to get some cash, and then start a new life when I got back home. But I fell in love with the twins that I looked after, and the rest is history. So, thanks to my gap year, I decided I didn't want to be a lawyer, but a primary school teacher. Mom and Dad were a bit surprised, but in the end they just accepted my decision.

Tina I've been in Scotland for six months[8] and it's been a nightmare. I got a part-time job at a big grocery store and have worked there for only three weeks[9], but I hate it. In the winter it gets dark at 4 p.m. and I think this is affecting my mental health. I'm getting really depressed and all I do is cry night and day. I really want to get on a plane and go back home soon. Luckily, my cousin has just come to visit, so I hope to have some fun with her.

C ▶3.11 Quickly reread and match 1–6 to the correct person. Then listen and, after each paragraph, repeat the pink-stressed words.

Who:

1 wants to go home as soon as possible?
2 changed her mind about her future?
3 stayed with family during the gap year?
4 doesn't have to pay for their apartment?
5 is visiting more than one country?
6 mentions language learning?

D 👤 Make it personal The time of their lives? In groups, take turns saying if you or someone you know has had one of experiences a–f in **A**. Answer questions about it. Any similarities? Were any experiences a waste of time?

My sister's worked as a volunteer in Africa.

Wow! What did she do?

She helped to build a school.

38

2 Grammar Present perfect 3: unfinished past

I have run, I have crawled, I have scaled these city walls, These city walls, Only to be with you. But I still haven't found, What I'm looking for.

3.4

A Who's still on their gap year in **1B**? Write *present* or *past* next to each underlined phrase.

B ▶3.12 Listen to two interviews with Rita and Tina. Find two incorrect details in their paragraphs in **1B** based on the interviews.

C Complete the grammar box. Is the present perfect similar in your language?

a Read **Common mistakes** and the four example sentences, and look at the graphics. Then circle the correct options in rules 1–3.

Simple past	Present perfect
I worked there from 2015 to 2018.	We've been married since 2018.
I finished reading the book yesterday.	We've been married for two years.
The action **started** and **finished** in the past	**started** in the past and still **continues**.

1 Use the present perfect for actions that started in the past and **have** / **have not** finished.
2 Use **for** / **since** + a time expression for the duration of the action.
3 Use + **for** / **since** to say when the action started.

b Complete the expressions with *for* or *since*.

_____ a long time   _____ many years   _____ I met you
_____ a few weeks   _____ 2011   _____ a period of time
_____ I moved here   _____ April   _____ a point in time

→ **Grammar 3C** p. 142

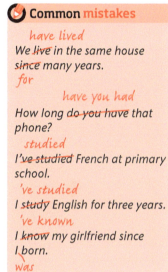

Common mistakes

have lived
We ~~live~~ in the same house ~~since~~ many years.
for

have you had
How long ~~do you have~~ that phone?

studied
I ~~'ve studied~~ French at primary school.

've studied
I ~~study~~ English for three years.

've known
I ~~know~~ my girlfriend since I ~~born~~.
was

D ▶3.12 In pairs, use the prompts to write questions and sentences about Tina and Rita's gap year. Listen again to check.

1 How long / you / be / UK?
2 I / be / UK / September.
3 How long / you / work there?
4 I / see / her / long time.
5 How long / you / live / Barcelona?
6 I / live / there / seven months.
7 I / work / au pair / four months.
8 Mom and Dad / in**sist** / long time.

E Meet Sam Same. He doesn't like change. Use pictures 1–6 to talk about him. Imagine his other habits.

Sam's probably had the same food every day for 30 years.

same house / 1990

same **hair**style / many years

foreign language / he was 20

same TV / 15 years

his girlfriend / 1995

same kind of music / many years

F 🔊 **Make it personal** Have you changed a lot? In pairs, ask and answer *How long …?* questions to find out. Change pairs and ask and answer about your previous partner. Did you learn anything new?

How long have you had the same hairstyle?

Oh, since I was 15. I like my hair the way it is.

How long has Joe had the same hairstyle?

Since he was 15.

39

3.5 Do you write reviews?

ID Skills Using evidence for your answers

Common mistakes
disappointment
It was a big ~~deception~~.

A Put these words in the correct category. Add the opposites of the underlined words.

cheap	a coffee maker	dirty	economical	filthy	friendly
good value	helpful	a kitchenette	near the beach	near the center
polite	a pool	quiet	reasonable	spotless	wifi

price	cleanliness	amenities	location	service

B Read these reviews and give an overall rating for each hotel.

○○○○○ excellent
○○○○○ very good
○○○○○ average
○○○○○ poor
○○○○○ terrible

We stayed at the Central Hotel for one night and I have to say I don't think it's good value for money, which was a big disappointment. The rooms are very basic and there's no coffee maker in the room and the wifi signal is too weak to use. The biggest problem for us was that the pool was empty, so we couldn't swim. The room was generally clean, but the bathroom was filthy – like they didn't clean it at all! There was hair in the tub and in the sink. On the plus side, the hotel is very central and you can walk everywhere, which is fantastic. Check-in and check-out were very easy and the staff were responsive to our needs, but the hotel really needs renovation urgently! And more entertainment – the only thing in our room was an old television.

Rating _____

We stayed at Golden Sands in October and the weather was amazing – warm, but not too hot. We had a dramatic ocean view room with a super comfortable bed. The service was the best we've ever had on vacation – staff and management were phenomenal. The food and drinks were excellent and the prices were very reasonable for a big resort like this. The hotel was not expensive at all for the service and amenities, and its location in front of the beach was superb. Everything in the room worked perfectly, from the wifi to the hairdryer. The only problem was that the room was a little small for a family of four, but that's kind of logical when you book one room for four people! Next time we'll get two rooms.

Rating _____

C ▶ 3.13 Listen, reread, and underline the parts in each review that relate to each category in **A**.

D In pairs, use the parts you underlined in **C** to decide on a star rating for each category in each hotel. Compare with another pair. How similar are your ratings?

	price	cleanliness	amenities	location	service
Central Hotel					
Golden Sands					

We've given this only two stars for price.

Once we stayed in a fantastic hotel on the beach. It wasn't cheap ...

E 👤 Make it personal

1 Have you ever stayed in a hotel like either of these? Were you paying?
2 In accommodation reviews, what is the most important category for you? Order the categories 1–5 (most to least important) and find someone with the same list.

Price is number 1 for me. I always look for the cheapest places.

Really? Sometimes the cheapest place is really awful and far away from the center.

3.5 Are you a logical person? 3.5

 Look what you made me do, I'm with somebody new, Ooh, baby, baby, I'm dancing with a stranger

ID in Action Reacting to unexpected information

A Read the paragraph and find 14 Latin words in it.

About 50 percent of all **En**glish words are **La**tin in **or**igin. So if you're a **na**tive speaker of Spanish, Portuguese, French, etc., you can understand and express many ideas using these words, even if your English is still **li**mited. The reviews you just read on p. 40, for example, con**tain** ap**prox**imately 50 Latin-based words.

B Scan the hotel reviews again and find three examples of each suffix.

-ic	-ment	-al	-ion
dramatic			

C Study the words in B and complete rules 1–3.

1. The suffixes _____ and _____ are **ty**pical of nouns.
2. The suffixes _____ and _____ are typical of adjectives.
3. Suffixes _____ usually stressed.

D Complete 1–6 with the correct form of the words. Write one more question using a word from the chart in **B**. In pairs, ask and answer the questions. Would you ask a stranger these questions?

Fun questions to ask a **STRANGER**!

1. Is there a lot of el**ec**trical *equipment* in your bedroom? (**equip**)
2. Do you think TV is still good _____? (**entertain**)
3. Has anyone ever considered you an _____? (**intellect**)
4. Is it possible to have too much _____? (**inform**)
5. Were you _____ as a child? (**music**)
6. Are you a _____ person? (**romance**)

First one. Is there a lot of electrical equipment in your bedroom?

Oh, yeah, lots. A TV, a reading light, my laptop, my phone ... what else? Oh, and my alarm clock.

Common mistakes

~~expect~~ to
I didn't ~~wait~~ you say that.
    un
That was ~~an~~ inexpected news.

E ▶3.14 Listen to two conversations. Which question in D is each one about?

F ▶3.14 Listen again and complete 1 and 2 with two words in each gap.
1. Barry learned how to play _____ when he _____ and _____ very first song when he was nine . It was called "_____ and the Stars."
2. Linda dislikes TV. She says there are one _____ good shows, and they're mostly late _____ or on cable. She doesn't let _____ watch TV, but she lets _____ time on the Internet.

G ▶3.14 Complete 1–5. Listen again to check. In pairs, practice different ways of reacting to surprising information.

Meaning	What you actually say	Or just ...
I don't understand. / Please explain.	1 What do you _____ nothing?	What?
I'm surprised to hear this.	2 You've never _____ me that.	Wow! Really? You're kidding me!
Please confirm what you said.	3 Wait a _____. Did I hear you say that ...?	What?
That is not logical.	4 But that makes no _____.	No way!
I have a different opinion.	5 I don't _____.	Oh, come on!

Wow! You have much less equipment in your bedroom.

H 🔘 **Make it personal** Change partners. Repeat activity D. Use sentences from G. Try to do it a little faster. Are your new partner's answers similar?

41

Writing 3 — An internship application

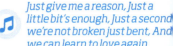

Just give me a reason, just a little bit's enough, Just a second we're not broken just bent, And we can learn to love again

A Read internship ads a–c and Marcia's email. Answer 1–3.
1 Which internship is she applying for?
2 Does she have the necessary experience and qualifications?
3 Complete the email with the correct country.

a

Kenya
Sports science graduate wanted for a six-month athletics training program. This is an opportunity to develop a career in top-level coaching. Must have a relevant degree and be fluent in English. Ability to drive essential.

b **Mexico**
Our marine conservation project has a vacancy for a suitably qualified intern. Get valuable career experience while contributing to important marine conservation work. Must be able to scuba dive and have a good command of Spanish.

c

Jamaica
Join our news team in the Caribbean, filming reports on local issues for our online video channel. Experience is not necessary as training will be given, but you must speak English and be a good communicator.

Dear Ms. Walton,

I would like to apply for the internship in _____ listed on the internship page of your website.

As you will see from my résumé (attached), I have recently graduated from Miami University with a degree in environmental science. I am a qualified scuba diver. I am also fluent in Spanish and English, and have a good command of Portuguese.

I am currently employed by the local environment agency, where I have worked for the past six months. I am responsible for testing water quality on local beaches, and helping to keep our beaches clean.

I am looking for a new opportunity to develop my experience of marine conservation. I have always been interested in everything related to the oceans, and I am sure I can make a positive contribution to your program.

Thank you for considering my application. I am available for interview at any time. If you have any questions, please feel free to call me on (1) 8989-7888. I look forward to hearing from you.

Sincerely,
Marcia Fernandez Ruiz

B Order the topics in the email, 1–5.
☐ education and qualifications
☐ work experience
☐ availability for interview
☐ position interested in
☐ reasons for applying

C Study the email and **Write it right!**, then complete tips 1–7 with *Do* or *Don't*.
In formal emails and letters:
1 _____ use an informal, conversational style.
2 _____ address the reader by his / her first name.
3 _____ include your contact information.
4 _____ thank the reader.
5 _____ end with your first name only.
6 _____ refer to your résumé.
7 _____ use contractions (*It's, I'm,* etc.).

✓ **Write it right!**

There are specific ways to open and close a formal email or letter.
Opening: *Dear Mr. Lee (Mrs. / Ms. + last name); Dear Sir / Madam*
Closing: *Sincerely, Kind regards, Best wishes*

D Complete 1–8 with the correct preposition. Scan the email to check.
1 Apply _____ a position or job.
2 Graduate _____ (name of university) _____ a degree _____ (subject).
3 Be responsible _____ something at work.
4 Be fluent _____ / Have a good command _____ (a language).
5 Have experience _____ something.
6 Be interested _____ something.
7 Make a positive contribution _____ something.
8 Be available _____ an interview.

E 🔵 **Make it personal** Write an email applying for an internship in 150–200 words.

Before	Choose an internship in **A** or imagine one you'd like to apply for. Brainstorm why you would be the right person for the job.
While	Write an application following the order in **B**. Include five paragraphs and follow the tips in **C**. Compare each paragraph carefully with the one in Marcia's email.
After	Exchange emails with another student. Decide if you will give each other the internship.

3 Under the moon

 Café

1 Before watching

A In pairs, check what's important for school / work projects.

I think it's important to …

- [ ] be creative
- [ ] have a good memory
- [ ] have experience
- [ ] have inspiration
- [ ] know how to write well
- [ ] have good research skills
- [ ] have a strong Internet connection

B 🎤 **Make it personal** In pairs. Have you ever had to do a big project?

I worked on a big project for my art class. *What was it about?*

C Guess how Andrea feels and why.

- [ ] homesick - [ ] not inspired - [ ] sleepy - [ ] tired

Maybe she's been up all night?

2 While watching

A Watch up to 2:40 to check. Complete 1–6 with the correct numbers. What else did you pick up?
1 Andrea's had _____ cups of coffee.
2 She has _____ more designs to complete.
3 She has to design _____ rooms in total.
4 The twins lived in Argentina when they finished _____ grade / just before their _____ birthday.
5 They lived in France _____ or _____ years ago.
6 They lived in Mexico from _____ to _____ grade.

B Watch again and complete 1–6.
1 Her designs have to be about places _____.
2 The last time the twins were in Argentina was when _____.
3 According to them, Andrea is _____ and August is _____.
4 French kids made fun of August's _____.
5 After leaving France, they moved back to _____.
6 The inspiration for her difficult design came from _____.

C Read 1–8 then watch the rest. Check August (Au), Genevieve (G), or Andrea (A).

		Au	G	An
1	comes from Montreal and misses it			
2	doesn't really have one home			
3	has got a lot of inspiration from travel			
4	recognizes where the design is from			
5	sent a postcard from Australia			
6	imagined she lived on the moon			
7	inspired a song to be written			
8	asks a question about the moon			

D Who says 1–10, Andrea, August, or Genevieve? Watch again to check.
1 Hey, you could tell?
2 Those were good times!
3 You are way more talented than I thought.
4 Hey! That was, like, a strange kind of compliment.
5 You know what I mean.
6 What does it remind you of?
7 They were just picking on you.
8 You have a good memory.
9 I get homesick sometimes.
10 We don't really have one home.

3 After watching

A Complete 1–6 with the correct form of these verbs.

| be | do | have | live | see | think |

1 You've _____ four cups already.
2 Let me see what you've _____ so far.
3 We haven't _____ back in years.
4 These are some of the best rooms I've _____.
5 It has to be a place you imagine you've _____ in.
6 I haven't _____ about that in a long time.

B Complete 1–7 with *has / have* or *'s / 've*.
1 _____ you worked out today?
2 I _____ got two more to do.
3 You _____ always been the pretty, fun, popular twin, and I _____ been the nerd.
4 This _____ been difficult for Andrea.
5 How long _____ it been since we lived there?
6 Andrea _____ always wondered about Genevieve's song title.
7 Well, we know man _____ walked on the moon …

C 🎤 **Make it personal** Have you ever been homesick? If so, what did you miss most?

When I went to college, I missed my grandmother's cooking.

43

4.1 Were you spoiled as a child?

1 Vocabulary Childhood

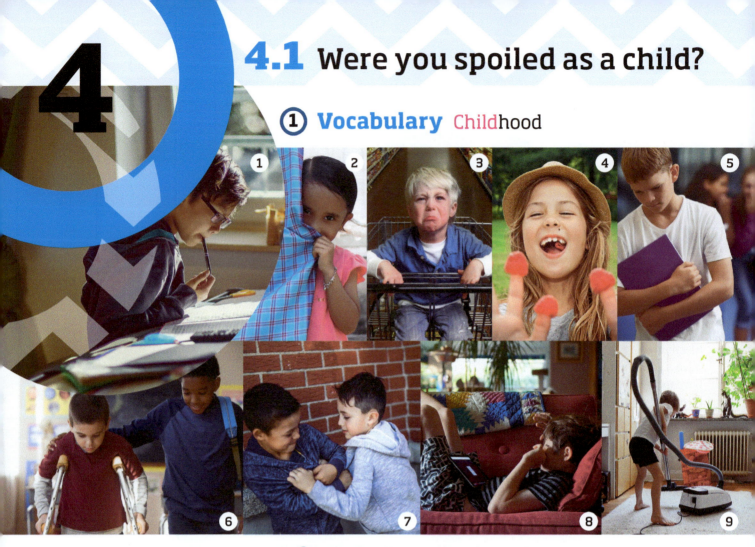

A ▶4.1 Read and listen to the website and match photos 1–9 to the **bold** words.

What kind of child were you?

Which group best describes you as a kid? Based on years of intensive study, psychologist Donald Elliot has created five categories to describe children aged 4–10. Here's a summary of his study.

	These kids are …	So they …
Group 1 Party kids	funny	like to **laugh** and entertain people.
	active and creative	do many activities at the same time and never get tired.
	sociable	make lots of friends – their own age or older – very easily.
Group 2 "Please love me" kids	**kind**	are always helping people in trouble.
	hardworking	like to do well in school to make their parents happy.
	sensitive	cry if other kids **make fun of** them.
Group 3 "But why?" kids	**shy**	like to be alone sometimes.
	curious	like to know how machines work, for example.
	independent	like to explore the world on their own.
Group 4 Explosive kids	honest	don't hesitate to tell people what they think of them.
	spoiled	won't stop until they get what they want.
	aggressive	**fight** more often than most other kids.
Group 5 Mini adults	obedient	wash their hands and take showers without a fight.
	critical	hate **lazy** people and always expect perfection.
	responsible	take the initiative to **do chores** around the house.

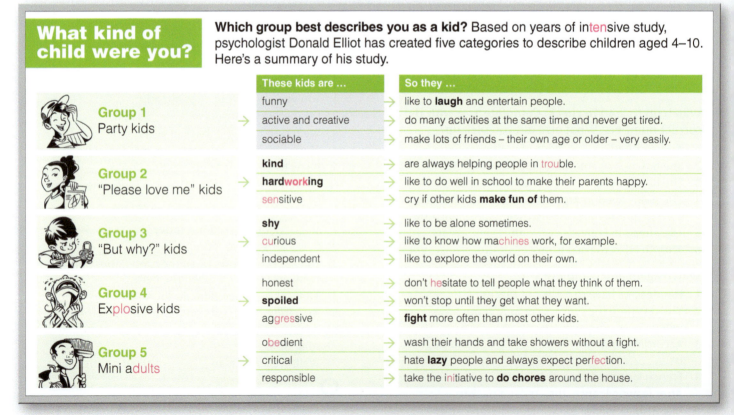

B ▶4.2 Listen to the children and say the correct bold word(s) after the beep.

C ▶4.2 **Listen and reread. Which kind of child would say a–g?**
Write the group number, 1–5.

a "I want the new iPad right now, Daddy, not next week." ☐
b "Mmm ... what happens if I put my watch in the microwave?" ☐
c "Go to bed? Mom, but it's only 11 p.m. I want to play video games. Please!" ☐
d "What? I only got 95 percent on that easy test? What was I thinking?" ☐
e "Grandpa, you look sad. What's wrong?" ☐
f "Mommy, can I help you wash the dishes? Please?" ☐
g "Yes, you're my aunt, I know, but I still don't like your voice." ☐

🎵 *My father said, Don't you worry, don't you worry child, See heaven's got a plan for you Don't you worry, don't you worry now, yeah*

4.1

D ▶4.3 **Complete the word stress chart with adjectives from the second column in A.**
Listen to check. Then circle the correct option to complete the rule.

Adjectives					
●	●●	●●●	●●●	●●●●	●●●●
kind	funny	sociable	creative	obedient	

Suffixes like *-able, -ible, -ive, -ent, -al, -ous* are **sometimes** / **never** stressed.

E 👤 **Make it personal** **What kind of child were you? In pairs, use the**
adjectives in A to find two similarities and two differences.

First one, funny ... Yeah, that was me.

Not me. I was very serious, and didn't laugh a lot.

② Listening

A ▶4.4 **Listen to two conversations. Which group from 1A does each child belong to?**

Michael ☐   Susan ☐

B ▶4.4 **Listen again. Are 1–6 True (T) or False (F)? Correct the false ones.**

1 Some of Michael's friends have wireless headphones.
2 His mother thinks wireless headphones are too expensive.
3 He probably helped his mother with the housework recently.
4 Susan wants to get an A on her test.
5 She likes to eat at McDonald's.
6 Her parents are young.

C ▶4.5 **Complete opinions 1–4 with *do* or *make*. Listen to check. Do you agree?**

1 If you _____ a promise to a kid, you can never, ever break it.
2 It's important to make children _____ the dishes, _____ the bed
  and help around the house.
3 Children who _____ a lot of of homework every day don't necessarily
  _____ well in exams.
4 Young parents usually _____ more mistakes with their children.

D **Complete the text with *make* or *do*. Then find and add seven more *make* / *do* phrases**
from this lesson to the chart.

Romance languages only have one verb for *make* and _____. Sadly, there are no
concrete rules for when to use _____ or *do* in English. So _____ this
exercise and _____ a big effort to remember the phrases.

Make			Do		
money	an effort	a decision	the laundry	a project	a favor

🔴 **Common mistakes**

make
I still commit mistakes when I speak.

I can't talk to you now, I have to make my homework.
do

do
Mike, can you make me a favor?

make
I never do my bed in the morning.

Use *do* for work, jobs, or tasks and *make* for creating.

E 👤 **Make it personal** **Complete 1–5 with *do* or *make* phrases. In small groups,**
compare and choose the one that is true for most people in your group.

When I was young,
1 I had to _____ every day / week. I hated that!
2 my parents never asked me to _____.
3 I went to a good / bad school. For example, _____.
4 I was / wasn't spoiled. For example, _____.
5 I found it difficult to _____.

When I was young, I had to wash the car every week. I hated that!

My dad washed our car. But I had to do the dishes every day, and I hated that!

45

4.2 What did you use to do as a child?

1 Reading

A What embarrassing things do children do? Use pictures 1–4 to guess what the stories are about. Then read the online forum and match the pictures to stories a–d.

How embarrassing is that!?

Tell us your stories and let our members decide how embarrassing they are!

a When I was in third grade or something, I used to sit in the back row, near the fish tank. When I was hungry, I ate the fish food flakes. Oh, boy, I loved fish food. No one knew about my secret eating habits, except my best friend, Sue. One day, she told everyone. I was so embarrassed and humiliated I had to move to another school. I think the fish food did me good though because a few years later, I became a swimming champion. Pretty ironic, isn't it? **Orbit606** posted at 2:30

b When I was around six, I had a phase where I only wanted to be called "Adele." You see, I knew an older girl called Adele and I liked her, so on my sixth birthday I decided to adopt her name. Mom almost went crazy! She used to wake me up calling my real name and I said, "Go away, I'm Adele, you know that!" This Adele phase lasted like an entire year. Then, after my seventh birthday, I got tired of Adele, so I chose a different name: Lisa. Guess what TV show I used to watch? **Ex789** posted at 8:00

c When I was about two, one of my favorite things to do was open Alfredo's mouth and pull his tongue out. Did he like that? Well, every time he saw me, he ran to my mother's bedroom and stayed there for hours, so I guess the answer is no. But, poor Alfredo, we used to love him! Oh, by the way, Alfredo was our Labrador Retriever. **Weirdo9** posted at 10:15

d When I was a child, I didn't like school, so I made lots of excuses to stay home. One morning, when I was about seven or eight, I woke up and told my parents I couldn't move my left leg. They took me to the hospital immediately and I spent the entire day in the emergency room. Obviously, the doctors didn't find anything wrong with me. After a few hours, my leg "magically" started to work again. I still don't know if my parents believed that story. **Smith7** posted at 12:49

B ▶ 4.6 Listen, reread, and rate the stories, 1, 2, or 3. In groups, compare opinions.
   1 Normal for a kid   2 A bit embarrassing   3 Seriously embarrassing!

C 🔵 **Make it personal** In pairs, share stories about embarrassing things that you or someone you know did as a child. Which is the most embarrassing?

When he was four, my brother once ate all the dog's food from her bowl!

That's seriously embarrassing!

2 Listening

A ▶ 4.7 Listen to part one of a conversation about one of the stories in 1A. Who's talking?

B ▶ 4.7 Listen again. True (T) or False (F)? Correct the false ones.
   1 Julia still hates her school days.
   2 Her brother enjoys school.
   3 She was always sick when she was a teenager.
   4 She used to eat bird food every day.

C ▶ 4.8 Read options 1–3 and guess how her dad is going to react. Listen to part two to check.
   1 Happy she wasn't sick.   2 Pleased she confessed.   3 Angry she lied and wasted time.

D 🔵 **Make it personal** In pairs, role-play Julia's parents talking about her. Decide what to do next. Who has the best solution?

I can't believe she did this to us!   *I think we should take away her phone for a week.*

She needs her phone. And it was a long time ago …

3 Grammar *Used to* and simple past

*We don't talk anymore, Like we used to do,
We don't laugh anymore, What was all of it for?
Oh, we don't talk anymore, Like we used to do*

4.2

A Check if 1–6 happened one time (OT) or over a period of time (PT).

	OT	PT
1 Did you use to like school?		
2 You used to be sick all the time, Julia.		
3 I didn't use to do it all the time.		
4 One day you ate bird food, remember?		
5 But, Julia, we took you to the hospital!		
6 I never lied about the serious stuff.		

▶ **Common mistakes**

~~I'm use~~ *usually* to download music.
You ~~use~~ *used to* call me on my cell phone.
Did you ~~used~~ *use* to have a CD player?
Who did you ~~used~~ *use* to play computer games with?

B Study 1–6 in **A** and **Common mistakes** and complete the grammar box.

> 1 Complete a and b with simple past (SP), *used to* (U), or both (B).
>   a To describe repeated past habits, facts, and states, you can use _____.
>   b To describe actions that happened once, you can only use _____.
>
> 2 Circle the correct options to complete the rule.
>   *Where did you use to study English before?*
>   *Just on my own. I didn't use to go to classes.*
>   Form questions and negatives using the auxiliary **did(n't) / do(n't)** + **use to / used to**.
>
>   ➔ **Grammar 4A** p. 144

C Study 1–6 and, if possible, rephrase the underlined words using *used to*.
1 When I was hungry, I <u>ate</u> the fish food flakes. I <u>loved</u> fish food.
2 One day, she <u>told</u> everyone.
3 On my sixth birthday, I <u>decided</u> to adopt her name. Then I <u>got</u> tired of Adele, so I <u>chose</u> a different name.
4 <u>One of my favorite things to do was open</u> Alfredo's mouth and pull his tongue out. <u>Did he like that?</u> Well, every time he saw me, he <u>ran</u> to my mother's bedroom.
5 When I was a teenager, I <u>didn't like</u> school.
6 I <u>couldn't</u> move my left leg. They <u>took</u> me to the hospital immediately.

D In pairs, using only pictures 1–4 in **1A**, take turns retelling the stories.

> *When this horrible child was two, he used to pull the dog's tongue.*

E In pairs, look back at the photos on p. 44 and ask and answer questions with *used to*. How many things do you have in common?

> *Did you use to make fun of other kids?*   *Oh yeah. I used to call my brother Bart Simpson.*

F 🟢 **Make it personal** **Childhood memories!** Read the speech bubbles, then in pairs:
A: Draw a memory about something you used to do when you were young.
B: Try to guess **A**'s memory while she / he's drawing.
A: Respond with *Yes* or *No* until **B** guesses correctly. Mime or give clues if **B** can't guess. Change roles.

> *Mmm ... maybe you used to listen to music walking to school.*   *No!*
>
> *OK, but did you use to listen to music when you exercised?*   *Yes. Here's a clue – we used to have a pet.*
>
> *Did you use to listen to music when you walked the dog?*   *Yes!*

4.3 Has your taste in music changed?

1 Listening

A In pairs, answer survey questions 1–6. Are your answers similar?

I never listen to CDs. I usually stream music, but I download things that I love.

Neither of us listens to CDs. We both prefer downloading music.

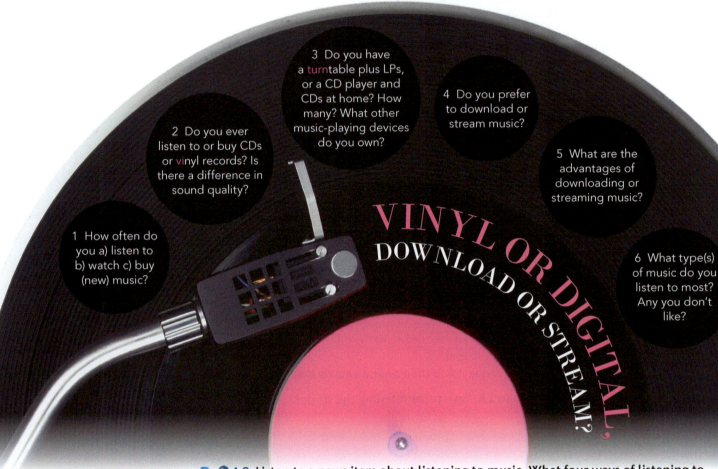

1 How often do you a) listen to b) watch c) buy (new) music?
2 Do you ever listen to or buy CDs or **v**inyl records? Is there a difference in sound quality?
3 Do you have a **turn**table plus LPs, or a CD player and CDs at home? How many? What other music-playing devices do you own?
4 Do you prefer to download or stream music?
5 What are the advantages of downloading or streaming music?
6 What type(s) of music do you listen to most? Any you don't like?

VINYL OR DIGITAL, DOWNLOAD OR STREAM?

Common mistakes
I don't have the same taste ~~like~~ my parents.
  as

B ▶ 4.9 Listen to a news item about listening to music. What four ways of listening to music are mentioned?

C ▶ 4.9 Circle the correct options in 1–6. Listen again to check.
1 The program associates vinyl records with the '50s / '60s–'70s / '80s.
2 Young people today think records are **boring / cool / weird**.
3 Jack Lowenstein prefers to listen to **CDs / MP3s / records**.
4 Sarah Griffith is buying more **punk / rock / pop** records.
5 In the early 2000s, most people used to **buy CDs / buy vinyl / download**.
6 The most important revolution in music is strea**m**ing / vinyl LPs / digital **for**mats.

D 🎤 **Make it personal** Take turns role-playing an interview with your parents or an older family member. Are the types of music they're into and their habits very different from yours? Why (not)?

A: You're the interviewee. Choose to be someone you know well.
B: Ask questions 1–6 in **A**, and follow-up questions.

I usually stream music, but my parents have CDs or they download. They like rap and dance music, but I like contemporary pop.

② Reading

Have your friends collect your records and then change your number, I guess that I don't need that though, Now you're just somebody that I used to know

4.3

A ▶ 4.10 Read tweets 1–8 and choose the correct hashtag for each. Listen to check.
  a #love2download   b #streaming4ever   c #cantbeatCDs   d #vinylisthebest

1 **Peter Ince** @Pince • 3m
Vinyl is back. I can see why – LPs are more authentic – you can hear everything – even the mistakes! Digital songs don't sound as good as LPs.

2 **Claire Sayer** @SayClare • 15m
My parents have thousands of CDs. They're more expensive and not as cool as new music! As soon as it comes out I love to have the newest music on my phone.

3 **Sam Same** @Ssame • 17m
I used to like to sit in front of the turntable for hours and watch the LP go around – it's more relaxing than just listening. I love old music and I love to hear how it was played originally. And the covers are works of art!

4 **NicoleMcArthur** @DrNic • 36m
The quality is better, without a doubt! And no need to pay for a streaming service when you can download the music.

5 **Candy** @Candy1256 • 41m
Digital music is the best – the sound is crisp and clear – with a good quality stereo you can't beat a compact disc – and they're prettier than LPs!

6 **Luke Johnson** @JustLuke12 • 50m
Why would you want to buy music when you can just "rent" it? I stream any music I want at any time using a cheap streaming service – it's much more practical and ecological in every way.

7 **James Marshall** @jamesmarshall • 53m
I love collecting music – how can you collect something that you are just borrowing? Give me something I can hold in my hand – in a digital format that I can put on my shelf and play whenever I want to.

8 **Syreeta Singh** @SySings • 57m
Downloading music is as ridiculous as buying CDs and records. I just want to hear the music I want when I'm in the mood and when it's new. The best way to do that is to use an online service.

B Reread, then match a–h to 1–8 in **A**. Cross (✗) those you disagree with.
  a doesn't want to pay for a streaming service
  b doesn't want to own or collect music
  c likes to collect music
  d likes to hear musicians make mistakes
  e thinks CDs have the best quality
  f says that streaming is better for the environment
  g thinks watching LPs improves the experience of listening
  h thinks CDs cost a lot of money

C In groups of three, talk about opinions a–h in **B**. Which ones do you disagree with? Which one is closest to your opinion?

I don't agree that LPs sound better than digital songs.

D 🎤 **Make it personal** Write a tweet giving your opinion. Share it with the class. Choose the best hashtag for each one.

In my opinion, CDs are the highest quality music.   *The best hashtag for that is " #cantbeatCDs."*

4.4 Do you speak English as often as possible?

1 Grammar Comparatives and superlatives, as ... as

A ▶ 4.11 Listen and write six phrases from the tweets on p. 49. Compare in pairs. Which are comparatives and which are superlatives? How do you pronounce the -est ending? Listen again to check.

B Complete the grammar box. Which group, A–D, is most similar in your language?

1 Complete the chart.

Type	Adjective	Comparative	Superlative
A	big	_____	the biggest
	fast	faster	_____
B	ugly	_____	_____ ugl_____
	crazy	crazier	_____ craz_____
C	expensive	_____	the _____ expensive
	practical	more practical	_____
D	good	_____	_____ best
	bad	worse	_____

(not) as ... as ...

2 Choose the best meaning for a and b.
  a *Downloading music is **as** ridiculous **as** buying CDs and records.*
     Only downloading is ridiculous. / Only buying is ridiculous. / Both are ridiculous.
  b *Digital songs **don't** sound **as** good **as** old LPs.*
     Digital songs sound better. / Digital songs sound worse.

➔ Grammar 4B p.144

> **Common mistakes**
> Cats are smaller than dogs.
> A cat is ~~more small~~ than a dog.
>   **highest**
> Everest is the ~~most high~~ mountain ~~of~~ the world.
>   **in**
>   **as**
> I'm not as big ~~like~~ my brother.

C Classify adjectives 1–14 by their type, A–D, in **A**. Then test a partner.

1 cheap   5 exciting   9 pretty   13 thin
2 com**pli**cated   6 funny   10 rich   14 light
3 con**ve**nient   7 heavy   11 sleepy
4 easy   8 nice   12 small

D In pairs. How many different ways can you compare 1–3? You have one minute for each.

1 a tablet / a laptop   2 your country / the U.S.   3 your language / English / Chinese

> OK, let's think. A tablet is not as big as laptop.   A laptop is more useful than a tablet. That's two.
> But I think a tablet is as useful as a laptop, so that's three.

> The guy on the left looks funnier than the one on the right.

E Do you recognize the actors? Use the adjectives to compare the actors and the cars.

funny
tall
good-looking
successful
young

good
modern
fast
expensive
damaged

F ▶4.12 Listen to 10 examples. How many are the same as yours in **E**?

🎵 *Makes me that much stronger, Makes me work a little bit harder, It makes me that much wiser, So thanks for making me a Fighter* 4.4

G 🟢 **Make it personal** Play *Who? What? Where?*
1. Write answers for a–d on separate pieces of paper.
   a two cities or places in your country?
   b two electrical items?
   c three celebrities?
   d three common objects?
2. In groups of three, put all your answers on the table.
3. Take turns comparing two or more of the items without saying the answers. Who can guess correctly which items are being compared the fastest?

It's smaller, but I think it's more interesting than this other one.   *Temuco and Santiago?*

Not Temuco. It's nearer to the coast.   *Valparaíso and Santiago?*

Correct!

2 Listening

A ▶4.13 Listen to Jason interviewing his grandmother. Then match 1–6 to a–f to make phrases. Listen again to check.

1 get   a dating / learning English / eating healthier food
2 start   b your first pet / job / phone
3 learn to   c the Internet / apps / VR goggles
4 go on   d driving lessons / evening classes / exams
5 take   e a trip alone / a boat / a date
6 use   f ride a bike / swim / get dressed by yourself

B ▶4.13 True (T) or False (F)? Listen to check. What else did you pick up?
1. Grandma was more social as a child.
2. Benji was a little duck.
3. Her father was more patient than her mother.
4. She used to go dancing frequently.
5. She got better at Spanish during her trip to Mexico.
6. She was 15 when she took her driving test.
7. She used the Internet before she started her master's.

C ▶4.14 Ask Jason's questions using the verbs in **A**. Listen to check. Notice which words are stressed and the pronunciation of "did you".

D 🟢 **Make it personal** Do you remember the first time? In pairs, interview your partner using the ideas in **A**. How similar / different are your experiences? Any surprises?

When did you get your first pet?

When I was about six. We got a parrot called Lola.

I wanted to get a pet, but I couldn't because my dad is allergic.

▶ **Common mistakes**

~~How many years did you have~~ *old were you* when you first rode on a motorbike?

4.5 How many pets have you had?

ID Skills Understanding an **an**ecdote

A Read the story as fast as you can and match pictures 1–6 to paragraphs a–f. Then identify the **bold** words / phrases in the pictures.

Weird Sophie

a ☐ The only pet I've ever had was a neurotic cat named Sophie. When Sophie was still a **kitten**, she accidentally drank half a bottle of detergent. Mom and I were worried, of course, so we took her to the **vet** immediately. Sophie didn't die, but she started to behave very strangely after that.

b ☐ For a long time, I was reluctant to let Sophie leave the house, (1)_____ I knew I couldn't keep her inside forever. One day, when she was an adult, I finally decided that it was time for her to be brave and explore the outside world, (2)_____ I opened the front door.

c ☐ Sophie took a few steps and then completely lost her mind. She had never felt grass, (3) _____ she didn't know what to do. She started to jump up and down like crazy and wouldn't stop. Sophie only ran back to the house when she heard Toby's **bark**. Toby was only a small, four–month old **pup**py, (4) _____ Sophie was terrified of him. Yes, my cat was afraid of a baby poodle.

d ☐ Sophie used to sleep in the sink from time to time, (5) _____ , for some mysterious reason, she never noticed when the water was running. One night, I was getting ready to go to bed and went to the other room to answer the phone. When I came back a few minutes later, Sophie was submerged in the sink, hypnotized. Cats are supposed to be afraid of water, right? Not Sophie.

The kitten is the baby cat in picture 4.

e ☐ She also loved to sleep in the washing machine, especially if there were dirty towels inside. One day, Mom didn't know she was there, (6) _____ she almost closed the door and turned on the machine. That was Sophie's second near-death experience.

f ☐ As time progressed, Sophie started to believe that she was a guard dog. She used to follow strangers around the house and **make weird noises**. Trouble is, she couldn't always differentiate between strangers and her owner, (7) _____ she used to **bite** and scratch everyone – including me. Sophie died at the age of 21. Can you believe it? I wonder how she's doing in Cat Heaven. She was a weird, weird cat, (8) _____ she was the only true friend I had during my entire adolescence.

B ▶4.15 Study the use of *so* and *but* in paragraph 1 and complete the rules. Then complete paragraphs 2–6 with *so* or *but*. Listen, check, and repeat the pink-stressed words.

Use _____ for consequences.
Use _____ for contrast.

C In pairs. Cover the text and uncover a line at a time. Guess the next word(s), uncover, and check. How many did you get right?

D 🔵 **Make it personal** In groups, share stories about pets you and your friends have had. Choose your favorite. Use these ideas:

kind of pet?	he or she?	name?	color?	intelligent?	friendly?
noisy?	aggressive?	weird?	"almost human?"	favorite moment?	

⊘ **Common mistakes**

~~He died at the 12 years.~~ *age of 12*

We had a cat when I was a kid. I remember it used to eat grass. *Was it a he or a she?* *A she. She was called Cupcake.*

52

4.5 Have you thought about moving abroad?

in Action Making recommendations

A ▶4.16 Roy and Brenda are at an animal shelter, looking for a pet. Listen and answer 1–3.
1. Who's more reluctant to adopt a pet? Why?
2. What pet does the owner of the shelter recommend initially?
3. What pet does the man want for his daughter?

B ▶4.17 Listen to the rest. True (T) or False (F)? Do you empathize more with him or her?
1. Brenda probably prefers cats to dogs.
2. Poodles bark more than Labradors.
3. Roy and Brenda like the idea of having a house rabbit.

C ▶4.16 & 4.17 Complete 1–4 with *get* or *getting*. Listen again to check and circle the correct option to complete the rule.
1. You should definitely _____ her a pet.
2. Have you considered _____ a cat?
3. Why don't you _____ a dog that's easy to train?
4. Have you thought about _____ a house rabbit?

Use **to + infinitive** / **verb + -ing** after prepositions and certain verbs (*enjoy, consider, keep, mind, finish*).

D ▶4.18 Listen and notice the stressed words. Listen again and repeat. Then, complete the rules with *usually* and *rarely*.
Words that carry the message, like nouns, adjectives, and verbs, are _____ stressed.
Grammar words, like articles, prepositions, and auxiliary verbs, are _____ stressed.

E Complete the email with the correct form of the words and circle *make* or *do*.

To: **Martin** Today at 09:05
Subject: Re: Hello from London All Mail

Hi Martin
Sorry to hear you _____ _____ (**feel**) a bit lonely in London! Not really surprising in such a big city. It can be difficult to **make / do** friends in a new city. You need to **make / do** something positive fast. You should think about _____ (**contact**) Valentin or Sally. Valentin lives _____ (**close**) to you than Sally, but Sally's _____ (**sociable**) than Valentin. Or _____ you _____ (**think**) about _____ (**join**) a club or evening class? Why _____ you _____ (**learn**) French? 😃 You should think about _____ (**visit**) me in Paris! That would definitely **make / do** you feel much _____ (**good**). You might even _____ (**move**) here instead!
Call me soon. I miss your voice. Lots of love Sophie xx

F 🔵 **Make it personal** **Recommendations!** In pairs, role-play situations 1 and 2. Choose one to perform for another pair.

Why don't you ...

Situation 1:
A: You need a new computer to download / watch movies and write short college papers.
B: Compare options (desktops, laptops, tablets ...) and make a recommendation.

Situation 2:
B: You're under a lot of stress and you need to get away for a few days, alone.
A: Compare options (the beach / mountains, a spa / retreat ...) and recommend somewhere.

Common mistakes

Have you thought about ~~to move~~ to another place?
moving

Jake should think about ~~to quit~~ his job.
quitting

I don't enjoy ~~to take~~ care of animals.
taking

🎵 *And I don't mind bleeding, Any old time you keep me waiting, Oh, oh-oh I got a love that keeps me waiting, I'm a lonely boy, I'm a lonely boy*

53

Writing 4   A social media post

 All we know is that we don't know, How it's gonna be, Please brother let it be, Life on the other hand, Won't make us understand, We're all part of the masterplan

A Read the two social media posts and answer 1–3.
1 What's Lucy's request?
2 What's Maya's recommendation? Do you agree?
3 Think of four positive and four negative aspects of working as a server.

B In which paragraphs a–e does Maya:
1 compare two different options? ____
2 suggest an option and discuss its pros and cons based on her own experience? ____
3 suggest a type of job and say why ____
4 make a recommendation? ____
5 talk about the pros and cons of a second option? ____

C Read **Write it right!**, then match the **bold** expressions in Maya's post to uses 1–5.
1 suggest an option
2 introduce a positive (pro)
3 introduce a negative (con)
4 add information
5 make a recommendation

> ✓ **Write it right!**
>
> Use linking expressions to compare options.
> **Introduce a pro:** *The good thing about … is, One advantage is*
> **Introduce a con:** *On the other hand, However*
> **Add another point:** *Another thing is, What's more*

D Complete the post with suitable expressions.

> ¹____ a bar called Valiani. I used to work there. ²____ Valiani is always busy, so you'll never get bored and the manager is nice. ³____, the customers are really friendly and give good tips. ⁴____, it's hard work and it can be tiring. ⁵____, the hours are very long. ⁶____ give them a call?

E Choose two restaurants or cafés you know in your city. List two pros and one con for working in each.

F 🎯 **Make it personal**   Write a post in about 150 words replying to Lucy about working as a server in your city.

Before	Use your notes in **E**. Look back at the post in **A** and underline any words or phrases you want to use in your own post.
While	Follow the paragraph structure of the post in **B**. Include five paragraphs and use appropriate linking expressions.
After	Exchange posts with another student. Do you agree with their recommendations?

Hi Maya,
I'm moving to San José in the fall for my gap year to improve my English and volunteer at a charity for homeless people. I need some part-time work to support myself there, but I don't know what kind of job would fit around my volunteer work. Can you help me with some ideas?
Thanks,
Lucy

Hi Lucy,

a **Have you thought about working** as a server in a restaurant? There are lots of restaurants and bars in the center of the city and they're always looking for new staff. They can usually offer flexible hours, so it's not difficult to fit the work around your studies.

b **One option is** a restaurant called La Cantina. I used to work there in the evenings and at weekends. **The good thing about** La Cantina is it's nearly always full and the work is fast-paced, so you never get bored. The customers are mostly young professionals and they usually give good tips. **Another thing is,** you get free food! **On the other hand,** when you're very busy, it can be stressful and tiring, especially if customers are rude.

c **An alternative is** Café Rio. It's more of a café bar that serves food. **One advantage is,** it's quieter, with a more relaxed atmosphere, so it's not as stressful as working at La Cantina. **What's more,** if you work late the manager gets you a taxi home. **However,** if you're not busy it can sometimes be boring, and the tips are not as good.

d Anyway, you need to decide what you really want from the job. Personally, I think La Cantina is a more enjoyable place to work, but if you just want to earn money and have an easy time, Café Rio is probably the better option.

e **Why don't you** contact both of them and see what they say?

Good luck!
Maya

54

4 Animal instincts

 Café

1 Before watching

A 🔘 **Make it personal** In pairs, define *instinct*. Write an example sentence to illustrate its meaning. Which is the class favorite?

B Rate each job by level of stress, danger, and difficulty, 1–5. Compare and choose the most and least for each category.

Jobs	Stressful	Dangerous	Difficult
an animal trainer			
a cowboy			
an environmental scientist			
a pet shop owner			
a veterinarian			
a zookeeper			

C 🔘 **Make it personal** When you were a child, did you ever want to work with animals? Why (not)?

> When I was little, I used to want to be a …

> Really? That's cool. I wanted to be …

D Using A–C as clues, guess some of the phrases August and Daniel will say.

2 While watching

A In pairs, try to pronounce these words. Then watch to check. Did you guess correctly?

to consider	a gecko	a golden retriever
a labrador	a ranch	surprised totally
a zebra		

B In pairs, try to answer 1–7. Watch again to check.
1 Which five other animals do they mention?
2 Who gets lonely?
3 Whose dog was bigger than him?
4 Who loves big dogs?
5 Which animal was a) Hector b) Gordon c) Morris d) Bruno?
6 Who insists on one condition for getting another pet?
7 Who used to have lots of land before moving to Missouri?
8 Why do you think they choose to go to a shelter and not a pet store?

C Which animal(s) …
1 uses a litter box in their house?
2 lived a) in a big glass tank b) a long life c) outside? (4 answers)
3 was smart and fast but got sold?
4 was the best of its kind – ever?

3 After watching

A 🔘 **Make it personal** In pairs, remember all you can about Daniel and August: their pets, where they lived, and their old jobs. Are you like either of them? If so, how?

> Like Daniel, I used to own a rabbit.

B Check the correct situation for 1–9.

Jobs	Breaking the news	Reacting to news
1 Oh, it's so cool.		
2 That sounds amazing.		
3 You won't believe …		
4 Alright, check this out!		
5 Bummer!		
6 Tell me this is a joke.		
7 Does / Would that bother you?		
8 I'm totally OK with that.		
9 As long as (you clean the litterbox).		

C 🔘 **Make it personal** In pairs, compare pets you or someone you know used to have. What's the best / worst aspect of each one? Would you consider getting a pet now? If so, where from? Any surprises?

> I used to have a big dog but we moved to a smaller apartment. We had to find him a new home.

> What a shame! Did you think about replacing him?

55

R2 Grammar and vocabulary

A **Picture dictionary.** Cover the words on these pages and use the pictures to remember:

page	
32	7 travel words / expressions
39	6 sentences about Sam Same
40	10 adjectives to describe the hotels
44	9 words to describe children and childhood
50	5 comparisons about the actors / cars
52	Sophie's story
158	5 pairs of picture words for the 5 diphthongs

B Look at the chart in **2D** on p. 45. In pairs, take turns miming four *do / make* expressions for your partner to guess.

Are you making your bed?

C Read the product reviews of a new tablet and circle the correct tenses. Have you had any similar experiences with technology?

★★★★★ **Pure Perfection!**
I've had / had my iTab for two weeks and I absolutely love it. It's fast, practical, and not very expensive. Some people say the screen freezes, but that hasn't happened / doesn't happen to me yet. ▾More

★★★☆☆ **It's just OK.**
I have bought / bought my iTab in April and it's an OK product – nothing out of this world. It has never frozen / never freeze or anything, but the battery doesn't last long and it's just too slow. ▾More

★☆☆☆☆ **Worst tablet ever!**
My life has been / was hell since I bought this stupid machine. The iTab is the worst product I have ever bought / ever buy. Guess what, mine has exploded / exploded this morning! Can you believe it? The warranty has already expired / already expires, so now I don't know what to do. ▾More

I've had my laptop for a year and it's been fantastic!

D 👤 **Make it personal** Think of your favorite device. Complete 1–7 with the verbs. In pairs, ask and answer. Can you guess the device?

1 How long _____ this product _____ on the market? (**be**)
2 How long _____ you _____ it? (**have**)
3 Where _____ you _____ it? (**buy**)
4 _____ you _____ it yesterday? (**use**)
5 What _____ you _____ it for? (**use**)
6 _____ it ever _____ working? (**stop**)
7 _____ the product warranty _____ yet? (**expire**)

E 👤 **Make it personal** In pairs, compare 1–6 using some of these adjectives or your own. Give reasons. How many can you agree on?

bad	difficult	easy	expensive	famous
good	healthy	modern	nice	
popular	practical	repetitive	talented	

1 English / Chinese / my first language
2 laptops / tablets / smart watches
3 Japanese / Italian / Mexican food

4 Jennifer Lawrence / Seth Rogan / Chris Pratt
5 Samsung / Apple / Huawei
6 rap / pop / rock

I think English is easier than Chinese.

Yeah, you're right. I think Chinese is the most difficult language to learn. And Spanish is the easiest for me!

F Correct the mistakes. Check your answers in units 3 and 4.

⏱ **Common mistakes**

1 Maybe I'll stay home. It depends of the traffics. (2 mistakes)
2 My sister have never been to Australia. (1 mistake)
3 My son doesn't call me yet. (2 mistakes)
4 I study English during three years. (2 mistakes)
5 How long do they live in Brazil? (1 mistake)
6 David Bowie has died on 2016. (2 mistakes)
7 I learned how to drive when I had 18 years. (2 mistakes)
8 Did you watch a lot of TV when you was younger? (1 mistake)
9 I use to go to the beach on weekends. (1 mistake)
10 Tablets are more small than laptops. (1 mistake)

Skills practice

 'Cos baby, now we've got bad blood, You know it used to be mad love, So take a look what you've done

R2

A ▶R2.1 Listen to six sentences from units 3 and 4. What does each person mean? Circle the correct options in 1–6.
1 I **know** / **am in** Australia.
2 We checked in **a few minutes** / **a long time** ago.
3 The weather is **the same** / **different**.
4 I **am** / **was** an au pair.
5 Digital songs sound **better** / **worse** than old LPs.
6 She **follows** / **followed** strangers around the house.

B ▶R2.1 Read AS R2.1 on p. 167. Listen again and repeat each sentence. Pay attention to the connections.

C ▶R2.2 Read the survey question, then listen and number the sentences, 1–4. There's one extra sentence.

Which sentence best describes your **childhood**?

- Dad, I wasn't kicking him!
- I'm going to wash your mouth out with soap!
- It wasn't my fault!
- Hey, I was watching that!
- Good night, God bless.

D Write two sentences that best describe your childhood. Share them in pairs and try to guess the details.

Hmm ... let's see. I think you used to be a very shy child and ...

E ▶R2.3 Read the travel article and cross out two sentences that shouldn't be there. Listen to check and repeat the **bold** words.

4 Travel Tips
to help you eliminate travel stress

A good vacation is a break from real life, but sometimes vacations can be extremely stressful. Here are some hot ways to help **keep you cool** when traveling:

1 Reducing stress starts before you leave home. Try to book direct flights so that you can escape those awful connections. By doing that, you can **avoid** long **layovers**, missed connections, or the worst problem: canceled flights.

2 Traveling can be stressful on any day, but Mondays and Fridays are a nightmare, especially between 7 and 9 a.m. and 4 and 7 p.m. Friday is actually my favorite day of the week. So do yourself a favor and don't travel then. Period.

3 Bad things are going to happen when you travel, so don't try to control everything. If you're angry, try to **lose** your anger in a calm way. Drink a cup of tea, practice deep breathing, or, if you can, try to find some humor in the situation.

4 Give yourself **plenty of** time for things right from the start: taking a **cab** to the airport, checking in at the airport, boarding your flight, renting a car, and finally checking in at your hotel. Remember you can book online. Remember: the less you **rush**, the less stressful your vacation will be.

F Match the bold words in E to meanings 1–6.
1 stay calm   4 eliminate
2 lots of   5 stops between two flights
3 do things quickly   6 taxi

G **Mini role-play. A:** It's Christmas Eve. You're having lots of problems at the bus station. You're afraid you won't make it to your parents' house. **B:** You're A's mom / dad. Ask for details and try to help.
Use at least two of these phrases:
What do you mean ... ?
Wait a second. Did I hear you say that ...?
You should definitely ... Have you thought about ...?

H ▶R2.4 **Make it personal** Question time!
1 Listen to the 12 lesson titles in units 3 and 4.
2 In pairs, practice asking and answering. Use the book map on p. 2–3. Ask at least two follow-up questions. Try to answer in different ways. Can you have a short conversation about all the questions?

How often do you travel?
When I take a vacation, one or two times a year.
Do you enjoy traveling alone?

57

5 5.1 What would you like to study?

1 Vocabulary and pronunciation
School subjects

A ▶5.1 Read pronunciation rule 1, and try to pronounce the nine school subjects. Listen to the first part of the ad for Marlbury College to check. Then match the subjects to icons a–i.

1 The suffix *-ology* means "the study of," e.g. techn*ology*, e*cology*. The stress is on the third syllable from the end (●●●).

biology geography
history psychology /saɪˈkɒlədʒi/
philosophy languages
sociology chemistry /ˈkɛməstri/
politics

2 Another common suffix is *-ics*: e*thics*, sta*tistics*. The stress is on the second syllable from the end (●●●●).

economics physics
business /ˈbɪznəs/
math(ematics) engineering
computer systems

3 Romance language speakers sometimes find these school subjects hard to pronounce:

art /ɑrt/
(rhymes with *heart*, *smart*)
law /lɔ/
(rhymes with *draw*, *saw*)
literature /ˈlɪtərətʃər/
(rhymes with *si*gnature, adventure)

What's this school subject in English?

B ▶5.2 Read rules 2 and 3, and try to pronounce the nine school subjects. Listen to part 2 of the ad to check. Then match the subjects to icons j–r.

C Test a partner using the icons.

D Put the subjects into the categories in the chart. Compare in groups. Do you all agree? Which subject(s) could be in more than one category?

Arts	Sciences	Social sciences	Others

E ▶5.3 Listen to final part of the the ad and check the items you hear. Which item doesn't the college have?

🎵 Numbers, letters, learn to spell
Nouns, and books, and show and tell
Playtime, we will throw the ball
Back to class, through the hall

5.1

an at**trac**tive **cam**pus   **ba**bysitting fa**cil**ities   **ba**chelor's de**grees** (BA, BS)
evening classes   free public **lec**tures   good teachers and ad**min**istrators
master's degrees (MS, MA)   modern facilities   online classes
vo**ca**tional education

✏️ **Common mistakes**

'*s*   *in*
I have a bachelor degree of history.
Our professor gave an excellent
conference on human rights.
  lecture

F ▶5.3 Listen again and circle the best answers. What else did you hear?
1 You can get a catalog **by phone** / **online** / **in person**.
2 There**'s only one** / **are two** / **are many** professional qualification(s).
3 You **have to** / **don't need to** / **should** go to a classroom.
4 **All** / **Some** / **A lot of** classes are in the evening.
5 **The best classes** / **All the classes** / **Some classes** are free if you're not a student.

G 👥 **Make it personal** Imagine you're choosing a major at Marlbury College. Which factors in **E** are most important and not important for you? In pairs, explain why.

The two most important for me are good teachers and modern facilities, because I want the best education. Evening classes aren't important for me.

Evening classes and babysitting facilities are most important to me! I have a young son and I work during the day.

② Listening

A ▶5.4 ▶️ In pairs, listen to / watch this student. **A:** answer question 1. **B:** answer question 2. Share your answers, change roles, watch, and share again.
1 What did you learn about her and her personal life?
2 What did you learn about her university life and career plans?

B ▶5.4 ▶️ Listen / Watch again and order Zena's words, 1–9.
20 ☐   England ☐   Olympic Village ☐
Brighton ☐   London ☐   Queen Mary University ☐
British ☐   Marshall ☐   south coast ☐

C ▶5.4 ▶️ Listen again. Are 1–8 True (T) or False (F)? Correct the false ones.
1 Zena chose European Literature because she loves reading and writing.
2 She goes home to get her washing done and sleep.
3 It's one of two London universities with a campus.
4 It's very cosmopolitan and people are friendly.
5 Her boyfriend's French and he's called Didier.
6 She sometimes finds her major a bit boring.
7 The teachers can be strict, and are often difficult.
8 After university, she'd like to do one of three jobs.

✏️ **Common mistakes**
      on
Lima is in the coast.

D 👥 **Make it personal** **Life choices.**
1 In pairs, find out:
   • why your partner chose her or his school / university / current job;
   • the positive and negative aspects;
   • any future plans.
2 Make a simple video like Zena's to introduce yourself, your school or **work**place, and any career plans.

Why did you choose to study at this school?

Because it's close to home and it has a great reputation. And you?

59

5.2 What do you have to do tonight?

① **Vocabulary** Class activities

A ▶5.5 Match classroom activities 1–10 to examples a–j. Listen to 10 extracts to check.

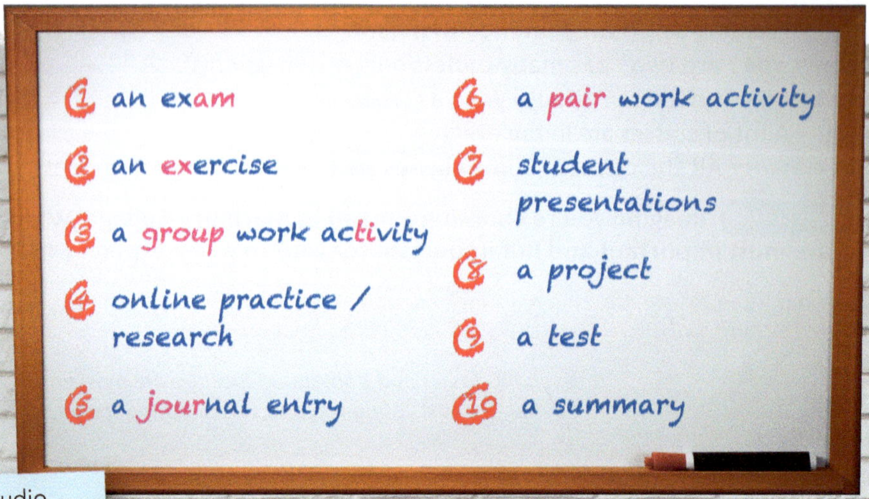

1 an exam
2 an exercise
3 a group work activity
4 online practice / research
5 a journal entry
6 a pair work activity
7 student presentations
8 a project
9 a test
10 a summary

a In your journal, write or record an audio about how you felt about class today. What were the things you understood? Write a question that you have for next class. ☐

b In a group of four, discuss the movie extract that we watched and find two things that you liked about it and two things you didn't like. ☐

c You have two minutes to write the past tense of these verbs. Then hand your answers to me. ☐

d You have ONE HOUR. Answer three out of five questions. You should spend about 20 minutes on each question. ☐

e Use PowerPoint to present your family to the class. ☐

f Write a one-paragraph summary of the last chapter of the book. ☐

g Talk about your plans for the weekend. Ask your partner what she or he is going to do. Then answer your partner's questions. ☐

h Complete these sentences with an appropriate word from the list below. Then listen to check. ☐

i Search online for a song line that you like featuring the words "used to." Bring a recording of it to the next class. ☐

j Houses: We'll look at the construction of houses in different parts of the world and we'll consider the materials used and why. ☐

B Which of the activities in **A** do you have in:
1 your English classes?
2 any other classes you take?

> In English class, we have pair work and group work activities. But we don't have these in my economics class.

C 🔵 **Make it personal** Which activities in **A** do / did you:
1 find useful?   2 hate?   3 love?

> I hated taking exams in college. It was so boring.

2 Which homework activities do you find most useful for learning English?

> I enjoy looking for examples of grammar in songs.

> I enjoy watching clips from movies, first with subtitles, then without.

60

2 Grammar Obligation and prohibition

Will we ever learn? We've been here before, It's just what we know, Stop your crying, baby, It's a sign of the times, We gotta get away

5.2

A ▶ 5.6 Listen to two students and answer 1–3.
1. How many obligations do they discuss?
2. What are they?
3. Who's the better student, Mark or Candy?

B ▶ 5.6 Listen again and complete Mark's notes for a friend.

Ms. Cosby's class:
You've _____ come to every class.
You _____ write a paper for _____ .
You _____ arrive late.
You _____ take notes. It's all _____ .

C Complete the grammar box with the verbs from **B**.

Obligation
Use _____ or _____ for obligations.
I've got to or *I gotta* is more informal.

Prohibition
Use _____ for prohibition. (This means it is not permitted.)

No obligation
Use _____ when you can do something if you want, but it's not essential.

▶ **Grammar 5A** p. 146

Common mistakes
doesn't have
He ~~hasn't~~ to work today.
do
You can't ~~doing~~ that here!
We gotta ~~to~~ go now.

D ▶ 5.7 Circle the correct options in the dialogue. Listen to check.
Mark: What are you doing tonight?
Candy: **I've got to / I got to** study, because I have a test tomorrow.
Mark: Another one! That's too bad! Do you **have got / have** to study on Saturday too?
Candy: Uh, I **can't / don't have** to study on Saturday, but I want to, because I really need to get good grades this time. Why?
Mark: Well, I wanted to invite you to a party on Saturday. Should be a good one!
Candy: Oh! Well, my mom gets worried so I **have to / can't** stay out later than 12, but I could go for a while. But **you'll have to / won't have to** ask my mom, and persuade her.
Mark: OK, pass me over. Hello, Mrs. McCormack. This is Mark.
Mrs. M.: Hello, Mark. Busy studying?
Mark: Yes, you know me! Er, can Candy come to a party with me on Saturday?
Mrs. M.: Sure, but she **doesn't have to / has to** be home by 12, please. I really worry if she stays out too late.
Mark: Not a problem, Mrs. McCormack. I **have to / can't** drive my dad's car after 11, so I have to be home by then, anyway.

E 🗣 **Make it personal** What are "the rules" where you live?
1. List five things you have to do and five things you (or others you live with) can't do.
2. Compare in groups. Which "rules" are the most restrictive? Who has the easiest and most difficult time?

I have to tell my mom when I'm going to be late, and I can't borrow the car if she needs it.

Well, I've got to pay all the bills and do all the shopping. I can't leave my kids alone at home.

My son can't use his PS4 during the week, only at weekends. He hates it!

5.3 Are you a good student?

1 Reading

A Read the college handout and match summaries 1–8 to the eight students.
1. Ask a classmate to summarize if you can't go to a class.
2. You need to study regularly and frequently.
3. You can't prepare for an exam in one night.
4. You shouldn't be timid or quiet if things are hard to understand.
5. It's important to be punctual and look interested.
6. You should be interested in what you study.
7. Make sure you're familiar with all the course program.
8. Teachers like students who prepare for class and get involved.

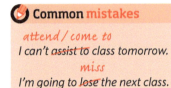

Common mistakes
attend / come to
I can't ~~assist to~~ class tomorrow.
miss
I'm going to ~~lose~~ the next class.

Streetway College

How to pass a college class – here's what our students say

"Take classes because you want to, not because you have to. You have to attend a lot of classes, so it's much better if you like the subject!" *Katia Browning* ☐

"Be on time and pay attention – that's really important! Your teacher will notice if you're always late or day-dreaming." *Jerome Manzanillo* ☐

"Ask questions when something isn't clear. Your instructor is there to help, so don't be shy about asking questions in class." *Charles Murphy* ☐

"You don't have to participate if you don't want to, but your teacher will notice you if you do volunteer or ask questions, and you're prepared. Research the next lesson – or at least take a look at it – before class starts." *Natalie Krazinski* ☐

"You have to read the syllabus. This is the most important document you'll receive from your professor." *George Smith* ☐

"You have to find time every day to study. A little and often is the best way. You don't have to study at the same time every day, but you can't leave it until half an hour before class." *Muhammed Burton* ☐

"If you miss a class, the easiest way to find out what you missed and catch up is to talk to someone who's also in that class." *Konstantina Spanos* ☐

"If you know you have to do an assignment, start working on it early. If you know you have a test, prepare for it early. You can't learn everything the night before an exam." *Charlotte Spalding* ☐

I can't choose between these two.
Which ones?

B ▶ 5.8 Listen to and reread the handout, and circle the four most important tips for you. In pairs, compare. Can you agree which two are the most important?

C 🙂 **Make it personal** List five tips for a new student at your English school. Read them out. Score a point for each original tip. How many points did you score?

Don't worry about making mistakes. Fluency is more important than mistakes and you have to make mistakes to learn!

Listen to some English every day.

2 Grammar too / enough, too much / too many

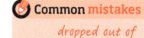
I'm not too shy to show I love you, I got no regrets. I love you much too much to hide you, this love ain't finished yet. So, baby, whenever you're ready, When you're ready come and get it, Na na na na

5.3

A ▶5.9 Why do people drop out of school? Listen and match ex-students' answers 1–4 to photos a–d.

a ☐

b ☐

c ☐

d ☐

Common mistakes
dropped out of
My sister ~~abandoned~~ college at ~~the~~ 17 ~~years~~.

B ▶5.9 In pairs, listen again for three phrases in each answer using *too* and *enough*. Pause after each answer to write the phrases.

C Study the nine phrases in **B** in AS 5.9 on p. 168 and complete the rules with *before, after, many, more, much*.

1. *Enough* means "sufficient" and goes _____ an adjective but _____ a noun.

   too + adjective = _____ than necessary: *This room's too hot.*

2. Use *too* + _____ for U nouns.
3. Use *too* + _____ for C nouns.

➔ Grammar 5B p. 146

Common mistakes
a lot of
I have ~~too many~~ friends.
enough
I'm not ~~enough~~ tall to reach the clock.

The first one is definitely work – unfortunately we don't get a salary for going to school!

D Complete the article with *too* or *enough*. Do the reasons refer to school (S), work (W), or both (B)?

Why do people quit?

The top 10 reasons why people drop out of school or quit their jobs.

a Their salaries aren't high *enough*.
b They don't have good communication or a strong _____ relationship with the boss.
c They don't have _____ money to continue what they're doing.
d Their workload is _____ heavy.
e They want better benefits like health insurance.
f They feel _____ isolated and homesick.
g They don't have _____ self-discipline.
h They have _____ many personal problems.
i They're not happy with the workplace.
j They're not interested _____ in what they're doing.

E ▶5.10 Listen to the conversation and order the reasons in **D** 1–5 for quitting a job (W) and 1–5 for dropping out of school (S).

F 🟢 **Make it personal** In groups of three, compare people you know who quit a job or dropped out of school. Was it for one of the reasons in **D**? Do your stories have happy endings?

A friend of mine dropped out of school last year because he really missed his family. He used to drive 200 kilometers every weekend to see them, so he never had enough time to study.

So did he go to a different school or get a job?

He got a great job near home!

63

5.4 What will you do when you pass this course?

1 Grammar Zero and first conditional

A ▶ 5.11 Listen to two conversations and complete emails 1 and 2.

1 To: All managers — Today at 10:23

Research shows that if employees _____ unhappy with their pay, they _____ the job well, or they find another job.

Note: We need to raise salaries. If we _____ more, our best employees _____.

2 To: Heads of Department — Today at 14:55

A recent study shows that if students _____ a lot of classes, they _____ of school.

Note: We need to check on our students who miss a lot of classes. If they _____ a lot of classes, they _____ of college.

⏵ **Common mistakes**

If I will go on vacation, I'll buy you a souvenir.

If you can't laugh at yourself, no problem. I'll laugh at you! That's what friends are for.

B Read about conditional tenses, then complete the rules in the grammar box.

If is one of the most common words in English because it's used to express conditions.
 Zero = *If you don't have photo ID, you can't fly.*
 First = *If we leave now, we'll arrive on time.*
Zero conditionals are generalizations. The speaker thinks it's a fact.
First conditionals refer to a specific future event that is probable or certain.
Both conditionals are formed and used in the same way as in Romance langauages.

Zero conditional
If you play sports, you meet athletic people.
If clause = _____ tense, result clause = _____ tense.

First conditional
If you play soccer tomorrow, you won't meet my best friend.
If clause = _____ tense, result clause = _____ tense.

You can invert the clauses without changing the meaning. When the *if* clause comes first, use a comma and rising intonation to indicate that there is more to come.

⏵ Grammar 5C p. 146

C Match the sentence halves. Do the sentences refer to general or specific situations? Write zero conditional (Z) or first conditional (F) for each sentence.

How to stay friends

Why do friends stop being friends? Here's our top advice to stay friends.

1 If you have things in common
2 You'll find it difficult to be friends
3 People stop being friends
4 If your friend complains a lot
5 Friends stay together
6 If your best friend gets married

a if they laugh a lot together.
b you'll find it difficult to stay friends.
c you have a lot of things to talk about.
d if you have different priorities.
e you won't want to see that friend.
f if they have a big fight.

D 🎤 Make it personal Do you agree with 1–6 in **C**? Give your own examples.

I don't agree with 6. My best friend got married and we still talk all the time.

2 Reading

5.4

> We've got to hold on to what we've got,
> 'Cause it doesn't make a difference if we make it or not,
> We've got each other and that's a lot for love
> We'll give it a shot, We're half way there, Livin' on a prayer.

A Read the brochure and match headings a–f to paragraphs 1–6.
- a Make work important
- b Show interest and appreciation
- c Be a good example
- d Help careers grow
- e Ask questions
- f Give people a chance to grow

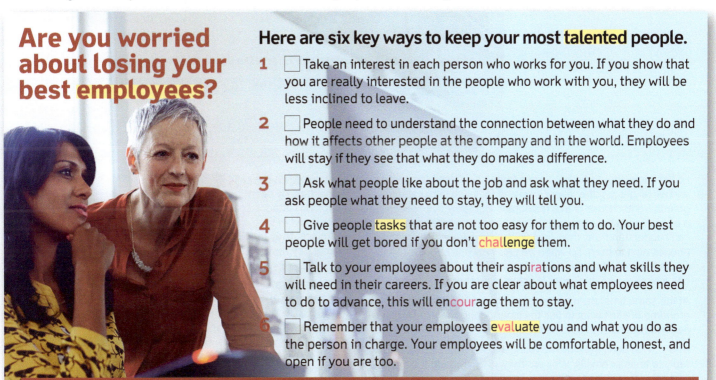

Are you worried about losing your best employees?

Here are six key ways to keep your most talented people.

1. ☐ Take an interest in each person who works for you. If you show that you are really interested in the people who work with you, they will be less inclined to leave.

2. ☐ People need to understand the connection between what they do and how it affects other people at the company and in the world. Employees will stay if they see that what they do makes a difference.

3. ☐ Ask what people like about the job and ask what they need. If you ask people what they need to stay, they will tell you.

4. ☐ Give people tasks that are not too easy for them to do. Your best people will get bored if you don't challenge them.

5. ☐ Talk to your employees about their aspirations and what skills they will need in their careers. If you are clear about what employees need to do to advance, this will encourage them to stay.

6. ☐ Remember that your employees evaluate you and what you do as the person in charge. Your employees will be comfortable, honest, and open if you are too.

B ▶5.12 Listen, reread, and match the highlighted words in **A** to their meanings.
1 employees   a naturally good at something
2 talented   b judge
3 tasks   c people paid to do a job
4 challenge   d give them a chance to test themselves
5 evaluate   e jobs or activities

C Do 1–6 encourage you to stay (S) at your job or leave (L)? In pairs, say why.
1 "What's your name again? I don't think I know you. Have we met before?"
2 "What you do will really help other people and make their lives easier."
3 "How are you feeling today? Is there anything I can do to make you more comfortable?"
4 "I have something really easy for you to do. You don't have to think at all."
5 "I think there are a lot of opportunities for you in this company."
6 "I'm not going to tell you why I made that decision. You'll have to guess."

I won't stay in my job if the boss can't even remember my name!

D Think about the places where you work, study, or socialize. What are its good and bad points?

A bad point at my school is that classes are really big and it's difficult to ask questions.

That's a shame. At my job, my boss is very friendly and he talks to me every day.

At my gym, the manager is really aggressive and everybody is afraid of her.

E 🔵 **Make it personal** Think of two changes you could suggest to your boss, school principal, or the manager of a local business or club. Compare in groups. Who has the best suggestions?

The owner of our local soccer club doesn't invest enough. If he doesn't buy some new players, we'll get relegated.

5.5 How do you usually get in touch?

Skills Understanding references

My grandma always calls on the landline. She still doesn't know how to use a smartphone.

A Think about your family and friends. Who prefers communicating …
1 face-to-face?
2 by phone (audio)?
3 by video call?
4 by email?
5 by text or instant messenger?
6 by social media?

B Read Maria's blog and complete the chart. Do you agree with these generalizations?

Generation	Born	Prefer to communicate
Millenials	after 1980	1
2	1965–1980	3
Boomers	4	5

I don't know about you, but I come from a big Greek family and we all get together every weekend for lunch either at my grandparents' house or in a restaurant. But lately I've noticed a bit of tension between **us** (1). For example, my grandparents can't understand why their grandkids always have to have their phones next to **them** (2) when we eat. Why don't people talk to each other or just do one thing at a time? And when everyone has a phone, why don't people actually call **them** (3) anymore?

At the same time, my mom and dad don't understand why grandma doesn't want to use the smartphone **they**'ve (4) given her and continues to use her old one.

And … **I** (5) don't get why my younger sister and cousins don't reply to texts or emails. Why are **they** (6) so rude to their family, when they're talking to their friends all the time on social media?

Then last week at work, we had online training about communication across generations, and **it** (7) all seems to make a bit more sense now. **It** (8) said that one of the biggest differences is the way "millenials" (that's anybody born after about 1980, like my sister and cousins) see technology compared with previous generations. For **them** (9), **it** is totally normal and an essential part of their identity. **They** (10) automatically use social media like Facebook and Instagram. Even Skype seems old-fashioned to them! That's why my sister won't put down her cell phone. It really seems like **it**'s (11) attached to her body! In the workplace, **they**'re (12) the majority now.

Then there's "Gen X" – the generation born between 1965 and 1980, like my parents. For **them** (13), technology is great for practical things like shopping, banking online, or making arrangements with friends. But **they** (14) don't message their friends just to chat or gossip as much as **we** (15) do. For **them** (16), email is the way to communicate, especially for anything important.

Finally, of course, there are much older people (like my grandparents, the so-called "boomers", born before 1965), who prefer to talk on the phone or even meet in person.

So, now I think I know why we sometimes misunderstand each other. Millenials know how to get things done quickly, but older generations want to focus more on personal relationships.

What do **you** (17) think? Have you seen this in your family too? I'd love to hear your experiences.

C ▶5.13 Listen, reread, and say who or what the **bold** pronouns 1–17 refer to.
us¹ = all of Maria's family

D ▶5.14 Listen to Zack and Vicky at work. Which of them do you think is older? Why?

E ▶5.14 Listen again and complete Zack's email.

Common mistakes
Please see the documents ~~annexed~~.
attached

Hi all
Our next staff meeting will be on _____ at _____ a.m. in the conference _____.
Attached is the draft agenda. Please send me any _____ for the agenda by the end of the day tomorrow.
See you there,
Zack

F **Make it personal** In groups, compare your generation with the ones before and after it. What are the biggest differences?

My parents watch a lot more TV than I do.   *Yeah, we usually watch shows online.*

66

5.5 Do you often take risks?

 But I've got a blank space, baby, And I'll write your name, Boys only want love if it's torture Don't say I didn't say, I didn't warn ya

ID in Action Giving warnings and making promises

A Imagine what these people are saying. Write speech bubbles for each cartoon.

 a

 b

 c

 d

> **Common mistakes**
> Whatever
> ~~Do what~~ you do, don't do that!

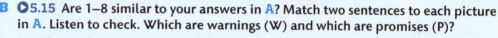

B ▶5.15 Are 1–8 similar to your answers in **A**? Match two sentences to each picture in **A**. Listen to check. Which are warnings (W) and which are promises (P)?

1 Whatever you do, don't eat that ice cream. If you do, you'll have to go to your room!
2 I won't buy you a new bike if you don't get good grades. You'd better do your homework.
3 Watch out! If you're not careful, you'll fall in.
4 Be careful. If you don't improve your work, you'll be fired.
5 If you stay late, I'll give you the day off tomorrow.
6 If you help me get in, I'll row the boat.
7 If you eat all your dinner, I'll give you some ice cream.
8 If you finish your homework, I'll take you to the movies.

C Complete these expressions. Then make warnings and promises for pictures 1 and 2 using the expressions and your own ideas.

Warnings	Promises
Be _____!	If you (don't) …, I'll …
Watch / Look _____!	If you (don't) …, I won't …
Don't move!	
You'd _____ (not) do that!	
Whatever you do, don't (forget to) …	

D **Make it personal** Write captions for photos 1–3. Write a warning and a promise for each and share with the class. Which is the best caption?

> The boy in picture 1 is probably saying, "If you sit, you'll get a treat."

Writing 5 A personal statement

 You know that I could use somebody, Someone like you, and all you know, and how you speak

A Read Matt's statement and number questions a–c in the order he answers them, 1–3.
  a What do you want to study, and why? ☐
  b How would you describe yourself and your interests? ☐
  c What useful experience do you have? ☐

B Are 1–5 relevant (R) or not relevant (NR) to Matt's statement? Which paragraph, a–c, would you put the relevant sentences in?
  1 I worked in a hotel in France for three months.
  2 My parents were both teachers before they bought the hotel.
  3 I'm very good at playing video games.
  4 I like taking courses that are about physical health.
  5 I want to know more about sustainability.

C Read **Write it right!**, then do 1 and 2.
  1 Look at the highlighted expressions in Matt's statement and circle the six verb +-ing forms that follow them.
  2 Underline seven more -ing forms in the text. Which
    • two are adjectives?
    • three follow a preposition?
    • two follow a verb?

> ✓ **Write it right!**
>
> To emphasize your abilities in a personal statement, use these expressions to add more information:
>   *along with, apart from, as well as, in addition to, on top of (that).*
> These expressions
>   • can be followed by a noun, a pronoun, or a verb in the -*ing* form.
>   • can come at the start or in the middle of a sentence, but *On top of that* usually comes only at the start.

D Rewrite 1–5 using the expressions in parentheses.
  1 I have a weekend job in a restaurant. I also deliver pizza. **(along with)**
  2 Ramona speaks Arabic and Russian. She is also fluent in Spanish. **(in addition to)**
  3 I enjoy running marathons. I also teach karate. **(apart from)**
  4 Alana works full-time. She also goes to college in the evenings. **(on top of)**
  5 I wrote a paper on ecotourism. I also gave a presentation. **(as well as)**

E 🔊 **Make it personal** Write a personal statement in 150–200 words to apply for a course you'd like to study.

Before	Brainstorm your positive qualities, relevant interests and experience, and the reasons you'd like to take the course.
While	Write your statement in three paragraphs that answer questions 1–3 in **A**. Use a polite, formal tone and include the five expressions from **Write it right!**
After	Exchange statements with two other students. Would you give them both a place on the course?

Personal statement: Matt Harper

a I'm a serious and hardworking person with an inquiring mind. I enjoy reading and learning about other cultures, as well as learning languages – I speak French, German, and Spanish. I'm also extremely sociable and I'm interested in meeting people from other countries.

b My family own a hotel and I have a lot of experience in many different roles. In addition to working in the kitchen and being a server, I have also been a receptionist and night manager. On top of that, I'm fascinated to see how hotels operate in other places. Apart from doing research into the industry, I have learned a lot about running a sustainable business. I'm passionate about conservation in tourism, along with providing top-quality food and accommodation.

c I want to study for a Master's in Sustainable Tourism Management, as well as working part-time in my family's business. I believe in developing my knowledge of the hospitality business and my ambition is to manage my own eco-hotel. This course sounds like the perfect way for me to combine my passion for tourism and travel with a career that I love and have experience in.

5 Man and cyberman!

1 Before watching

A Match four of words 1–6 to photos a–d.
1 to blot
2 a crow
3 a deadline
4 napkins
5 a towel
6 a schedule

B Match words 1–6 in A to definitions a–f.
a a bird which sings badly
b a plan of events and the times they should happen
c paper items you get with takeaway food
d the end date for something
e what you do after spilling (liquid) on clothes
f you use it to dry yourself after a shower

C Use photo a in A to imagine Genevieve and Rory's conversation.

Maybe she saw his jacket was dirty and offered to clean it?

2 While watching

A Watch up to 1:17 to check your answer in 1C. Did you imagine correctly? How upset was Rory?

B Complete what Genevieve says to 1) apologize and 2) respond to a compliment. What's the opposite of *coordinated*? Watch again to check.
1 I'm sorry, I d_ _ _ _ _ _ m_ _ _ _ t_ _.
2 T_ _ _ _ _ _ s_ _ _ _ _ _.

C Watch up to 2:37. True (T) or False (F)? Correct the false ones.
1 August's finished his robot project.
2 Genevieve wants a website to get a bigger audience.
3 Genevieve thinks August will be able to help.
4 August doesn't want to involve Rory in the website.
5 Genevieve's not in a hurry and Rory's not busy.
6 August offers to rearrange his schedule to help.

D Imagine how the episode ends. Then order these events logically, 1–7. Watch to check. Were you right?
☐ August tells him not to worry if he can't do it.
☐ August offers to help him build the website.
[1] August apologizes for suggesting Rory can help.
☐ Genevieve loves the website and wants to thank Rory.
☐ Rory's too tired to go to Genevieve's gig after not sleeping all week.
☐ Rory regrets his offer as he's too busy.
☐ Rory says August should invent a "Robot Rory."

3 After watching

A Match *get* expressions 1–6 to meanings a–f.
1 What can I get you?   a be given
2 Can I get a coffee?   b bring
3 Got any napkins?   c Do you have
4 I can get more people to come. d find and bring
5 Let me get my ideas.   e persuade
6 I haven't been getting enough sleep. f receiving

B Check 1–6. Zero or first conditional?

		0	1st
1	If I don't sleep enough, I sing like a crow.		
2	If I have a website, I can get more people to come to the café.		
3	If there's someone who's great at building websites, it's you.		
4	If I have a website, I can get more publicity.		
5	If he rearranges his schedule, he'll be able to work on her website.		
6	If I build Genevieve's website too, I'll have to stay up all night.		

C Match expressions 1–6 to their opposites a–f.
1 exhausted   a don't tell me
2 let me know   b unite and liberate
3 I've done enough   c asleep
4 awake   d fresh and relaxed
5 you're only human   e it's the least I can do
6 divide and conquer f try to do the impossible

D Summarize the episode and explain the title.

E 🔵 **Make it personal** In groups, discuss 1 and 2. Anything in common?
1 Does your behavior change when you
   a) have too many projects?
   b) don't get enough sleep?
2 Have you ever volunteered but then regretted it?

I don't feel sociable when I'm tired.   *Once, I offered to help a friend move house and ended up in hospital!*

69

6

6.1 Have you ever been to Florida?

1 Vocabulary Leisure time activities

A ▶6.1 Use the clues to complete the verb phrases, then match them to photos 1–9. Listen to an ad to check. In pairs, use the photos to share your experiences. Any surprises?

bowl	camp	climb /klaim/	club	dive
fish	hang out	hike	work out	

☐ go __ __ s __ __ __ __ __
☐ go h __ __ __ __ __ __
☐ go __ __ __ p __ __ __ __
☐ go __ i __ __ __ __ __
☐ go __ __ __ l __ __ __ __

☐ go __ __ i __ __ __ __ __ __
☐ go __ __ __ __ b __ __ __ __
☐ __ __ n __ __ __ __ with friends
☐ __ __ __ __ __ __ __ __

I've worked out many times, but never on the beach.

I hang out with friends all the time. A group of us ride our bikes every Sunday.

Common mistakes

~~Let's go to club!~~ *clubbing*

~~Yesterday I ran with some friends.~~ *went running*

I've been surfing but I've never been parasailing.
~~I surfed but I never went to parasail.~~

B ▶6.1 Listen again and write down the 13 adjectives you hear. Have you been to Florida? Where would you most like to go in the U.S.?

> *I haven't been to Florida, but I'd love to go!*
>
> *When I was a kid, we went to Orlando. I remember being in a great theme park.*

🎵 *I got my hands up, They're playin' my song, I know I'm gonna be OK, Yeah, it's a party in the USA, Yeah, it's a party in the USA*

6.1

C In pairs, try to divide the activities in **A** into two groups: high risk (H) and low risk (L). Does the whole class agree?

> *I guess going bowling is usually safe.*   *Not always! Once, I pulled a muscle bowling.*

⚠ **Common mistakes**

~~Climbing is a high risk activity.~~
~~The climbing is an activity of high risk.~~
~~Skating~~
~~To skate~~ is fun and good exercise.
Use the verb + *-ing* as a noun.

D 👤 **Make it personal** Read, then do the Florida visitor questionnaire. In pairs, compare and find at least two similarities and two differences between you.

Visitor Feedback

Here in Florida, we want our visitors to have the best possible time, so we'd like to know exactly what you love doing on vacation.

Which are your two favorite:
- **out**door activities? *going hiking*
- **in**door activities?
- cold weather activities?
- warm weather activities?
- exciting or adventurous activities?
- child-friendly activities

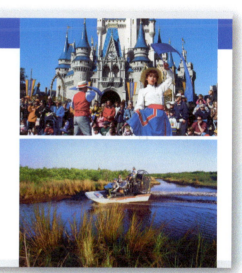

> *My favorite outdoor activities are going hiking and swimming.*   *Mine are sunbathing and swimming in a pool.*

② Grammar *Go* + gerund (verb + *-ing*)

A ▶6.2 Listen and check the activities from **1A** that Rosie did in Florida.

B ▶6.2 Listen again. True (T) or False (F)? What else did you pick up?
1. They caught a fish.
2. They saw four different animals.
3. The rain came on the last day of their vacation.
4. They enjoyed the end of the vacation.
5. The tent survived the rain well.
6. Her friend seems very **jea**lous of her holiday.

C Read the examples and complete the grammar box.

> *I always go shopping on Friday.*   *I'm going skating tonight.*
> *I went skiing last year.*   *What are you doing at the moment? I'm sightseeing.*
>
> **True (T) or False (F)?**
> 1. Verbs like 1–7 in **1A** can be used with or without *go*.
> 2. The *-ing* form after *go* is a noun.
> 3. Two of the examples are in the present continuous.
> 4. *Go* + *-ing* is often used for routines, completed, and future actions.
> 5. Use *go* + *-ing* to talk about what someone is doing right now.
>
> ➡ **Grammar 6A** p.148

D 👤 **Make it personal** Which parts of Rosie's vacation sound like fun? What would you do in Florida for a week? In groups, compare. Who has the same ideas as you?

> *The first part doesn't sound like fun to me. I hate camping.*   *Really? It's not so bad if there are showers and a restaurant at the camp site.*

6.2 Would you like to try hang gliding?

① Vocabulary Verbs of movement

A ▶6.3 Listen to the ad for an extreme sports company. Number the verbs in the order you hear them, 1–12.

☐ climb _____   [1] get _____   ☐ race _____
☐ dive _____   ☐ get _____   ☐ run _____
☐ fall _____   ☐ hang _____   ☐ swim _____
☐ fly _____   ☐☐ jump _____

B ▶6.3 Match one or two verbs from **A** to each of photos 1–5. Listen to check, and write the preposition you hear after each verb in **A**.

C ◉ Make it personal **Mime against the clock!** In teams, use the verbs and prepositions in **A** and take turns miming actions for your team to guess. Which team can mime and guess them all the fastest?

Are you getting into the pool?   No.   *I know. Are you getting into the bath?*   Yes!

Common mistakes

~~I ran to the pool and dived into.~~ *the water*

~~I ran to the pool and dived into.~~ *in*

dived into the water = prepositional phrase (preposition + noun).
dived in = adverb.

2 Reading

🎵 *I came to get down, So get out of your seat and jump around! Jump around! Jump around! Jump around! Jump up, jump up and get down! Jump! Jump! Jump! Jump!*

6.2

A ▶6.4 **Read and complete the website with these extreme sports. Listen to check. Notice which part of each compound word is stressed. Which word is different?**

bungee jumping   **cliff** diving   **hang** gliding
snowboarding   underwater **hock**ey

THIS WEEKEND: Five wild extreme sports!

1 | _____

It's kind of like surfing or skateboarding, but you do it on snow. For those who can't **stand** waiting for the good weather to go surfing again – this is a good option.

2 | _____

Do you like holding your breath? Divers who miss being in the water during the winter months, love this. When the outside water is too cold for diving, you just need a **snor**kel, a stick, and a puck, and you're ready to dive into to the local swimming pool for a game!

3 | _____

How about this? You run off the edge of a cliff or any very high place and hang from a bar with a sail inside a kind of big bag and fly like that. If you feel like flying – without a plane – this may be for you!

4 | _____

A person goes to the top of a steep cliff and dives off into the water below – how about that! Only for those who practice diving a lot! They say it's amazing!

5 | _____

Perhaps you prefer jumping off a bridge, building, or mountain attached to a thick e**las**tic cord that **boun**ces you up and down. Can you imagine doing this? A lot of people love it!

B Read again and name the sport or sports 1–6 refer to.
1 People do it when it's cold.
2 It involves flying.
3 It takes place in water.
4 You don't need any special equipment.
5 You need to jump from a great height.
6 It's a game.

C Read the rule then name the objects in the photos. Does your language have compound nouns?

Compound words are combinations: two words combine to make a new one, e.g. *boy* + *friend* = *boyfriend*. There's no strict pronunciation rule, but the main stress is usually on the part that describes the word, e.g. *boy*friend.

D 🔵 **Make it personal** In groups. Which is the most and the least dangerous of the sports? Why? Which activities would you like to do and which would you like to watch? Why? Who is the most adventurous person in your group?

> *I think hang gliding is the most dangerous because if you fall, you'll probably die!*

> *I'd like to try cliff diving because I like diving at the pool.*

> *Not me! I'd be too scared. But I'd like to watch it.*

75

6.3 Do you feel like going out tonight?

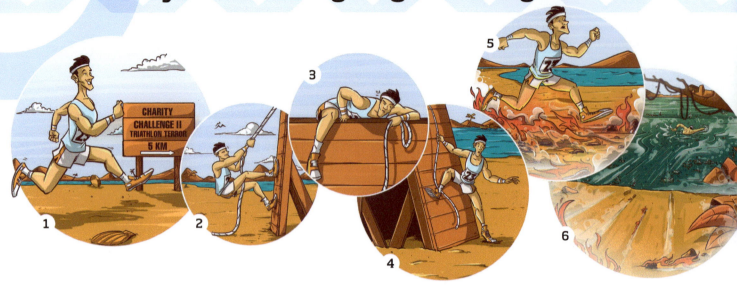

1 Vocabulary Prepositions of movement

A ▶6.5 Match the prepositions to pictures 1–12. Listen to a conversation about the event to check. Which six prepositions are exact opposites?

across ☐   along ☐   around ☐   down ☐   into ☐   out of ☐
over ☐   past ☐   through ☐   towards ☐   under ☐   up ☐

B In pairs, retell the story. **A:** as Charlie; **B:** as a TV commentator.

> First I ran along the beach …

> And away he goes! Now he's running …

C 🔵 Make it personal   In pairs. Which of the race activities can / can't you do?

> I can run five kilometers along a beach.

> Really? I don't think I can – it's difficult to run on sand.

2 Listening

A ▶6.6 Listen to Martin and Jo discussing their plans and note the activities they like (✓) or don't like (✗).

	Martin	Jo
surfing		
swimming		
bowling		
going to the movies		

⚠ Common mistakes

~~swimming~~
I can't stand ~~to swim~~.
~~playing~~
We adore ~~to play~~ basketball.
~~cooking~~
I'm responsible for ~~to cook~~ the dinner.
~~watching~~
She enjoys ~~to watch~~ Netflix in the evenings.

See Grammar 6A p. 148 for a list of verbs followed by gerunds.

B ▶6.6 Listen again and complete 1–8. Whose weekend plan would you prefer?
1 I don't feel like _____ hot and tired.
2 I don't really enjoy _____.
3 I really miss _____ to the beach.
4 I adore _____.
5 You keep _____ me that.
6 I can't stand _____.
7 When I met you, you started swimming and _____ with me.
8 I can't imagine _____ onto a surfboard.

76

I know you're really busy and I know you got plans, But are you really too busy for a sun tan? I ain't talking about walking down the high street, I'm talking about laying on a bright white beach

6.3

C Complete 1–6 with a gerund. Use your imagination! Then, in pairs, ask and answer. Were any of your questions similar? What was the most interesting answer?

1. Do you enjoy _____?
2. Do you ever feel like _____?
3. When you were a child, what was something you couldn't help _____?
4. What is something you can't stand _____?
5. Can you imagine _____?
6. Would you mind _____?

Do you enjoy eating ice cream at the beach?

D Play *Mad Libs!*

1. Complete 1–10 with nouns and gerunds.
   1. the name of a classmate _____
   2. an extreme sport _____
   3. an indoor activity _____
   4. a town / place _____
   5. something you often buy _____
   6. an outdoor activity _____
   7. the name of a friend _____
   8. your favorite activity _____
   9. an activity you hate _____
   10. a bad habit of yours _____

2. Complete the postcard with your words 1–10. In pairs, decide whose postcard is funnier.

Hi (1)_____,

I'm really enjoying (2)_____ here in California. Yesterday I took a break and I felt like (3)_____, so I went to (4)_____ and bought (5)_____. Not too many, don't worry! Tomorrow I'm going (6)_____ with my friend (7)_____ and we both like (8)_____, so we're going to do that. I hope we catch something!

The evenings are a little boring. I can't stand (9)_____, but everyone here loves it, especially The Big Bang Theory. I can't help (10)_____ when people are watching, so people get mad at me!

See you soon,

Gaby

E 🔊 6.7 **Make it personal** Listen and compare your postcards with Gaby's postcard. Did you use any of the same words?

I wrote "books" for number 5 because I love reading. How about you?   *I wrote "bananas", I think I'm addicted to them!*

77

6.4 What do you enjoy doing on your birthday?

Sports For All
2020–2021 Catalogue

1 Listening

A Match the sports equipment to catalog photos 1–10. Name a different sport for each item.

a bat ☐   fins ☐   gloves ☐   a **hel**met ☐   a mask ☐
a hoop with a net ☐   a puck ☐   a **ra**cket ☐   a snorkel ☐   a stick ☐

B ▶6.8 Watch / Listen and check the six items from **A** you need to play the game.

C ▶6.8 Watch / Listen again and order the instructions, 1–6.
Jump into the water. ☐   Line up on the wall. ☐
Swim fast to get the puck. ☐   Put your snorkel on. ☐
Put your mask on. ☐   Hold your breath until you score a goal. ☐

D ▶6.9 Listen and guess the sport after the beep.

E 🙂 Make it personal In pairs, write simple instructions explaining to a child how to play a sport. Read them to another pair. What sport is it?

You need a ball and a bat. The batter needs to hit the ball …

Common mistakes
score
You make goals by putting the ball in the net.

catch

hit

shoot

kick

2 Grammar Verb + infinitive / verb + gerund

🎵 *My loneliness is killing me (and I) I must confess, I still believe (still believe), When I'm not with you I lose my mind, Give me a sign, Hit me, baby, one more time*

6.4

A In pairs, use the photos to brainstorm five facts about Las Vegas.

> *It's the biggest city in Nevada.*

B Read Laura's email. Does she mention all your ideas?

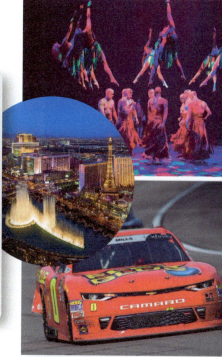

> Dear all,
>
> It's my 30th birthday in April and I've **decided** to do something really different! So, I'm writing to see if any of you **want** to join me on my adventure. You all know how I **adore** driving, especially at high speeds. Well, for the first time ever I'm going to Las Vegas! No, not to drive around the casinos – I hate **gambling**! I've chosen Vegas because they have an awesome **race**track there. Check it out on the website!
>
> So, who'd like to come with me? There's so much other stuff to do in Vegas too. If you'd **prefer** to catch a show, stay at the hotel and just swim and relax, get a helicopter across the desert to the Grand **Can**yon, or go to the casinos, whatever, that's fine.
>
> If you prefer watching me drive to driving yourself, that's fine too. But I really hope you all **agree** to come!! Oh, and remember, what happens in Vegas stays in Vegas! 😃 So, don't **forget** to message me soon to let me know if you can make it.
>
> Lots of love, Laura xxx

C ▶ 6.10 Listen, reread, and repeat the pink-stressed words. Are 1–5 True (T) or False (F)? Which of the activities she suggests would you prefer to do?

1. Laura loves driving, particularly when she can go fast.
2. She chose Las Vegas because there are great hotels and shows.
3. After driving with Laura, her friends can all do what they want.
4. She says she'd prefer her friends to go driving with her than stay at the hotel.
5. She tells her friends to look at the hotel website.

D Complete the grammar box with the highlighted words from the email in **B**.

> Some verbs combine with a gerund (the *-ing* form of the verb), others combine with the infinitive, and some verbs combine with both.
>
> | Verb + gerund | Verb + infinitive | Both |
> |---|---|---|
> | _____, dislike, enjoy, finish, keep, practice, quit | _____, ask, _____, choose, expect, _____, hope, _____ | begin, continue, hate, like, love, _____, start |

➡ **Grammar 6B** p. 148

Common mistakes
- I decided ~~do~~ *to* something.
- Don't forget ~~calling~~ *to call* me later.
- They insisted ~~to pay~~ *on paying*.

E ▶ 6.11 Complete Jack's reply using these verbs. Listen to check. Notice *to* = /tə/ or /tuː/.

come (x2)   drive (x 2)   gamble   invite   meet   stay

> Hi, Laura!
> It's Jack. What a great idea for your birthday! I really enjoy _____ too, so of course I'd love _____ with you to the racetrack. It looks amazing! I've talked to Margo and she's agreed _____ us in Vegas. She's decided _____ a day later than me as she doesn't want _____. But … she adores _____ – I hope she doesn't lose all our **sa**vings! – so she wants _____ at a hotel while we go. So … WE'RE COMING! Yay!
>
> PS As a birthday present, we'd like to _____ you for a helicopter trip. As long as you don't insist on flying it!

F 🎤 **Make it personal** Write a reply to Laura and record it. Compare in pairs. Do you want to do the same things?

> *You want to gamble, but I don't like to gamble.*

6.5 What's the highest place you've been to?

Skills Guessing meaning

A Read Margee's blog and check how she felt walking 356 m in the air.

	Before the walk	During the walk
confident and excited		
terrified and uncomfortable		
relaxed and thrilled		

Margee's blog

EdgeWalk in Toronto is the CN Tower's most thrilling attraction. It's the world's highest full circle hands-free walk on a 5 ft (1.5 m) wide ledge encircling the top of the Tower, 356 m / 1168 ft (116 stories) above ground.

I remember when I found out about the CN Tower EdgeWalk – I was Googling "terrifying experiences" and it was the first one to pop up. I thought that it would be quite an easy experience that wouldn't be too scary. I've never really been afraid of heights, so I felt confident I'd feel fine hundreds of feet in the air. I was very wrong.

The first thing that impressed me was the very thorough check and preparation for the EdgeWalk. This level of precaution usually means some very scary stuff is about to happen. At this point, I was excited, but not scared.

I was completely unprepared. It was terrifying. I stepped out onto the platform and felt a wave of fear wash over me. I felt like I forgot how to walk for a moment but at the same time I wanted to run away! The guide, Margo, started explaining what we were going to do and I realized I wasn't listening to anything she said. Then I was worried I'd do something wrong.

I had no idea I'd be as scared as I was, and I had a really, really hard time leaning out over that edge. Everything in my body was screaming "THIS IS A BAD IDEA! YOU CANNOT FLY!", even though rationally I knew I was safe and secure. I kept reminding myself that the harnesses are designed to hold hundreds of pounds and that it was impossible to fall. But then you start thinking, "What if THIS TIME the harness breaks?" It's ridiculous to think this – it's just not going to happen. But that's what my body was telling me – DANGER!

Each time I thought about falling, I could feel my entire body start shaking. It was terrifying and uncomfortable, but you have to take a breath, remind yourself you're safe, and relax. After about 10 minutes I leaned out over the edge and the feeling was out of this world!

Yes, I'd definitely do it, because I love feeling scared!

B ▶ 6.12 Listen, reread, and put the events in order, 1–9.
- ☐ She leaned out over the edge.
- ☐ The guide explained the instructions.
- ☐ She started to relax.
- ☐ She stepped out onto the platform.
- ☐ There was a detailed preparation for the walk.
- ☐ She felt excited.
- ☐ She thought she was going to fall.
- ☐ She started to feel very scared.
- ☐ She Googled the CN Tower EdgeWalk.

C Use context to circle the correct meaning of 1–8.
1. to pop up – to appear **suddenly** / **slowly**
2. heights – **high places** / **tall people**
3. a ledge – **narrow** / **wide** surface that projects from a wall or rock
4. to lean out – to **move your body from a vertical position** / **sit down on a chair**
5. a harness – a **part of the body** / **piece of equipment**
6. to shake – to **move uncontrollably** / **stay completely still**
7. stories – number of **floors** / **rooms** in a building
8. fear – **being afraid of** / **enjoy** someone or something

D Find five words in the blog that you don't use yet, but are similar in your language. Compare in groups and help each other with pronunciation.

E **Make it personal** Would you like to do the EdgeWalk? Why (not)? Are you or any people you know afraid of heights, spiders, snakes, dogs, open or crowded spaces, or thunderstorms?

6.5 Would you rather stay in or go out?

ID in Action Expressing preferences

Common mistakes

~~I'd~~ 'd
I rather stay at home.
The verb is would.

~~I'd like driving.~~ to drive
I'd like driving.

We can say *I like to eat* or *I like eating* but not "I'd like eating."

~~I prefer eat eggs than meat.~~ to
I prefer eat eggs than meat.

~~Would you prefer watching TV?~~ to watch
Would you prefer watching TV?

We can say *I prefer watching, I prefer to watch,* or *I'd prefer to watch* but not "I'd prefer watching."

A ▶6.13 What did they decide to do? Listen and circle the correct picture.

B ▶6.13 Complete the dialogue with these words. Listen again to check.

'd rather (x 2)   do (x 4)   feel like   like (x 2)   prefer (x 3)   would

A: What _____¹ you want to do this evening? _____² you want to go out?
B: I think I _____³ stay in.
A: _____⁴ you _____⁵ to cook or order in?
B: You know me, I always _____⁶ someone else's cooking!
A: Mmmm, yes. Well, _____⁷ you _____⁸ pizza or Chinese food?
B: I _____⁹ Chinese food better, but I _____¹⁰ eating pizza.
A: OK. _____¹¹ you _____¹² Alice's or Eric's better?
B: I _____¹³ order from Alice's. They're faster.
A: OK, great. Sounds good to me.

C Decide if 1–10 refer to a general preference (GP) or a preference on a specific occasion (SO). In pairs, ask and answer 1–7. Then complete the chart.

1 Do you prefer to read or listen?
2 Did you use to like to read comics?
3 Do you want to learn some new words?
4 Would you rather study at home or at school?
5 Would you like a hot or cold drink?
6 Would you like to see some apps?
7 Do you like speaking English?
8 I'd like to pass the English test.
9 I'd rather study at home.
10 I want to pass the English test.

Asking about general preferences	Asking about preferences on a specific occasion	Expressing general preferences	Expressing preferences on a specific occasion
_____¹ you prefer (to) …?	Would you like (to) …?	I like to + verb	I'd like to + verb
_____² you like (to) …?	Would you rather … ?	I like + _____⁵	I'd prefer to + verb
	_____³ you prefer (to) …?	I prefer to + verb	I'd rather _____⁷
	_____⁴ you want (to) …?	I prefer + _____⁶	I want to + verb
			I want + noun
			I feel like + _____⁸

D In pairs, use the dialogue in **B** as a model to talk about options 1 or 2.

1 watch TV / go to the movies
  see action / comedy
  eat popcorn / candy

2 go running / go for a walk
  in the country / in the city
  go for an hour / two hours

E 🎤 **Make it personal** **Difficult decisions!** Think of two options in any situation and ask classmates to decide between them and give a reason. Which is the most difficult decision to make? Who had the best reply and reason?

> Would you rather eat alligator or snake?

> I'd prefer to eat snake, because I think it would be more tender than alligator!

🎵 *Know with all of your heart, you can't shake me, When I am with you, there's no place I'd rather be, N-n-no, no no, no place I'd rather be*

Writing 6   An adventure vacation blog

If we've only got this life, then this adventure only I, wan to share with you, with you, with you, O sing it out, sing it out!

A Look at the photos and read the extracts from Adam's blog. Which activity would you prefer to do, and why?

Day 2: Hiking in the forest

Today we carried backpacks and all our camping equipment. At first it was easy, as we were walking along clear paths through trees. But after a while the path started to go up the side of the mountain. We walked uphill all afternoon – it was really tiring. Finally, we reached the top where we were going to camp. The views across the valley were absolutely magnificent. It was definitely worth the climb. We arrived at the campsite just before 5:00. By then, we were all completely exhausted, so we ate supper and then went straight to bed.

Day 4: On a glacier

What a day! Totally awesome. Before starting, the guides told us always to hold onto the ropes. They explained that during the day, the ice melts a little, so you have to be extremely careful. We actually walked inside the glacier. On the narrow ice paths, you could look down into deep crevasses – that was absolutely terrifying. In the afternoon, we tried ice climbing using ropes and special equipment. My friend Louis slipped and nearly fell, but the guides were amazing. When they saw what was happening, they were instantly there to help. Later, we laughed about it, but it made me realize that glaciers are not only beautiful, but also incredibly dangerous.

B Reread. Are 1–8 True (T) or False (F)?
1. The hike started out difficult but got easier.
2. It took a long time to reach the top of the mountain.
3. When Adam reached the top, he wished he hadn't made the effort.
4. They were already very tired when they got to the campsite.
5. The guides explained the risks of being on a glacier at the beginning of the day.
6. They spent most of the day ice climbing.
7. The guides were slow to react when Louis slipped.
8. Adam and Louis enjoyed most of their experience of being on a glacier.

C Look at the highlighted time expressions in the blog and read **Write it right!** Then reread the blog and find:
1. four more time expressions.
2. six adverb-adjective combinations describing a place or activity.
3. two adverb-adjective combinations describing how someone felt or behaved.

✓ Write it right!

When you're describing an experience:
- use time expressions to help the reader understand exactly when things happened: *at first, after a while, by then, during (the day), in the morning / afternoon, later.*
- use adverbs to intensify adjectives: *absolutely, completely, extremely, incredibly, really, totally.*
  - *absolutely, completely, totally* can be used only with non-gradable adjectives (*absolutely freezing, totally impossible*)
  - *very, extremely, incredibly* can be used with gradable adjectives (*extremely interesting, incredibly high*)
  - *really* can be used with any adjective

D Complete the blog with these expressions.

absolutely fantastic	after a while
at first	before starting	by then
during the morning	extremely useful
really hungry	totally amazing

Day 5: Kayaking

Today we went kayaking. Our guide was Lauren, and ¹she gave us a safety talk which was ²_____. Then we started paddling. ³_____ it was quite hard, but ⁴_____ things improved. ⁵_____ the weather was calm and we saw a lot of seabirds. At 1:00, we stopped for lunch – ⁶_____ we were all ⁷_____. In the afternoon, the weather got worse and we had to return to the beach. On the way, we met a family of dolphins, which was ⁸_____, as they are quite rare here. Later, we all agreed it had been an ⁹_____ day.

E Imagine you're on a two-day adventure vacation. Choose two or three experiences and make notes about what you did and how you felt about them.

F 🔵 **Make it personal** Write a blog about your adventure vacation in 150–200 words.

Before	Use your notes in **E**. Look back at the blog in **A** and underline any words or phrases you could use in your own blog.
While	Order your blog using a variety of time expressions. Use adverbs to intensify adjectives correctly.
After	Exchange blogs with another student. Check each other's use of time expressions and adverb-adjective combinations.

6 Brains vs. brawn

1 Before watching

A Read the definition. Is the example true for you? Do the sports in the chart require more brains or more brawn? Check the correct word for each sport.

brawn 🔊 /brɔn/ *n.* Muscular strength. Often used to compare physical strength to intelligence.
"Most people prefer brains over brawn."

	Brains	Brawn
boxing		
chess		
golf		
rock / wall climbing		
skateboarding		
skiing		
soccer		
swimming		
table tennis		
video games		

B 🔵 **Make it personal** Which are "real sports"? Which two do you like best a) to watch b) to do?

I love going swimming, and I love watching soccer.

C Guess which two activities Rory, Daniel, and August are each good at.

2 While watching

A Watch up to 3:08 to check. How do August (A), Daniel (D), and Rory (R) feel about these activities? Complete the chart. Some activities have two answers.

	Likes	Is good at	Hates
wall climbing			
playing golf			
playing video games			
playing table tennis			
using muscles / strength			
using speed and precision			
climbing quickly			
winning at games			

B In pairs, try to pronounce these words correctly. Watch again to check. Who's the most competitive? What else did you pick up?

en**e**my   ba**l**anced   **cou**rage   **pu**re
battle   pre**ci**sion   ho**n**estly   **pro**ven
ad**mi**re   **cha**mpion   **stra**tegy   **vic**tory
muscle   re**qu**ire   **cha**llenge

C Guess how the episode ends. Watch with sound off to check. Was your guess close?

Maybe August is too afraid to climb?

D Watch again with sound on, and note the five times you hear.

3 After watching

A True (T) or False (F)? Correct the false ones.

1 August loves de**feat**ing his enemies, and his friends.
2 August was high school golf champion three years in a row.
3 Daniel prioritizes balance, and really needed to get out of the house.
4 August challenges the others at two activities.
5 Daniel doesn't think he'll beat August on the wall.
6 Daniel and Rory aren't happy about August's victories.

B Check the correct situation for each phrase.

	Agreeing to participate	Reacting to someone's victory
You're on!		
Not again! I can't believe this.		
It's luck. It's gotta be pure luck.		
I don't know how he does it.		
Great job!		
OK … you win!		

C 🔵 **Make it personal** In pairs, compare "unexpected victory" stories you know. Which was the biggest shock?

I'll never forget the 2018 World Cup, when Germany lost to Japan, two nil.

Yeah! How did that happen?

R3 Grammar and vocabulary

A Picture dictionary. Cover the words on these pages and use the pictures to remember:

page	
58	18 school subjects
60	10 classroom tasks
67	a warning and a promise for 3 situations
72	9 leisure time activities
74	5 extreme sports
76/77	the 12 parts of Charlie's triathlon
78	10 items of sports equipment and the sports you use them for
79	5 attractions in Las Vegas
155	the first 8 pairs of picture words for the consonants

B ▶R3.1 Complete the sports club's poster. Listen to check.

Premier Sports Club offers _____ a fabulous variety of activities. You can go _____ on our new 15-meter wall, or maybe you would _____ to go _____ in our heated 25-meter pool. If you want to get in shape, why not _____ out in our fully-equipped _____? For more relaxing activities, we have 12 ten-pin lanes where you can go _____ with your friends, or you can just _____ out in our café and enjoy our delicious, healthy food and _____. All for just $49 a month!

C ▶R3.2 Use the photos to write the five pool rules. Listen to check. Which are good rules and which ones aren't? Change the ones you don't like.

Children have to ...   You can't ...

D Complete 1–4. Make a first conditional chain (minimum five steps) for each. Any funny ones?
1 If the weather's good this weekend, I'll _____.
2 I won't _____ if _____.
3 If I don't pass this class, _____.
4 I'll _____ if I don't _____.

If the weather's good this weekend, I'll play soccer.

If I play soccer, I'll see my friend Roberto and then if I see Roberto, .

E Match 1–5 to a–e to make facts about the human body.

1 If people eat too many calories,
2 If we don't get enough sleep,
3 If people have too much sugar,
4 When your body is too hot,
5 If we don't eat anything,
a your heart beats faster.
b we can survive for about 50 days.
c we can go crazy.
d they can lose their teeth.
e they get fat.

F ▶R3.3 Listen to the beginning of Clara's presentation and complete the chart.

Name:	Clara _____
Age:	
From:	
Living in:	
Reason:	
Leaving In:	

G ▶R3.4 Listen to the rest of Clara's presentation. After each pause, predict the form of verbs 1–8. Will it be *to* or *-ing*?

1 travel   3 study   5 speak   7 go
2 go   4 pay   6 pass   8 study

H Correct the mistakes. Check your answers in units 5 and 6.

⏱ **Common mistakes**

1 Do you have a master degree? (1 mistake)
2 How many homeworks do we have to make? (3 mistakes)
3 You have to assist to class every day. (2 mistakes)
4 Kim is too tall. She's enough tall to play basketball. (2 mistakes)
5 If you will lose any classes, you'll fail. (2 mistakes)
6 We haven't to read that book, but we can if we want to. (1 mistake)
7 We want go shop after work. (2 mistakes)
8 Before to eat dinner let's go to jog. (2 mistakes)
9 Jack can't stand to wait for her daughters. (2 mistakes)
10 You prefer stay at home or going out? (2 mistakes)

Skills practice

🎵 *I can't write one song that's not about you, Can't drink without thinkin' about you, Is it too late to tell you that, Everything means nothing if I can't have you?*

R3

A In pairs, play *Promises, promises!* Write an *If you* clause with a favor you want someone to do for you. Exchange papers and complete your partner's sentence with a promise. Read them out and vote for the funniest one in the class.

> *If you wash my car,*   *I'll let you borrow it.*

B ▶ R3.5 Complete Ben's directions with the correct prepositions. Listen to check.

> Hi Lena!
> So, here's how to get to my house again.
> First you go _____ a long street called York Street. Then you go _____ a tunnel. When you come _____ the tunnel you walk _____ a park and you go a footbridge. Then you walk _____ the street and my house is number 25 York Street. It's the purple one ____ the left. Call me if you get lost, OK?
> Can't wait _____ see you!
> Ben Xx

C Read the ad and answer 1–3.
1 Where's Crocosaurus Cove?
2 Can you touch a crocodile?
3 What other animals can you see there?

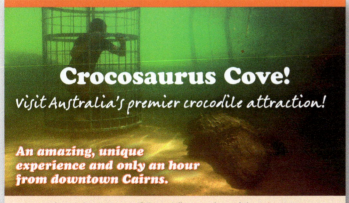

Crocosaurus Cove!
Visit Australia's premier crocodile attraction!

An amazing, unique experience and only an hour from downtown Cairns.

- Jump into the "Cage of Death" to swim with saltwater crocodiles (age 15+).
- Hold a baby saltwater croc for a magical selfie.
- Visit our aquarium, full of exotic fish, coral, and sharks!
- See the largest turtle sanctuary in Queensland.

D ▶ R3.6 Listen to a conversation about the "Cage of Death." True (T), False (F), or Not mentioned (N)? Correct the false ones.
1 The plastic cage is just one inch thick.
2 The man thinks it's a ridiculous idea.
3 You stay with the crocodiles for 50 minutes.
4 You can give food to the crocodiles.
5 Two people can get in the cage.
6 The crocodiles are very hungry.

E Write five warnings or pieces of advice about the "Cage of Death." Use these words. Compare in groups and choose the best five.

| break | calm | feed | get out of | open |
| take | touch | wear | | |

> *Don't open the cage to take a selfie!*

F **Mini role-play. A:** You're a visitor to Crocosaurus Cove. Use the ad in **C** and your imagination to interview B. **B:** You've worked there for 20 years and are a local celebrity. Answer and give A safety advice.

G Do the questionnaire. Compare answers. Which are the class favorites?

Would you rather ...
- stay at home or go out tonight?
- go clubbing or eat out on your birthday?
- walk on the beach or in the mountains?
- do writing exercises at home or in school?
- be married or single?

Do you prefer ...
- noisy places or quiet places on vacation?
- Mexican food or Peruvian food?
- to get up early or stay in bed on weekends?
- action movies or comedies?
- brains or brawn?

> *Marta would rather stay at home tonight but I'd rather go out, so we're different.*

> *Most people in class prefer Mexican food, but a lot of them haven't tried Peruvian food before.*

F ▶ R3.7 🔵 **Make it personal** **Question time!**
1 Listen to the 12 lesson titles in units 5 and 6.
2 In pairs, practice asking and answering. Use the book map on p. 2–3. Ask at least two follow-up questions. Try to answer in different ways. Can you have a short conversation about all the questions?

7

7.1 How often do you go to the movies?

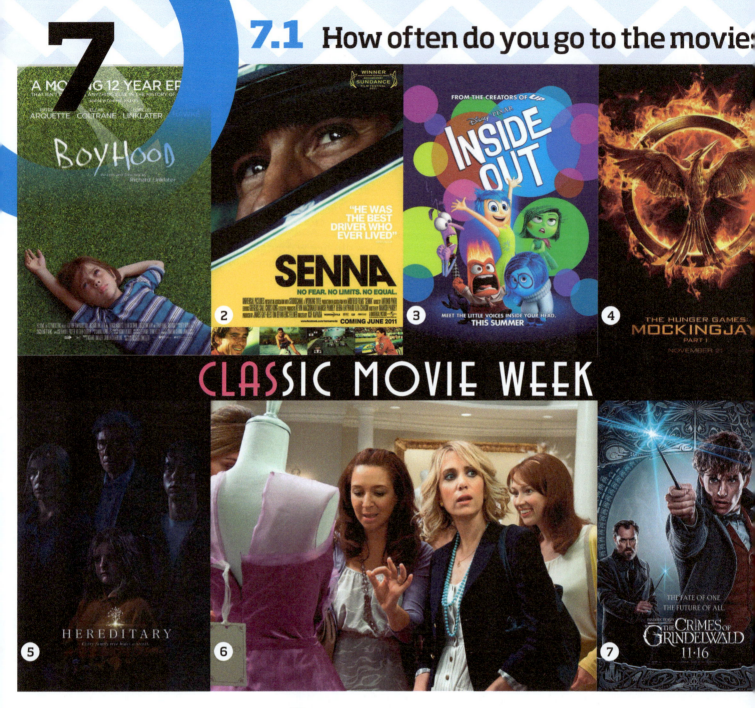

1 Vocabulary Movies

A ▶7.1 Complete the movie genres with the correct vowels. Match the movies in photos 1–7 to the best genre. Listen to check. Then think of another movie you know for each genre. Check its English title online if necessary.

__cti__n   dr__m__
__dventur__   f__nt__sy
__nimat__d   h__rr__r
c__m__dy   myst__ry
d__cument__ry   thr__ll__r

For action, how about Spiderman: Far From Home?

⚠ **Common mistakes**

I think the most the men enjoys the adventure movies.

Remember, the suffixes -or, -er, -ure, -ive, -y are never stressed.

B ▶7.2 Listen to two friends at the movies and number what they do in order, 1–6.

☐ buy the tickets   ☐ stand in line   ☐ buy the sodas
☐ go into the theater   ☐ buy the popcorn   ☐ choose the seats

C ▶7.2 Listen again and write if Kelly (K) or Jack (J) did each thing.

D 🎤 **Make it personal** In groups. Which kinds of movies do you like? Use questions 1–8 to talk about the last time you went to the movies. Who had the best experience? Who had the worst experience?

🎵 *I'll be your dream, I'll be your wish, I'll be your fantasy, I'll be your hope, I'll be your love, Be everything that you need*

7.1

1 What did you see? Who with?
2 Did you have any snacks?
3 What genre was it? One-off or a se**quel**?
4 Was it dubbed or subtitled?
5 Did it have good reviews?
6 Who were the main characters / actors?
7 What did / didn't you like about it?
8 Would you recommend it?

I like drama so we went to see A Star is Born. I went with my two sisters to the movie theater at the mall.

Did you have any snacks? *Yes, we bought popcorn.*

2 Reading

A Brainstorm five things any good movie needs. Then read the blog to find the movie critic's five choices. How many are the same as yours?

*How about origi**nal**ity? You know, so you don't feel you've seen it before.*

What makes a great movie?

Some people believe it's the director who makes a movie great – or not so great. Just think of all the directors who have made some terrible movies as well as brilliant ones! So making a great movie must involve more than the director.

I think that **plot** is the most important factor. A high quality movie needs a high quality story. Then there are the **characters** and the chemistry between them. A **sa**tisfying movie includes characters we're interested in, and who we care enough about to want to know what happens to them – even if we don't like them. This is why the actors who bring the **script** and the characters to life are so important. If the acting is bad, the movie will be bad too. Then, of course, the reason we watch a movie rather than read a book is for the **vi**suals. Is the cinema**to**graphy beautiful? Are there amazing special effects? And finally, we can probably all think of good movies that have been ruined by poor sound – when you can't hear the dialogue clearly or the sound effects are too loud – so sound quality is also **vi**tal to me in a good movie.

Other people may think that the **soundtrack** is just as important, or the **screenplay**, locations, action, and **stunts**, but, for me at least, these are the top five characteristics essential to any great movie.

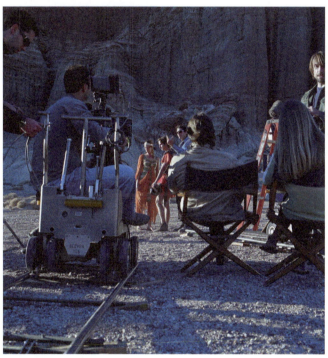

B ▶7.3 Listen, reread, and repeat the pink-stressed words. Match the highlighted words in A to definitions 1–6.
1 the story of the movie _____
2 the people in the story _____
3 the book that contains complete instructions for the actors and cinematographers _____
4 unusual, difficult, or dangerous pieces of physical acting _____
5 the music used in the movie _____
6 the words the actors have to say _____

C 🎤 **Make it personal** Choose the top three characteristics that make a movie great for you. Then, in pairs, analyze your favorite movies based on your criteria.

My favorite movie is The Green Book. It has a superb plot and characters and it's based on a true story. It's funny, has lots of surprises, and it makes you think.

Yeah, I've seen it too. It certainly holds your attention from beginning to end.

87

7.2 Are you crazy about music?

1 Reading

A Quickly read and match quotes a–g about passions to photos 1–7. Then match the photos to the labels.

a "We have to do **some**thing to save the planet – I campaign to raise a**ware**ness of the dangers of climate change and what we can do about it. I've been an activist all my life and I'm a big fan of getting involved." *Leila, Athens*

b "**Man**chester U**ni**ted! Does **any**one love them more than I do? I doubt it – I'm totally into the team and I go to all their games, even though it costs me a **for**tune. Some say I'm obsessed. I'm ec**sta**tic when they win and I'm de**vas**tated when they lose." *Jason, UK*

c "I play piano, sax, and guitar and practice about five hours a day and perform most evenings too. I rarely get a night off. It's my life – I'm crazy about music." *Marta, Brazil*

d "I volunteer in a pet hospital and I have five dogs, ten cats, a **tor**toise, and a rabbit. I love animals and I won't do **any**thing to harm them – ever!" *Jurgen, Germany*

e "There's a great atmosphere at the office – we work as a team on really sti**mu**lating projects. Sometimes I work over 80 hours a week! **Every**body says that's ridiculous and I'm obsessed with work, but I really love what I do and I'm per**sis**tent – and I make a lot of money!" *Rachel, the U.S.*

f "I'm a painter and spend all day looking at art or creating it – it's all I've ever wanted to do and now I'm living that dream – it's so ful**fil**ling to be an artist. I don't make much money, but **no**thing is as important to me as painting." *Claudia, Mexico*

g "I get up and run about five miles every day, then I go to a **spin**ning class. In the evenings I go to another fitness class and run two miles home – I run **every**where. I'm retired so I do all I can to stay in shape." *John, Canada*

an animal lover ____   an instru**men**talist ____   a worka**ho**lic ____
a com**mit**ted activist ____   an obsessive sport fan ____
a fitness fa**na**tic ____   a talented artist ____

B ▶7.4 **Listen, reread, and name the person(s) who:**

1 spends a lot of time practicing.
2 is probably not paid for what they do.
3 is really into sport.
4 thinks money is not important.
5 goes to classes every day.
6 mentions their work.
7 works with a group of people.

🎵 *Blow a kiss, fire a gun, We need someone to lean on, Blow a kiss, fire a gun, All we need is somebody to lean on*

7.2

C In pairs, practice the pink-stressed words and underline the expressions that each person uses to describe their passion.

> ⏱ **Common mistakes**
>
> *anybody*
> I don't know ~~nobody~~.
> *No one*
> ~~Anyone~~ can help me now.

D 🔘 **Make it personal**

1 Do you know anyone like the people in **A**?
2 Imagine you're being interviewed. What are you passionate about? Record your answer. In groups, listen to the recordings and decide who sounds most passionate.

> *I'm really into plants and I have my own garden.*

② Grammar Pronouns *some-, any-, every-, no-*

A **Answer 1–4 about the six phrases with a highlighted pronoun in 1A.**

1 Does the pronoun refer to a thing, a person, or a place?
2 Is the verb positive, negative, or a question?
3 Does the sentence have a positive or negative meaning?
4 Does the pronoun refer to a thing, person, or place that is **unidentified** or **a group** of things, people, or places?

B Complete the grammar box. Are the ➕ and ➖ forms different in your language too?

> **1** Complete the pronouns with *some-, any-, no-, every-*.
>
> | ➕ sentences | I know _____ one who's just like this.
_____ one (= all of us) knows _____ one like that. |
> |---|---|
> | ❓ questions | Do you know _____ one like this guy? |
> | ➖ negative | I don't know _____ one like this. |
> | ➕ verb with ➖ meaning: | _____ one wants to be like her at all. |
>
> **2** -thing   -one   -body   -where
>
> Use _____ or _____ for a person, _____ for a thing, and _____ for a place.
>
> ➡ **Grammar 7A** p. 150

C ▶7.5 **Complete 1–6 with the correct pronoun. Listen to check. In pairs, are they true for you? Add details.**

1 I always prefer _____ else's cooking to my own.
2 Radio used to be much better. There's _____ good to listen to these days.
3 You shouldn't go _____ if you have a cold or a cough.
4 There's _____ healthy to eat at fast food restaurants.
5 I don't love _____ or _____ as much as I love my pet.
6 There's _____ I've always wanted to do, but I haven't done it yet.

> *I definitely prefer my own cooking.*   *Are you a good cook?*   *I think so, yeah. I like to try new things.*

D 🔘 **Make it personal** Search online for a song line you like with *someone, nothing, anywhere,* etc. Share it with the class, and explain the use of the pronoun.

> *I like this one by Rita Ora. "Just take me anywhere, Anywhere away with you." She means, it doesn't matter where they go if they are together.*

> *I think there's a Queen song about "somebody."*

89

7.3 What do you have a lot of at home?

1 Listening

A ▶7.6 Listen to part one of a show about unusual collections. Match three of photos 1–4 to the people. In pairs, share what else you remember.

Barbara ☐   Percival ☐   David ☐

> ⚠ **Common mistakes**
>
> ~~Drake's songs~~
> I enjoy ~~the songs of Drake~~ but I prefer ~~the music of The Beatles~~.
> The Beatles' music
> Remember, possession is shown by 's or s'. Without the 's, the name becomes an adjective.

B ▶7.6 Listen again. Are 1–4 True (T) or False (F)? Correct the false ones.
1 The radio show started with number 1 on the list.
2 All Barbara's chairs are made from wood.
3 Percival 's collection includes over 50,000 toys.
4 David thinks traffic cones are important for safety on roads.

C ▶7.7 Use photos 5 and 6 to try to guess the unusual things Rainer and Nancy collect. Listen to check.

Rainer _____   Nancy _____

> Maybe he collects hotel doors?

90

D ▶ 7.6 and 7.7 Match comments 1–5 to Barbara (B), Percival (P), David (D), Rainier (R), or Nancy (N). Listen again to check.

♪ *Nobody said it was easy, it's such a shame for us to part, Nobody said it was easy, No one ever said it would be so hard.*

7.3

1 That's such a strange thing to collect!
2 Such a lot of little chairs!
3 They are so important for safety.
4 There are so many better souvenirs.
5 That's so sweet!

E 🟢 **Make it personal** In pairs. Which is the most unusual collection in the photos? Order them from 1 (most unusual) to 6 (least unusual). Then find another pair with the same order, or persuade a pair to change their order to yours.

I don't think the toy collection is very unusual. I know people who collect restaurant toys.

2 Grammar *So* and *such*

A Reread 1–5 in **1D** and study **Common mistakes** and the song line. Then complete the grammar box with *so* or *such a*.

⚠ **Common mistakes**
The hotel had such a̶ wonderful rooms!
Wow! Such a̶ nice weather!
Don't use *such a* with plural or uncountable nouns.

Use:
_____ with *much* and *many*.
_____ before an adjective followed by a noun.
_____ before an adjective.
_____ before a noun.

So / such + that is often used to express result:
The cat is **so** dirty **that** the flies love her.
They're **such** bad owners **that** the cat should find a new home.

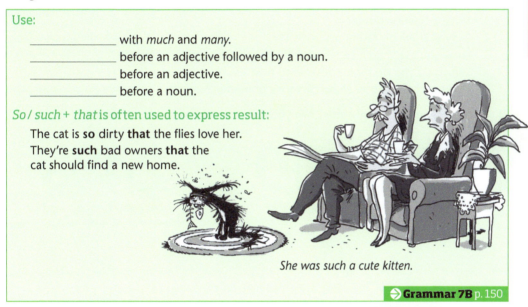
She was such a cute kitten.

➡ **Grammar 7B** p. 150

B ▶ 7.8 Add *so* or *such* in the correct places in 1–4, then match to endings a–d. Listen to check and repeat, stressing *so* and *such*. In pairs, talk about photos 1–6 on p. 90 using *so* and *such*.

1 Percival is careful with his toys that …
2 This man's a passionate traffic cone fan that …
3 Barbara is a huge fan of miniature chairs that …
4 She likes them much that …

a he has a collection of over 500.
b she has collected them from 50 countries in the world.
c he has over 15,000 of them.
d she has her own museum.

C In pairs, make sentences about the collectors in 1–5 using *so* or *such*.

1 Carol Vaughn: passionate about soaps / 5,000 bars in her apartment.
   She's so passionate about soaps that she has 5,000 bars in her apartment.
2 Rob Foster: huge fan of *Star Wars* / 3,000 *Star Wars* toys in his bedroom.
3 Leslie Rogers: in love with brown paper bags / names and numbers.
4 Randy Knol: enthusiastic about toy dinosaurs / more than 6,000 in his house.
5 Emeline Duhautoy: fan of toy cows / collected them for more than 10 years.

D 🟢 **Make it personal** In groups, share stories and ask questions about collectors and their collections. Who's the most obsessive collector? Who has the most unusual story?

My cousin used to collect Mexican wrestling masks. He still has about 200.

Where does he keep them?   *What does his wife think about them?*

7.4 Who was Instagram created by?

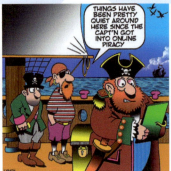

1 Reading

A Read / look at the cartoons. Did you find any of them funny? In pairs, answer 1–5.
1. What's the boy doing?
2. Do you think his father ap**proves**?
3. Have you ever had a conversation like this with family or friends?
4. Which do you do more: download or stream?
5. Do you often read or share cartoons or memes? /miːmz/

B Quickly read the infographic. Are you surprised by any of the figures?

3☠0bn
1. Over 300 billion visits were made to piracy websites last year – 106.9 billion to TV piracy websites, 73.9 billion to music piracy sites, and 53.2 billion to movie piracy sites.

71,600
2. Every year, 71,600 jobs are lost in the U.S. because of illegal downloads.

24%
3. About 24% of the global Internet bandwidth is used by Internet pirates to illegally download music and other content.

$850
4. An average mobile device contains something like $850 worth of pirated songs.

35%
5. 35% of music buyers get at least one song from an illegal source.

87%
6. Mobile devices are used for 87% of all piracy activities and desktop PCs are used in the remaining 13% of cases.

C ▶7.9 Read **Common mistakes**, then in pairs pronounce and write the underlined numbers in **B**. Listen to check, then check your spelling in AS 7.9 on p. 171.

D Circle the correct options in rules 1–3. Then dictate six large numbers to a partner.
1. Use and say **point** / **dot**, not *comma*, in numbers to separate decimal places.
2. In U.S. English, you **can** / **can't** omit *and* between numbers.
3. After numbers, use *hundred, thousand, million* and *billion* in the **singular** / **plural**.

> One million five hundred and fifty-two thousand.

🔥 Common **mistakes**

There are around eight billions of people on the planet Earth.
I have six hundreds friends on Facebook.
1,500 = one thousand and five hundred

Do Spanish and Portuguese speakers make the third mistake?

E 🎤 **Make it personal** What do you think of online piracy? Do you think it's possible to reduce online piracy? Can it be stopped? How?

> I think if they make downloading cheaper, there will be less piracy.

② **Grammar** Passive voice: present and past

🎵 *I'm beautiful in my way, 'Cause God makes no mistakes, I'm on the right track, baby, I was born this way*

7.4

A In pairs, try to remember the missing verbs in 1–4. Then complete the grammar box.

1 Over 300 billion visits ... to piracy websites last year.
2 71,600 jobs ... because of illegal downloads.
3 About 24% of the global Internet bandwidth ... by Internet pirates.
4 Mobile devices ... for 87% of all piracy activities.

> **1** Circle the correct options in sentences a–c about the passive voice.
>
> a The actions are **more** / **less** important than who did them.
> b *Be* (*is, are, was, were*) is **always** / **often** used in passive sentences.
> c The main verbs are in the **simple past** / **past participle**.
>
> **2** Look at sentence 3 in **A** and complete the rule.
>
> We use _____ + a _____ to specify who did the action.
>
> ➡ **Grammar 7C** p. 150

🔴 **Common mistakes**

were
Two billion songs ~~was~~ downloaded illegally last year.

are
A lot of movies ~~is~~ shared illegally every day.

B ▶7.10 Complete posts 1–4 on the forum with these verbs in the passive. There's one extra. Listen to check. Which opinion(s) do you disagree with?

create   invent   pay   reduce   share   upload

Downloading = Stealing?

1 Singers and movie stars _____ millions of dollars, anyway. Losing a few thousand dollars makes no difference to them.

2 People were recording TV shows and vinyl albums long before home computers _____ and the Internet _____. Downloading content illegally is basically the same thing.

3 The media industry should lobby to reduce download speeds. If speeds _____ , file sharing will drop too.

4 Every time a file _____ illegally, money is lost. End of discussion.

C ▶7.11 Listen to extracts from the infographic in **1B** and circle the correct option in the rule.

In the passive form, *are, was*, and *were* are usually **stressed** / **unstressed**.

D Read questions 1–5 and circle the correct answers. In pairs, ask and answer.

1 When were the first iPhones released?
  a 2006   b 2007   c 2008
2 What were the first words that were spoken on the moon?
  a God bless America.   b That's one small step ...   c Hi, Mom, look where I am!
3 Which music act is considered the best-selling of all time?
  a The Beatles   b Madonna   c Elvis Presley
4 Where's the Wimbledon tennis championship played?
  a New York   b Sydney   c London
5 When was the World Wide Web invented?
  a 1989   b 1990   c 1999

E 🔘 **Make it personal** In pairs, write a five-item trivia quiz to test the class. Ask about music, movies, TV, sports, history – you choose!

Where was the video for Luis Fonsi's "Despacito" filmed? Was it a) Cuba b) Dominican Republic c) Puerto Rico?

93

7.5 What do you think about reality TV?

ID Skills Listening for specific information

A In groups, answer 1–9. Who's the biggest fan of reality TV?
Which reality shows …
1 have you ever watched in English?
2 have a**dap**ted versions for your country?
3 have celebrity judges?
4 have you watched at least once?
5 have you contacted to vote?
6 do you like best / least?
7 would you eliminate forever if you could?
8 is the hardest to win?
9 do you think will last the longest?

I'd love to eliminate the "Got Talent" show, I can't stand it!

Tell us about it!
Have you ever auditioned for, or participated in, any of these shows? Call us at **637-8877** and leave a message describing your experience. The best stories will win an extraordinary – and unique – prize you'll never forget!

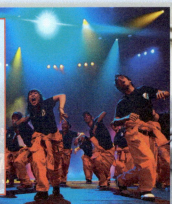
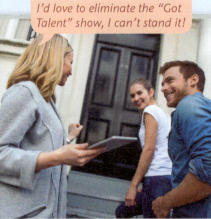

B ▶ 7.12 Listen to two callers to a radio station. Which shows from **A** are they talking about? Why did they want to be on the show? Did they appear on the show?

C ▶ 7.12 Listen again and complete 1–6 with numbers. Check in pairs.
1 There were _____ people standing in line outside the audi**tor**ium.
2 They were only allowed inside the building at _____ a.m.
3 Only _____ contestants perform in front of the celebrity judges.
4 About _____ people read Judy's blog every day.
5 If the woman appeared on the show, her family could be paid _____ dollars.
6 Judy tried to get in touch with the producer of the show at least _____ times.

D Rewrite 1–3 using *such* and 4–6 using the passive voice.
1 The place was so huge! It _____ !
2 I was so disappointed! This _____ disappointment!
3 My family is so con**ven**tional! I have _____ !
4 Someone chose me to be on TV. I _____ .
5 They paid families $20,000 to appear on the show. Families _____ .
6 They ig**nored** all my calls. All _____ .

E Read tips 1–3 and find examples of each in AS 7.12 on p. 171.
To improve fluency in a monologue, you can:
1 pause between ideas, or use phrases like *yeah* or *you know*.
2 repeat words and phrases from time to time for emphasis.
3 use words like *anyway* to help you change subject.

⬤ Common mistakes

auditioned
I once ~~made an audition~~ for a show.

contacted
I ~~put myself in contact with~~ the show.

F 🔵 **Make it personal** In pairs, answer 1–3. Can you use the phrases in **D** for any of your experiences? Do you have any similar answers?
1 Who do you feel most sorry for? Why?
2 Why is reality TV so popular?
3 Have you ever or would you ever audition for a show or movie? Which one?

I auditioned for a part in my high school play.

I'd audition as an extra in a movie, if I was paid well.

7.5 Are you a good singer?

🎵 *And I thought I was mistaken, And I thought I heard you speak, Tell me, how do I feel? Tell me now, how should I feel?*

ID in Action Giving your opinion

A Look at the picture of Bruce, who's on another talent show. In pairs, answer 1–5.
1 How confident do you think Bruce looks?
2 Do you think he's a good singer?
3 Has he already sung or is he about to sing?
4 Guess which judge will be more positive about his performance.
5 Guess what each of them is saying.

I'm not sure if he's crying or sweating. What do you think?

> **Common mistakes**
> We're ~~on the point of going~~ out.
> *about to*

B ▶ 7.13 Listen to check. Were your guesses correct?

C ▶ 7.13 Listen again and complete comments 1–5. Will Bruce try again?
1 You've just _____ my favorite song of all _____.
2 That was _____ an _____ version.
3 You have _____ a lot of _____!
4 You'll need to work very _____. You sounded like you had a _____.
5 Come back again when you're _____.

D ▶ 7.13 Match beginnings 1–4 to the endings. There are two extra endings. In pairs, listen and, simultaneously, repeat each sentence.

1 I thought …
2 I didn't think …
3 It wasn't as good …
4 I have to agree …

> **Common mistakes**
> I thought that performance ~~very~~ good.
> *was*

☐ … with Simon.   ☐ … it was all that great.   ☐ … as I expected.
☐ … than I thought.   ☐ … it was quite good.   ☐ … about Emma.

E ▶ 7.14 🔵 **Make it personal** In groups of three, imagine you're the judges. Listen to Joe and then Lisa and decide if they should progress to the next round of the show.

I didn't think Joe was all that great, but he was OK. Maybe we should give him another chance.

95

Writing 7 A TV series review

I will jump right over into cold, cold water for you, And although time may take us into different places, I will still be patient with you, And I hope you know

A Read the review and decide how many stars the reviewer gives the TV show.

B Which paragraph a–d answers 1–5?
1 Is there anything she doesn't like about the show?
2 Would she recommend the show?
3 What does she particularly like about it?
4 Why is it interesting and enjoyable?
5 What's the name of the TV show, and what is it about?

C Study the highlighted and underlined words in **A**, then complete the rules in **Write it right!**

> ✅ **Write it right!**
>
> Use _____ and _____ to add extra information. _____ can start a sentence, or go before the verb / adjective. _____ goes at the end of a sentence.
> Use _____ and _____ to introduce a contrast.
> Use _____ (that) with adjectives.
> Use _____ with uncountable nouns and _____ with countable nouns.

D Complete 1–4 with *also, although, however,* or *too*. More than one answer may be possible.
1 _____ the visual effects were amazing, the sound was too loud.
2 The leading actor was brilliant. The other actors were _____ very good.
3 The story is very complicated. It keeps you guessing right to the end _____ .
4 The violence was graphic. _____ , it was important to the story.

E Circle the correct options to complete 1–4.
1 Very few movies get **so / such** excellent reviews.
2 The ending was **so / such** unexpected – I couldn't believe it!
3 I love Tarantino's movies – I think he's **so / such** a great director.
4 The first series was **so / such** successful that they decided to make a sequel.

F 🎧 **Make it personal** Think of a movie or TV show you really enjoyed and write a review in 200 words.

Before	Brainstorm answers to questions 1–5 in **B** for you. Look back at the review in **A** and underline any words or expressions you want to use in your own review.
While	Follow the structure of the review in **A**. Include four paragraphs and a variety of adjectives. Check you use the connecting words from **Write it Right!** correctly.
After	Exchange reviews with another student. Does their review make you want to see the movie / TV show?

☆☆☆☆☆

a A TV show I've really enjoyed is *Killing Eve*, a spy thriller in eight episodes. It's about a secret service officer, Eve, played by the American actor Sandra Oh. Her mission is to find an international assassin called Villanelle (British actor Jodie Comer), who has killed a number of important people in different countries. As the series develops, both women seem to be looking for each other, which I think is such an original idea.

b I'm a big fan of action movies and TV shows, although the heroes always seem to be men. In *Killing Eve* I particularly like the idea that the two main characters are women. The story is fast-moving, with a lot of drama and excitement. It also has some surprising changes. Eve and Villanelle are both such unusual people that you want to find out more about them. This makes the story very interesting. The audience is meant to sympathize with Eve, however, Villanelle is so mysterious and charismatic that we really like her too.

c *Killing Eve* is quite violent, and I don't like this so much. In places, the violence is so graphic that it's difficult to watch. I think this might upset some viewers. However, it's always connected to the development of the story and isn't just for "entertainment."

d I'd definitely recommend this series to anyone who enjoys great acting and great storytelling. The two leading actors are extremely convincing and the director keeps you guessing what will happen all the way through. Also, the final episode was really unexpected. If you want to know what happens, you'll have to watch it yourself!

Sara T., Portland, USA

7 Sound tracks

1 Before watching

A In pairs, write the name of two movies you've seen (and enjoyed) for each genre, in English. Share and make a class list. Vote for the class favorite.

| action | comedy | horror | romance | science fiction |

I used to love those Die Hard films, with Bruce Willis.

B Classify these words. Some can go in both columns in the chart. When you hear the phrase "great soundtrack," what comes to mind?

| to edit | an MP3 file | to record | samples | scenes |
| a shot | a song | the soundtrack | that's a wrap |

Film	Music

As a kid, I loved the songs in Mamma Mia! I still do!

C Guess what Paolo and Andrea are doing / saying and why.

Maybe he's teaching her some karate moves?

2 While watching

A Watch up to 1:36 to check. Number these phrases, 1–4, in the order you hear them. Then use them to complete the sentences.

- ☐ lifesaver
- ☐ no big deal
- ☐ owe you one
- ☐ short notice

1 When someone doesn't give you enough time to plan something, it's _____.
2 If you do someone a big favor, they might say you're a _____.
3 After you do someone a favor, you can say it's _____.
4 If someone does you a favor, you can say, "Thanks, I _____."

B Watch the rest and check any movie titles on your class list from **1A** that you hear. Which others does Lucy mention?

C Complete extracts 1–8 with *so, such, so much,* or *so many*. Who said them? Watch again to check. What other phrases did you catch?

1 I'm _____ glad you could do this for me.
2 I know it was _____ short notice.
3 It took _____ longer to edit than I thought.
4 It takes me _____ tries to get one that I think sounds OK.
5 You and I are _____ much alike.
6 The romantic pieces are always _____ easier.
7 That was _____ scary.
8 Thank you _____.

3 After watching

A Order the story, 1–10. If necessary, watch again to check.

- ☐ The movie was edited and sent to Genevieve for the soundtrack.
- ☐ The monster was defeated by Paolo.
- ☐ Genevieve watched the film.
- ☐ Andrea's character screamed.
- ☐ 1 The movie was shot in a forest and in an alley.
- ☐ Lucy will tell her professor about Genevieve's music.
- ☐ Genevieve and Lucy listened to music samples.
- ☐ Three exciting music compositions were chosen.
- ☐ Several types of movies were discussed.
- ☐ They talked about the difficult aspects of their work.

B Present or past passive? Complete 1–5 with these verbs.

| finish | match | compose | shoot | write |

1 The film _____ in two days.
2 Genevieve says that sometimes a song _____ in half an hour.
3 The scenes _____ up with a few different samples.
4 Action and romantic pieces _____ by Genevieve.
5 When the music _____ Lucy was happy.

C Rewrite 2–5 using the passive.

1 Lucy's movie features Andrea and Paolo.
   Andrea and Paolo are featured in Lucy's movie.
2 They chose dramatic and classical music for it.
3 People know John Williams for his great soundtracks.
4 Genevieve created several music samples for it.
5 Lucy wrote the script and shot the movie.

C ● **Make it personal** In groups, choose either:
- a genre, then plan and script a short movie scene.
- a clip you like from a movie, and act it out yourselves.

Let's create a scary scene from a horror movie.

Can we do a scene from La La Land? I love the dance routine between Ryan Gosling and Emma Stone!

97

8

8.1 Are you into science fiction?

1 Vocabulary Technology

A Underline the **bold** words you recognize in extracts 1–6 from an audio journal. In pairs, guess their pronunciation. Then match 1–6 to photos a–f.

1 "**The facial recognition device** doesn't know who I am again, so I can't use my **GPS**."
2 "And I can see better too, thanks to the **active contact lenses** that I got at the same time."
3 "It sends this information to the **surveillance camera** in the kitchen, and now the smart refrigerator has locked its doors."
4 "I hope their **smart vending machine**'s not broken again. I'm dying for something to eat."
5 "Why are the **voice-activated speakers** always playing old Justin Bieber songs?"
6 "Oh, I miss the good old days when I could simply press a **button** on the remote and decide what to watch."

B ▶8.1 Listen to check, then cover **A** and test a partner with the photos.

C 🙂 Make it personal Which of the technology items do / don't you use? How many of each do you have at home? Compare in groups. Any surprises?

I have facial recognition on my phone.

Oh really? I don't – I prefer to use my fingerprint.

> **Common mistakes**
>   *miss*
> I ~~feel a need~~ for my old phone.

98

② Reading

♫ *Futures made of virtual insanity now, Always seem to, be governed by this love we have, For useless, twisting, our new technology, Oh, now there is no sound for we all live underground*

8.1

A ▶8.2 **Insert sentences 1–6 from 1A in the journal. Listen, check, and repeat the pink-stressed words.**

9:00 a.m. Thursday's finally here, after a relatively busy working week. So, why on earth did the home entertainment system decide it should wake me up at 9? (a) _____ I specifically requested Mozart!

9:30 a.m. Smart bathroom seems worried about my health. Apparently, I've gained two pounds in the past week. So, here's what it does: (b) _____ No breakfast for me today, thanks to the bathroom-fridge conspiracy. How about that?

10:00 a.m. The kitchen appliances are still refusing to cooperate, so I'm on my way to get a breakfast burrito at the store now. Yes, fast food for breakfast, of all things! (c) _____ I never thought I'd say this, but sometimes I miss human attendants and their inefficiency.

11:00 a.m. I get into the car. (d) _____ That's the third time this week. Could it be the two extra pounds? I guess I have no choice but to answer the same old security questions it asks me.

2:00 p.m. After three hours stuck in the car, trying to prove that I'm not an impostor, I get home, sit down, and tell the TV I want to watch soccer. Guess what, it looks like it has decided that I'm in the mood for classical ballet today. (e) _____

6:00 p.m. I'm having a great time at my brother's birthday party, especially with the sound cancellation ear plugs I bought last week. What a fantastic device! It makes everything sound much nicer. (f) _____

B **What do the underlined pronouns refer to? Draw connecting arrows, like the example.**

C **In pairs, use only the photos in 1A to reconstruct the main events in the journal.**

> *When he woke up the smart speakers were playing classical music, right?*   *No, they were playing Justin Bieber!*

D **Which technology items 1–8 are mentioned in the text in A? In pairs, talk about the three you would most like to have. Are your choices the same?**

1 decision-making devices
2 voice-changing devices
3 identity-checking devices
4 self-driving cars
5 self-locking appliances
6 house-cleaning robots
7 sleep-monitoring cameras
8 conversation-making robots

E **In groups, use these verbs (or your own) to create five innovative technologies. Use tips 1–3 to help you. Share your lists and choose your two favorite devices.**

changing   cleaning   controlling   doing   learning   making   monitoring

1 Use the *-ing* form of verbs to describe what things do: *a money-making scheme; a fitness-tracking watch.*
2 In compound nouns, the stress is usually on the first word.
3 Use *self-* when no one else is involved in operating a machine: *a self-updating program.*

> *My first one is an English-learning device. I'd love to become fluent automatically!*

> ⚠ **Common mistakes**
>
> *money-counting*
> The bank uses ~~money-count~~ machines.
>
> *self-cleaning*
> This oven is ~~self-clean~~.
>
> You don't need to worry, this is a ~~self-updated~~ app.
> *self-updating*

F 🔊 **Make it personal** **In pairs, answer 1–3. Do you mainly agree with each other?**

1 What are the advantages and disadvantages of the technology in the journal?
2 What problems does technology cause for you and humanity in general?
3 Do you think we will live more and more like this in the future?

> *I think technology can make life more complicated, not easier.*   *No way! Technology is progress!*

99

8.2 Do you ever switch off from technology?

1 Grammar Phrasal verbs

A ▶8.3 Listen and match conversations 1–4 to pictures a–d.

B ▶8.3 Match a–i to speech bubbles 1–9 in **A**. Listen again to check.

a I'll get up in five minutes.
b Let me plug you in.
c I'm going to switch you off.
d Please turn the thermostat down! Turn it down!
e Don't turn on the coffee maker!
f You know you can't switch me off!
g I'm going to turn on the coffee maker.
h I'm going to turn up the thermostat.
i It's time to wake up.

C Complete the grammar box.

> **Common mistakes**
>
> Why are the speakers off?
> Switch ~~on them~~.
>   *them on*
>
> The volume's too low. Please turn ~~up it~~.
>   *it up*

1 Match phrasal verbs 1-7 to meanings a-g.

1	get up	a	to decrease
2	wake up	b	to increase
3	plug in	c	to stop (a light or machine)
4	turn up	d	to connect to an electrical outlet
5	turn down	e	to get out of bed
6	turn on / switch on	f	to start (a light or machine)
7	turn off / switch off	g	to stop sleeping

2 Circle the correct options in a-c.
   a The TV is too loud! **Turn down it.** / **Turn it down.**
   b The lights are very bright in here! **Turn them off.** / **Turn off them.**
   c In phrasal verbs, pronouns usually come **after** / **between** the verb and the particle.

➡ Grammar 8A p.152

D ▶8.3 Listen again and repeat a–i in **B**. Stress the particle (adverb or preposition), not the verb.

E In pairs, cover a–i in **B**, use the pictures in **A**, and try to remember the sentences.

F 🟢 **Make it personal** Complete 1–5 with phrasal verbs from **C**. Create two more questions using phrasal verbs from the box. Then ask and answer in pairs. Did you learn anything new?

🎵 *Come on, come on, turn the radio on, It's Friday night and I won't be long, Gotta do my hair, I put my make up on, It's Friday night and I won't be long*

8.2

1 What time do you usually _____ _____ in the mornings, during the week, and at weekends? How long is it usually before you _____ _____?
2 How often do you _____ _____ your cell phone completely? How long before you _____ it _____ again?
3 When your favorite songs are playing do you usually _____ _____ the volume?
4 Do you have any devices that you _____ _____ and _____ _____ with your voice?
5 How many devices do you have _____ _____ to an outlet now at home?

What time do you usually wake up at weekends?

go out / stay in   pick up / put down   put on / take off   stand up / sit down

Do you normally ask people to take off their shoes at your house?

Do you prefer to stand up or sit down at pop concerts?

② Pronunciation Intonation in questions

A ▶ 8.4 Listen to more of Michael's conversation with his car computer from **1A**. What do 1–5 refer to? Check with a partner.
1 Huff   2 July   3 Canada   4 a white T-shirt   5 October

B ▶ 8.5 Listen and mark if the intonation goes up ↗ or down ↘ at the end of 1–4. Then circle the correct options in the rule.
1 What's your full name?
2 Are you American?
3 May I ask you a few security questions?
4 Why are you doing this to me?

Intonation usually goes **up** / **down** at the end of *Yes* / *No* questions and **up** / **down** at the end of *Wh-* questions.

C ▶ 8.6 Remember the car's questions. Write them using prompts 1–7, then listen, check, and repeat.
1 what / full name?
2 how / spell "Huff"?
3 American?
4 when / born?
5 how long / have / this ve**hi**cle?
6 use / this car / Tuesday?
7 what / wearing?

Good morning surveillance camera. Did you have a busy night? Did you miss me?

D In pairs, choose a device and role-play a conversation with it. Which pair can create the funniest conversation?

E 🟢 **Make it personal** Share your experiences with technology. What do you think about devices, appliances, and apps that speak? How many in the class like them and how many don't?

I love that I can talk to my phone and ask it questions!   *I don't talk to my phone.*

101

8.3 Will space vacations be popular soon?

1 Reading

A In pairs, answer 1–3 about the cartoon. Give both a "real" answer and a fun one too.
1. Why is the woman surprised?
2. How do you think she should a) react and b) reply?
3. Do you think machines will ever have any human emotions?

She should react positively. After all, it's a compliment!

Maybe. Lots of robots in movies get emotional.

B ▶8.7 Quickly read the article and match three of questions 1–4 to replies a–c. Listen to check.
1. Will we be able to communicate through thought transmission?
2. Will computers have emotions or some sort of consciousness?
3. Are we ever going to travel through time?
4. Are computers going to be more intelligent than us?

Future Perfect?
Penny Duff and Harry Reid

Last week we asked you to tweet us your questions about life in 30 years' time. This is what futurists Penny Duff (PD) and Harry Reid (HR) have to say about the top three questions.

a PD: Probably not. Consciousness is an exclusive attribute of the human brain and we probably won't be able to teach robots how to feel until we know much more about our brain and how it functions.

HR: Probably. We've built robots that can, for example, identify themselves when they look in a mirror or even mimic our emotions according to the quality of our voice, so, yes, I think machines will be able to feel human emotions.

b PD: Maybe. Synthetic telepathy seems like science fiction, I know, but I think it will be possible to establish some form of rudimentary communication through electric signals, not words.

HR: Definitely. Scientists have actually created a computer program that can decode brain activity and put it into words. So it's going to be relatively easy to capture thoughts and transmit them to another brain, I suspect.

c PD: Certainly. Time travel to the future is an essential characteristic of Einstein's theory of relativity, and this has been investigated many times by lots of scientists worldwide, so maybe there will be some form of future time travel. But traveling back to the past is a whole different story. There's no evidence that this is possible. So, who knows?

HR: Possibly. As I've said on a number of occasions, I think computers will probably be as intelligent as humans by 2040 or so. If that happens, I'm pretty sure they're going to help us find a way to travel through time.

C ▶8.7 Try to pronounce the highlighted cognates in the text. Listen again and reread to check. Did any of the pronunciations surprise you?

D Say the first word(s) in each of Penny and Harry's replies in B. How confident are their predictions? Complete the Venn diagram with the words.

maybe	definitely
probably	probably not
certainly	possibly

Most confident — Least confident

102

E **Make it personal** In pairs, say which scientist you agree with for each question in B and why. Are your opinions the same or different?

🎵 They will not force us, They will stop degrading us, They will not control us, We will be victorious

8.3

First question ... Who do you agree with?   *Penny Duff. I don't think machines will ever feel anything.*   *I agree, so that's a similarity.*

2 Grammar Future forms 1

A Study example sentences 1–7. Then decide if a–e in the grammar box are True (T) or False (F). Correct the false ones. Any similarities to your language?
1 Will we be able to communicate through thought transmission?
2 Are computers going to be more intelligent than us?
3 Machines will be able to feel human emotions.
4 We probably won't be able to teach robots how to feel.
5 I think it will be possible.
6 It's going to be relatively easy.
7 There will be some form of future time travel.

> a Use both *going to* and *will* to make future predictions.
> b Word order = *will* + adverb (e.g., *probably, certainly*) + verb; adverb (e.g. *definitely*) + *won't* + verb.
> c Use *will / won't be able to* for something that will / won't be possible.
> d *There is / there are* has no future form.
> e Use verb *be* for questions with *will*.

➡ Grammar 8B p. 152

⏰ **Common mistakes**

There will be
~~Will have~~ no more 4G technology by 2030.

be able to
Computers will ~~can~~ read our minds one day.

B Circle the correct options. Check in pairs and say if you agree with the predictions.
1 The Internet **don't / won't** change substantially in my lifetime.
2 There will **have / be** fewer languages in the world a century from now.
3 Printed newspapers **probably will / will probably** disappear before 2040.
4 Ordinary people will **can / be able to** travel to the moon very soon.
5 Chinese **is going to be / will to be** the official world language at some point.
6 There **won't maybe / probably won't** be another outbreak of Ebola in the next five years.

I disagree. There's a good chance it might be much more controlled.

Really? I don't think it'll change, but we'll probably find more uses for it.

C Correct mistakes of word order or form in tweets 1–5. Which of these mistakes have you made?

1 **Gabriel Aguiar** @bielaguiar
Robots will replace teachers?

2 **Lin Jung** @linjung92
Will it be enough food and water in the world?

3 **Javier Blanco** @javiwhite
We gonna to have computers in our brains?

4 **Anna Baum** @cuteanna
People is going to be able to learn languages faster?

5 **Khalef Nassar** @naskhalef
We will ever to find life on other planets? And will survive humans another 1,000 years?

D **Make it personal** In small groups, ask and answer questions 1–5 in C. Who's the most optimistic person in your group? Who's the most certain?

Will robots replace teachers?   *Possibly for some subjects, but not all of them.*

⏰ **Common mistakes**

Will fossil fuels be prohibited soon?   I think ~~that~~, yes.
so

not
Well, I hope ~~that no~~. We just bought a new gasoline car!

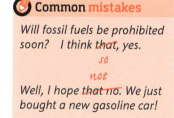

103

8.4 Is technology making us more, or less, social?

① Reading

A Read the article quickly and choose the best title.

1 Technology is making us antisocial
2 The art of making bad conversation
3 Here's how to make more friends
4 It's all about you!

Over the last 30 years or so, technology has created a world of instant and fast communication. We're easily accessible and online all the time. Some argue that it's making us less social, while others say it's actually connecting us more and expanding our opportunities. Whichever you believe to be true, here are four sure-fire ways to ruin a face-to-face conversation today. Which ones do you recognize?

1 You get a notification and that's all you need! It doesn't matter if you're in the middle of a very interesting **discussion**, you just have to look at your screen immediately. You make the other person wait while you look at your phone. Good way to lose a friend. 👎

2 You're just trying to be "helpful" – or perhaps "judgmental" is a better word? If you think the person you're talking to is doing something that you consider wrong – unhealthy, impractical, or immoral – you tell them. And of course, you always **assume** that the other person wants your **sensible** advice. 👎

3 When your friend is talking, you start talking, too – probably in the middle of the sentence – even if you say something that doesn't make sense. Also, it doesn't matter if you change the subject completely – you're not **actually** listening anyway. 👎

4 When someone introduces a subject, you find a way to talk about you and your life and experiences. For example, a friend tells you they're going to **attend** an important meeting. You don't ask who, when, or where. Instead, you talk about the last meeting you went to and why it was the most important meeting in the world. You always make it about you! You just need to hear a recording of your conversations. One listen, and you'd be too **embarrassed** ever to speak about yourself again! 👎

B ▶8.8 **Listen and reread a paragraph at a time. Match each one to ways to ruin a conversation, a–e. There's one extra.**

a keep interrupting
b keep checking your phone
c be the center of the universe
d judge the other person
e break eye contact and slowly turn away

C Over 90% of Latin-based words are "cognates", with similar meanings in your language. However, there are a few "false cognates", like the **Common mistakes**. In pairs, match definitions 1–6 to the **bold** words in **A**. Do they mean the same in your language?

1 a conversation
2 in reality
3 based on good judgment
4 suppose
5 be present at
6 feel uncomfortable about yourself

⚠ Common mistakes

intends
Marcia ~~pretends~~ to become a doctor.

success
Sue had a lot of ~~exit~~ in her last project.

At the moment
~~Actually,~~ I'm a student, but I'll get a job when I graduate.

kept
She ~~was staying~~ checking her phone all the time.

D 🔊 Make it personal In small groups, answer 1–3. Any big differences?

1 Which is the most annoying way to ruin a face-to-face conversation?
2 Are online written "conversation killers" similar or different?
3 Does anyone you know have any of the habits described in the article?

I don't like it when people interrupt … … me all the time!

I know what you mean! It really annoys me.

② Grammar Future forms 2

A ▶8.9 Listen to three conversations and identify the "conversation killers" from **1B**.

B ▶8.9 Listen again. True (T), False (F), or Not mentioned (N)?

1 Sue's car is brand new.
2 Sue's dad is loyal to a particular car model.
3 Regis has talked to Ann about her health before.
4 Ann sees a doctor regularly.
5 Yuko was about to leave for the airport when Sally called.
6 Yuko has been to New York before.

C ▶ 8.9 Complete 1–5 with the verbs in the correct tense. Use your intuition. Listen again to check.

1 "I _____ to sell mine in October or November." (**try**)
2 "I _____ him right now and tell him." (**call**)
3 "I _____ the doctor on Friday." (**see**)
4 "I _____ a check-up too." (**get**)
5 "The plane _____ at two and I haven't started packing yet." (**leave**)

♪ *All our troubles, We'll lay to rest, And we'll wish we could come back to these days, These days*

8.4

D Study the verb forms and uses in **C** and complete the grammar box.

Match verb forms a–d to uses 1–5. Use 4 has two answers.

a	simple present	1	prediction based on evidence
b	present continuous	2	quick decision
c	*going to*	3	events on a timetable
d	*will*	4	future arrangement / fixed plan
		5	intention

➡ **Grammar 8C** p. 152

E Match pictures 1–5 to quotes a–e. Circle the best future forms and explain why.

"DO YOU WANT TO SEE A MOVIE TONIGHT?"

Five irritating types to watch out for …

a ☐ "Yeah, but the movie **starts / is starting** in three hours. We've got to leave now!"

b ☐ "Oh, what a pity! I'd love to, but I'm **taking / will take** grandma to her karate class tonight. Maybe some other time."

c ☐ "Hmm … I don't know. I mean, look at those clouds. It looks like it's **going to rain / raining** tonight … And you know how bad the traffic gets when it rains."

d ☐ "Thanks, but Bob and I are **going to watch / will watch** it in Paris next week."

e ☐ "You mean a movie? Tonight? Well, **I'll think / I'm thinking** about it and get back to you, OK?"

1 The excuse inventor
2 The punctuality freak
3 The non-decider
4 The pessimist
5 The boaster

F ▶ 8.10 Listen to check. Then cover the text and use the pictures to remember each quote.

G 🔵 **Make it personal** **Irritating types!** Role-play in pairs. Then change roles.

A: choose a personality type from **E** and answer B's questions.
B: choose a situation below and ask A. Can you guess A's personality type?

- It's your grandma's birthday on Sunday and all her friends will be there. Invite **A**.
- You need to borrow **A**'s new car to take your mom to the doctor.
- You want **A** to help you paint your bedroom.
- You want **A** to organize a class party with you.

My grandma's turning 90 on Sunday and we're having a party. Would you like to come?

I'd love to, but I'm not sure what I'm doing yet. I'll let you know, OK?

8.5 Who do you talk to when you need help?

 **Skills** Understanding ads

A Scan and match ads a–e to the areas of life below. How many ads offer coaching in more than one area?

☐ finances ☐ relationships ☐ health and diet
☐ personal development ☐ professional

Coaching Professionals in the Manhattan Area

a Good Life Services
Our health and fitness experts will show you how to stay in good shape and feel healthy and full of life. We'll analyze your diet and lifestyle, and prepare a personalized program for you. Check our website for much more information, or call to speak to one of our personal advisers.

b Money Wizard
Do you have money problems? Credit card bills you can't afford to pay? Need a quick, guaranteed solution? Just send $50 and your details to receive my amazing, exclusive guide to transforming your finances. Millions of dollars already saved for my customers! Get your money back if you're not 100% satisfied.

c Jenny Brook Coaching
Are you trying to get your life back on track? I'll look at you as a whole person and can help with all aspects of your life. I can offer you the benefit of my experience as a grandmother, mother of nine, and someone who has also had a lot of problems in their life. 50% discount on first session.

d Matt Jones
If you need help deciding on a career, or advice about whether to stay in your current job or move on, I can help you to work out the right answer. Specialist in sales and marketing jobs worldwide. See website for references and contact information.

e Heart to Heart Coaching Services
Do you have a history of failed relationships? Are you afraid of love? Do you constantly argue with the people you love most? Don't despair! Understanding how to improve your relationships with loved ones, friends, and colleagues will also help you to understand how to be a better, happier, and more successful person. Call today or make an appointment online.

B ▶ 8.11 Listen, read, and, after each ad, repeat the pink-stressed words. Underline words you recognize as cognates.

C Reread the ads and choose the best coach for the people in 1–5. Would you recommend each coach after reading or listening to their ad? Why (not)?
1 "I can't decide whether to wait for promotion or look for a different job."
2 "My finances are a mess! I owe a lot of money and don't know what to do."
3 "I need to make a lot of changes in my life, but I don't know where to start."
4 "I keep arguing with everyone I know. I feel like everybody hates me."
5 "I always feel tired or sick. How can I lead a healthier life?"

> I'd recommend Good Life Services. They seem professional and have an informative website.

D 🗨 **Make it personal** In pairs, answer 1–3.
1 Are you usually more convinced by reading or listening to ads?
2 Which areas of life in **A** do people usually need most help with? Order them 1–5. Any differences?
3 Do you know anyone who pays for coaching? Would you ever pay?

> My brother pays for a personal fitness trainer at the gym. I don't think it's necessary. It's obvious what to do to keep fit.

> But sometimes you need someone to motivate you!

8.5 Will you ever get married?

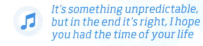
It's something unpredictable, but in the end it's right, I hope you had the time of your life

ID in Action Making predictions

A ▶ 8.12 Joe's going through a difficult time, so he talked to three coaches from ads a–e on p. 106. Listen and match the coaches to their ads.

coach 1 _____   coach 2 _____   coach 3 _____

B ▶ 8.12 Listen again and check what you think Joe will do. Give reasons.

Joe's future	Yes	No	Maybe
1 get a promotion			
2 move to a new job			
3 sleep better			
4 check social media at night			
5 tell Emma how he feels			
6 marry Emma			

I think he'll get a promotion. He deserves one beacuse he's been with the company a long time.

I disagree! He needs to look for a new job. He's already waited too long for a promotion.

Common mistakes

Did your boss talk to you?
~~You will~~ get a promotion?
W

C ▶ 8.12 **Test your memory!** Circle the five words / expressions the coaches use. Then listen again to check.

yes	Definitely. / For sure. / Absolutely.
	Probably. / There's a good chance.
fifty-fifty	Maybe. / Perhaps. / Possibly. / That depends.
no	Probably not. / I doubt it.
	Definitely not. / No way. / Not a chance.

D **Make it personal** **Fortune Telling!** In pairs.

A: Write three questions about your future (money, love, family, travel, career, studies …) and give each question a random number between 1 and 6. Ask B your questions.

B: You're an inexperienced fortune-teller. Listen to A's question and number and make a prediction based on the photo on the corresponding card. Use your imagination and expressions from **C**.

Am I going to marry my boyfriend? Number 4.

No, not a chance! He's going to get a great job abroad and you'll meet someone better.

1. I — THE WARRIOR
2. II — THE TRAVELLER
3. III — THE UNLUCKY
4. IV — THE LUCKY
5. V — THE SUN
6. VI — THE CLOWN

Writing 8   A formal inquiry email

Trapped in a prism, In a prism of light, Alone in the darkness, A darkness of white. We fell in love, Alone on a stage, In the reflective age

A Read ads 1 and 2 and the email. Which ad is the email responding to?

B In which paragraphs, a–d, does Kiera:
1. ☐ express interest in talking to the coach
2. ☐ make an inquiry about the coach's work
3. ☐ explain why she needs help
4. ☐ thank the coach and request a response
5. ☐ say where she saw the ad
6. ☐ give details about exactly what she wants to know

C Look at the highlighted examples in the email and read **Write it right!** Then correct the mistakes in 2–5.

> ✓ **Write it right!**
>
> In a formal inquiry, you need to sound very polite to build a good relationship. Use indirect forms to request information.
>
> Add *if* in Yes / No questions and remove the auxiliary *do*. Notice that the word order sometimes changes.

Direct (less polite)	Indirect (more polite)
Do you work in the evenings?	Can / Could you tell me if you work in the evenings?
Where do you work?	Can / Could you tell me where you work?
Can you see me next week?	Do you think you could see me next week?
What are your fees?	I'd appreciate it if you could tell me your fees.
Can I meet you to discuss this?	I'd be interested in meeting you to discuss this.

1. I'd appreciate ^it if you could explain what your work involves.
2. Do you think could you recommend someone to help me?
3. Can you tell me when do you open?
4. I'd be interested to knowing more about your plans.
5. Could you tell me what are your fees?

D Rewrite direct questions 1–5 using more polite, indirect forms.
1. Can I have your phone number?
   Do _____?
2. Do you have an office in Boston?
   Could _____?
3. Who are your clients?
   I'd _____.
4. Do you have any clients in Brazil?
   Could _____?
5. Can you get back to me by tomorrow?
   I'd _____.

---

1 **Get the career you want**
Becky Smith, professional careers coach. Experience of working with students from all backgrounds. Specialist in the financial and business sectors. 95% success rate. Contact me for a confidential consultation.

2 **Change your life for good**
Do you want to improve your employment prospects, become more socially confident, or take control or your life? Lifestyle coach **Toby Wilde** can help you succeed in all aspects of your life. Call or email today.

Dear _____,

a. I saw your ad on the university website. I'd be interested in talking to you about my situation.

b. I'm 19 years old and studying law. My parents want me to work in a big city law firm. The problem is, I don't want to be a lawyer, but I feel that I'm trapped in my situation. I'm really interested in science, and I'd like to work in research. I'm ambitious, but there are very few job opportunities for someone without a science degree. I know the pay and benefits for lawyers are very good. I want to develop my career, but I'm worried that if I do what my parents want, I'll be unhappy.

c. I'd like to know more about the work you do. Firstly, you say in your ad that you specialize in the financial and business sectors. Can you tell me if you also have experience of working with scientific research? You also said you have a very high success rate. Do you think you could give me the names of some people you have helped? Finally, could you tell me what the cost is for a consultation?

d. Thank you in advance for taking the time to answer my questions. I'd appreciate it if you could reply to my questions as soon as convenient. I look forward to hearing from you.

Sincerely,

Kiera Jones

E 🎧 **Make it personal** Choose an ad from **A** or p. 106. Write an email in 150–200 words inquiring about the services of the coach.

Before	Decide why you need to hire the coach and what exactly you need to know.
While	Write an inquiry following the structure of the email in **A**. Include four paragraphs and at least three questions using indirect forms.
After	Exchange emails with another student. Check each other's emails, paying attention to the requests for information. Is the email polite?

108

8 Back to your future

1 Before watching

A Match 1–6 with definitions a–f. Which words do you already know and use? Give examples.

1 a fair
2 make stuff up
3 a (higher) plane
4 scare
5 tag along
6 a trick

a make someone afraid
b a (su*pe*rior) level of thought, e.g., *spi*ritual
c a large exhibition, full of fun things to do
d go somewhere with someone
e an action designed to de*cei*ve (someone)
f invent things / stories

I have a friend who's always making stuff up.

I was tricked into paying too much for my car!

B Check what each character will be interested in at the fair.

	August	Andrea	Daniel	Lucy
futu*ri*stic science exhibits				
being with Daniel				
going somewhere with Lucy				
seeing horses				
the *pie*-eating con*test*				

2 While watching

A Watch up to 0:50 to check your answers in 1B. When are they all meeting up again?

B Listen without image up to 1:36. Number these items in the order you hear them, 1–8.

☐ coming back
☐ environmental reporter
☐ experience at least
☐ getting people la*ttes*
☐ internship in Washington
☐ Los Angeles
☐ pretty im*pres*sive
☐ this summer

C Watch to check. What else did you hear and notice?

I think they held hands at the end!

D Watch the rest. True (T) or False (F)?

1 They're both keen to hear their futures.
2 The fortune teller surprises them.
3 Both of them have doubts and ask questions.
4 Daniel shows her his hand then gets angry.
5 He thinks it's some kind of trick.
6 She knows where they're both going.
7 She predicts they'll go far away and never meet again.
8 Neither of them believe anything she says.

E Complete 1–9 with *will* or *be going to* according to the video. Who said each sentence?

1 I _____ go see the horses.
2 What _____ you guys _____ see?
3 I _____ tag along with you if you don't mind my company.
4 So we _____ all _____ meet back here in an hour or so.
5 You _____ be a wonderful environmental reporter.
6 I think you _____ be a fabulous *film*maker!
7 I _____ be running around and trying to find or*ga*nic chocolate for some crazy actress.
8 You _____ go very far. And you _____ be on many planes, both spiritual and physical.
9 But in the end, you _____ come back together.

3 After watching

A Complete 1–6 with the verbs in the simple present or present continuous.

come back   go (x2)   think   try   wait

1 August _____ to the science exhibits.
2 August _____ all year for the pie-eating contest.
3 What _____ Lucy _____ about doing this summer?
4 Lucy says, "You know I _____ to L.A., right?"
5 Lucy wants to know if Daniel _____.
6 What _____ you _____ to do? Scare us?

B Watch again to check. As you do, whenever your teacher pauses the video, tell your partner the next thing the character is going to say.

C 🔘 **Make it personal** Are you good at predicting (results, weather, etc.)? Any experience of fortune telling, or being tricked?

I guess soccer scores every week, but I'm hardly ever right!

My grandmother used to read coffee cups. I loved it!

I was given false money once. I didn't know what to do.

D 🔘 **Make it personal** In groups of three, role-play Lucy, Daniel, and the fortune teller.

1 Role-play the video as closely as you can.
2 Change roles and do it again. But this time, believe everything she says.

Show me your hands, my dears. Ooooooh! I see many things, good and bad.

109

R4 Grammar and vocabulary

A **Picture dictionary.** Cover the words on these pages and use the pictures to remember:

page	
86	7 movie genres
87	6 key aspects of movies
88	7 labels for passionate people
90	6 unusual collections
95	4 phrases for giving your opinion
98	6 technological items
100	7 phrasal verbs
155	the 8 pairs of picture words in lines 3 and 4 of the consonants chart

B ▶ **R4.1** Complete the quiz with these verbs in the passive, then circle the correct answers. Listen to check.

call   consider   find   sell   write

1 "Imagine" _____ by **John Lennon** / **Paul McCartney** in 1971.
2 About 1.5 billion **smartphones** / **iPhones** _____ around the globe every year.
3 Beyoncé's first solo album _____ **Dangerously in Love** / **Irreplaceable**.
4 Amy Winehouse was only **27** / **31** when she _____ dead in her apartment.
5 **Canadian** / **American** singer Ariana Grande _____ to be one of the world's best vocalists.

C In small groups, write a five-question quiz using passive sentences. Use the verbs in **B** or choose your own. Give two answer options for each question. Exchange with another group. Any "killer" questions?

> Love in the Time of Cholera was written by Gabriel García Márquez / Isabel Allende.

> Machu Picchu was constructed by the Aztecs / Incas.

D Complete 1–3 with *so*, *such* or *such a / an*. Choose the best (✓) and worst (✗) line each time. Compare in pairs.

E 🔊 **Make it personal** Circle the correct options in 1–5. Do you agree with the predictions? In pairs, compare and give reasons.

Life in the Future

1 CDs and DVDs _____ disappear before 2030.
  a probably won't   b won't probably
2 People will _____ travel in self-driving cars soon.
  a can   b be able to
3 _____ less online piracy by 2030.
  a There will have   b There will be
4 Apple _____ disappear in the next 20 years.
  a will   b is going
5 In 100 years, there won't be _____ to live on dry land.
  a anywhere   b nowhere

> I think CDs and DVDs are going to disappear before 2025.

> Right! They've already disappeared in my house.

F Correct the mistakes. Check your answers in units 7 and 8.

🔶 Common mistakes

1 I'm really into watch horror movies. (1 mistake)
2 We didn't do nothing on the weekend. (1 mistake)
3 I'm lucky to have so intelligents parents. (2 mistakes)
4 Thousands of songs is downloaded illegal every day. (2 mistakes)
5 I thought the latest Shawn Mendes album great. (1 mistake)
6 "Where did you born?" "On 1988." (3 mistakes)
7 How long do you study here? (2 mistakes)
8 "Do you go to the party tonight?" "I think yes." (2 mistakes)
9 Will have less pollution 100 years from now. (2 mistakes)
10 I will ever find true love? (1 mistake)

Meeting someone for the first time? The right and wrong things to say!

1 A blind date
☐ I'm _____ happy to finally get a chance to meet you.
☐ Wow! It feels like we've known each other for _____ long time.
☐ Hmm … You didn't look _____ short in the photos.

2 Your girl / boyfriend's parents
☐ It's _____ honor to meet you.
☐ I've heard _____ great things about you.
☐ I've heard _____ many great things about your food that I have to try it myself.

3 Your boss
☐ It's _____ privilege to work with someone like you.
☐ You look _____ much younger in person.
☐ It's _____ great to finally meet you.

> I think the worst one for a blind date is …

110

Skills practice

♪ *And I've missed your ginger hair, And the way you like to dress. Won't you come on over, Stop making a fool out of me. Why don't you come on over Valerie?*

R4

A ▶ **R4.2** Listen to conversations 1–4. After the beep, you have four seconds to write the number next to the correct sentence. There are three extra sentences.

I'll turn it down. ____
I'll turn it up. ____
I'll plug it in. ____
I'm going to get up at 5 a.m. ____
I'm going to wake up at 5 a.m. ____
I'm going to turn it on. ____
I'm going to turn it off. ____

B ▶ **R4.3** Listen to the news stories and circle the correct options in 1–4.
1. **More** / **Fewer** people are out of work.
2. This news item is about **a power outage** / **politics**.
3. Pineapple is probably a **computer** / **car** company.
4. This news item is about **a natural disaster** / **alien life**.

C ▶ **R4.3** Listen again and write the numbers in 1–4. Practice saying the sentences. Don't stress the gray words.
1. Unemployment has increased by _____.
2. _____ cities were affected.
3. _____ of all iTabs produced in May were considered defective.
4. The town, with a population of only _____, was visited by UFOs in the past.

D ▶ **R4.4** Listen, read, and match review extracts 1–3 to the correct genre. There's one extra genre.
action ☐   mystery ☐   documentary ☐   drama ☐

E Reread. Which review is about a movie with …
a. a lot of emotional conversations?
b. very few words?
c. a story we've all seen many times?

F 🎙 **Make it personal** In groups, play *Guess the movie!* Take turns thinking of a movie or TV series plot you can describe in one sentence, like Review 1. The others ask *Yes* / *No* questions to try to guess the movie / TV series.

> *A rich girl meets a poor boy on a boat, they fall in love, the boat hits an iceberg, he dies, but she survives.*

> *Did it win an Oscar?*   *Is it an American movie?*

G ▶ **R4.5** 🎙 **Make it personal** **Question time!**
1. Listen to the 12 lesson titles in units 7 and 8.
2. In pairs, practice asking and answering. Use the book map on p. 2–3. Ask at least two follow-up questions. Try to answer in different ways. Can you have a short conversation about all the questions?

Review 1 ★☆☆☆☆
The plot is so unintelligent that it can be described in a sentence: Girl falls in love with boy, boy dies, girl gets depressed. Think of all the Hollywood clichés you've ever heard. They're in this movie. But it's guaranteed to be a box office success in the U.S. and abroad.

Review 2 ★★★★★
This movie is truly spectacular. If you think a silent movie about an unsolved murder in 1870 is a recipe for disaster, think again. The main character (Lucy Barnes) is played by Jennifer Lawrence with such skill that, honestly, you don't miss hearing her voice. *The Trap* is a classic example of images speaking louder than words, which perhaps explains why subtitles are used only five times in this movie.

Review 3 ★★★★☆
What do you expect from a movie starring Mark Wahlberg? Lots of action scenes, right? Well, wrong. In *Gone*, Wahlberg reconstructs the events leading to the Boston Marathon bombing in 2013 with such sensitivity, precision, and attention to detail that you instantly forget who he is. The interviews with paramedics alone are worth the price of admission. *Gone* is a masterpiece of factual movie-making and it truly deserves to win an Oscar.

111

9.1 What do you think of marriage?

How to plan the perfect wedding
- plan the **enga**gement party ☐
- plan the **ho**neymoon ☐
- book a place for the wedding **ce**remony ☐
- make the guest list and send wedding **invi**tations ☐
- create a **gift** registry ☐
- choose clothes for the **bride**, **groom**, and **brides**maids ☐ ☐ ☐
- plan the re**cep**tion ☐
- choose the **flo**wers and deco**ra**tions ☐ ☐

⚠ Common mistakes
George got married ~~with~~ *to* Amal in 2012.
We need a ~~local~~ *place / venue* for the wedding.
They ~~compromised themselves~~ *got engaged*.
Use *get* for all the stages in a relationship: *get together, get engaged, get (re)married, get divorced*!

1 Vocabulary Weddings

A ▶9.1 Which **bold** words in the wedding checklist do you recognize? Guess the pronunciation. Then match them to a–k in the photos. Listen to a wedding planner and number them in the order you hear them, 1–11.

B ▶9.1 Listen again. Which two things on the checklist doesn't the planner do? Which three things do you think are the most difficult to organize?

For me, one of the hardest would be choosing ...

C 🔵 **Make it personal** In small groups.
1 Would / Did you / your parents use a wedding planner? Why (not)?
2 Search online for a quote you like about weddings and marriage. How does it reflect your opinion?

Here's a good one: "Six words for a successful marriage: I'm sorry, it's my fault!". I totally agree!

2 Listening

🎵 *My head's under water, But I'm breathing fine, You're crazy and I'm out of my mind 'Cause all of me, Loves all of you*

9.1

A ▶ 9.2 Listen to Michaela and her wedding planner. Does the photo show the wedding she wants or the one the wedding planner wants?

B ▶ 9.2 Listen again and complete the chart with what each of them wants.

		Wedding planner	Michaela
1	color of invitations		
2	ceremony at …		
3	reception in a …		
4	number of bridesmaids		
5	number of wedding guests		
6	type of rings		
7	place for honeymoon		

C 👤 **Make it personal** In pairs, answer 1 and 2 then share your best ideas in groups.
1 Which wedding in **A** would you prefer? Agree three things that are essential for a good wedding. Does the class agree?
2 Describe the best wedding you've been to. Why was it so special?

> *My sister's wedding was amazing. They got married in a beautiful church and I was a bridesmaid.*

3 Reading

A Read the website and identify three things that are different from a traditional wedding. Compare in pairs. Did you identify the same three things?

A wedding that is up in the air!

Are you looking for a way to make your wedding more interesting and memorable? Last Saturday, a crane lifted Helen Gomez and James Brandon up onto a platform in the air for their wedding ceremony. They got married up there, 160 feet (50 meters) in the air with the officiant, who conducted the ceremony, and 20 of their friends and family. There was even a platform for musicians to play the music the couple wanted. After they shared their marriage vows, Helen and James did an exciting bungee jump over the side of the platform.

After the ceremony, the wedding party all went back down to earth, but then they all went back up again for the reception. At the reception, guests ate a three-course meal wearing seatbelts so they were safe and couldn't fall. The idea of this kind of wedding is to create an experience that really will be unforgettable. You're probably asking yourself, "is this safe?" Marriage in the Sky, the company who organized the wedding, insist that it is. They operate in more than 40 countries, including ones that have strict rules about safety, such as the U.S., Canada, and Australia.

B ▶ 9.3 Listen and reread. Are 1–7 True (T) or False (F)? Correct the false ones.
1 A large elevator took the bride and groom up in the air.
2 The other people at the ceremony were strangers.
3 The couple chose their own music.
4 They made their marriage promises while they did a bungee jump.
5 The guests stayed up in the air after the ceremony, then did a bungee jump at the end.
6 When the guests ate, they couldn't walk around.
7 The company operates only in Europe and Asia.

C 👤 **Make it personal** In pairs. What's similar / different in your culture about weddings and the weddings described in this lesson? Do other pairs agree? Who in class has been to the most unusual wedding?

> *Here, most people get married in a church.*

> *Yes, that's true, but not everyone does that anymore.*

9.2 Do you think romantic movies are entertaining?

1 Vocabulary Romance

A ▶9.4 Listen to two conversations and match them to photos a and b.

1 I met Abby about two years ago and immediately **had a crush on her**. We **dated** for about a year and then we **broke up**. She's seeing someone else now, but I'm still in love with her. I'm really worried that I'm going to lose her forever. What should I do?

2 I found out that my partner **cheated on me** in the past. He says that he fell in love with someone else, but that it's over now, it was a mistake, and he wants to stay with me. Now we **argue** all the time. It's absolutely exhausting! Should I **dump him**? Or try again?

B ▶9.4 Read problems 1 and 2 and match the **bold** phrases to meanings 1–6. Which ones are more informal? Listen to check their pronunciation and remember the listener's responses.

1 _____ = stopped seeing each other
2 _____ = saw each other
3 _____ = was unfaithful to me
4 _____ = was very attracted to her
5 _____ = end the relationship
6 _____ = express different opinions, often angrily

> **Common mistakes**
> *fell*
> She ~~felt~~ in love.
> *felt* = past tense of *feel*;
> *broke up*
> They ~~terminated~~.
> She *likes* me. (I *like* her.)
> You *like* me. (I *like* you.)
> **Subject** + *like* + **object**

C 🔵 **Make it personal** **Giving advice** In pairs, take turns role-playing the situations in **A**. What's the best advice you can think of?

A: Explain what has happened.
B: Listen sympathetically and give advice.

> *You have to tell her how you feel. Maybe she'll respond positively.*

114

2 Grammar -ed and -ing adjectives

🎵 *Seasons change and our love went cold, Feed the flame 'cause we can't let go, Run away, but we're running in circles, Run away, run away*

9.2

A ▶9.5 Match sentences 1 and 2 to photos a and b. Listen to the conversations to check.
1 The man is bored.   2 The man is boring.

> ⚠ **Common mistakes**
>   *interested*
> I'm ~~interesting~~ in math, but this class was ~~bored~~.
>   *boring*
>   *excited*
> I'm really ~~exciting~~. I'm going to be an aunt.

B Circle the correct options in examples 1 and 2 and the rules in the grammar box.

> 1 They were **amazed** / **amazing** by the **amazed** / **amazing** fireworks.
> 2 Sci-fi movies often include **frightened** / **frightening** monsters. As a child, I was really **frightened** / **frightening** by The Xenomorph in the movie *Alien*.
>
> Adjectives ending in:
>   *-ed* / *-ing* are used for a feeling.
>   *-ed* / *-ing* are used for something that causes the feeling.
>
> → **Grammar 9A** p. 154

C ▶9.6 Complete 1–8 with the correct form of the words. Listen to check. In pairs, which sentences are true for you? Explain why.
1 Watching TV alone is _____. (**depress**)
2 I usually find English classes _____. (**interest**)
3 My family is _____ (**surprise**) when I get good grades.
4 The last movie I saw was _____. (**confuse**)
5 I get _____ (**tire**) after I've eaten.
6 Horror movies aren't usually very _____. (**frighten**)
7 I get _____ (**embarrass**) when people talk about me.
8 Falling in love is always _____ (**excite**), but it can be _____ (**terrify**), too!

> *Number 1 is true for me. I like to have company when I'm watching TV.*

D 🗨 **Make it personal** Intense experiences! In groups, answer 1–3.
1 Choose the two adjectives from **C** or below that best describe your opinion of 1) work 2) school 3) weekends 4) going on a first date 5) learning English.

| amazing | boring | entertaining | exhausting | relaxing | stressful |

2 Find someone who chose the same adjectives as you. Are your reasons similar?

> *My work is exciting, because I travel a lot.*
>
> *Lucky you! My work is boring, because I do the same thing every day.*

3 Describe and compare the last time you had these feelings. Who has the best example for each?
  • very irritated
  • really bored
  • extremely excited
  • absolutely exhausted
  • completely relaxed
  • totally terrified

> *The last time I was absolutely exhausted was after going clubbing on Saturday. I danced nonstop all night!*

115

9.3 If you had three wishes, what would they be?

1 Grammar Second conditional

A ▶9.7 Listen to the first part of a conversation.
1 What do you think the relationship is between:
   a Sarah and Max?   b Sarah and Tony?   c Tony and Max?
2 What do you think Max is going to ask Sarah?

B ▶9.8 Listen to part two to check. What else did you pick up?

C ▶9.8 Listen again and circle the correct options in 1–6. In pairs, do you think Tony is cheating on her? Why (not)?
1 What **would** / **will** you do if Tony **cheats** / **cheated** on you?
2 If I **see** / **saw** him with another person, I'**ll** / '**d** confront him.
3 What if a friend **tells** / **told** you, what **will** / **would** you do?
4 If I **didn't** / **don't** know for sure, I'**d** / '**ll** ask Tony first.
5 **Would** / **Will** you follow him, if you **think** / **thought** he liked someone else?
6 I'**ll** / '**d** trust him to tell me the truth, if he **wants** / **wanted** to date someone else.

D Complete the grammar box. Are both form and use similar in your language?

I'd be an architect.

> **1** Match *if* clauses 1-3 to result clauses a-c. In pairs, ask and answer the questions.
>
> | *If* clause | Result clause |
> |---|---|
> | 1 If you were a bird (but you're not), | a what would it be? |
> | 2 If the Internet didn't exist (but it does), | b where would you fly to? |
> | 3 If you could choose any job (but you can't), | c how would your life change? |
>
> **2** Circle the correct options. Use the second conditional for:
> – future situations that are **possible** / **impossible** but **not very** / **very** likely to happen.
> – imaginary present situations: If we **were** / **are** rich, we'd buy a yacht. But we're not …
>
> ➔ Grammar 9B p. 154

🔥 **Common mistakes**

~~d~~
If I met him, I'~~ll~~ tell him.

If I had more free time,
I'd ~~I'll would~~ learn English more quickly.

E Complete second conditional questions 1–6 with the correct form of the verbs.
1 If your parents _____ (**not like**) your partner, _____ you _____ (**dump**) him / her?
2 If you _____ (**be**) president, what _____ you _____ (**change**) first?
3 If you _____ (**have**) a superpower, which one _____ you _____ (**choose**)?
4 What three items _____ you _____ (**take**) if you _____ (**be**) exiled to a desert island?
5 If you _____ (**have**) a time machine, _____ you _____ (**travel**) back to the past or into the future?
6 If you _____ (**see**) that the person next to you _____ (**have**) a gun in their belt, what _____ you _____ (**do**)?

F 🟢 **Make it personal** Ice breakers! In groups, ask and answer 1–6 in **E** and give reasons. Then decide on one answer for each question. Do other groups have similar answers?

I'd choose to be invisible when I want. Then I'd be able to go anywhere!

I'd be Superspeed and do everything faster.

116

2 Reading 9.3

🎵 *Even if I could, I wouldn't turn on you, And I would stop the world for you, You know I I wanna let you know, I'll never let this feeling go, This love has no ceiling, I cannot deny*

A Take the questionnaire and read about your score. Is it a fair **ver**dict on you?

💬 *Well, yes and no. I'm a bit like that but …*

Are you the jealous kind?

1 Your friend wants to talk about her latest success. Would you …
 a) listen enthusi**as**tically?
 b) listen, but try to change the subject?
 c) avoid your friend for a few days?

2 You're supposed to visit a friend who has a new house. Would you …
 a) go immediately – you'd be very happy for your friend?
 b) go soon, but don't say much about the house?
 c) try to meet your friend in another place?

3 If you had some really great news, would you …
 a) not tell anyone, because you wouldn't want them to feel **en**vious?
 b) tell your closest friends, but you'd be very modest?
 c) tell all your friends, because you want them to feel envious?

4 Your best friend wants you to go out with their new friend. Would you …
 a) go along happily? You'd love to meet your friend's friend.
 b) go, but you'd feel jealous of your friend's friend?
 c) make an excuse and not go?

5 If you saw your partner talking and laughing with someone else, would you …
 a) do nothing? You'd be happy that your partner was having a good time.
 b) go and interrupt and join them?
 c) in**ter**rogate him / her later at home.

6 If you and your friend ap**plied** for the same job (or the same school) and your friend was ac**cep**ted and you weren't, would you feel …
 a) happy for your friend?
 b) disap**point**ed, but still happy for your friend?
 c) very unhappy and you wouldn't want to see your friend?

How many
As? _____
Bs? _____
Cs? _____

Mostly As – You're never jealous and tend to trust others and feel genuinely happy for their success.

Mostly Bs – You have a tendency to get jealous and envious of others, but you're not always this way.

Mostly Cs – You definitely have a jealous nature. You feel jealous of others and you want others to be envious of you.

B ▶9.9 Listen, reread, and repeat the pink-stressed words. In pairs, compare your answers. Any big differences? Do you usually enjoy questionnaires like this?

💬 *The quiz says that I'm a jealous person.*
💬 *Do you think that's true?*
💬 *Yes, sometimes. For example, if my boyfriend wants to go out with his friend and not me, I get jealous.*
💬 *Maybe the quiz is right then!*

⚠️ **Common mistakes**
jealous / envious
He's ~~with envy~~ of her.

C 👤 **Make it personal** In pairs, complete 1–6. Which pair has the most original answers?
1 If my partner were jealous, I'd …
2 If I could be any famous person, I'd be …
3 If I could live anywhere in the world, …
4 If I could invite any three people to dinner, …
5 If I had $50,000 to spend in 24 hours, …
6 If I could change one thing about my life, …

💬 *If my partner were jealous, I'd tell her not to worry.*
💬 *If I could be any famous person, I'd be Lionel Messi because …*

117

9.4 Have you ever performed for an audience?

1 Vocabulary Performers

A ▶9.10 Listen to two friends fantasizing and count the different types of performers they mention. Which ones would they like to be?

B ▶9.10 Complete the names of the performers. Listen to check, match them to photos 1–10, then add to the correct place in the chart. Add two or more words to each column.

an act__ __   a gymn__ __ __   a danc__ __   a comed__ __ __
a music__ __ __   a sing__ __   a skat__ __
a magic__ __ __   an athl__ __ __   a clo__ __

-or	-er	-ian	other
actor			

C ▶9.10 Listen again. True (T) or False (F)?
1 He thinks she's a good singer.
2 Maybe she has musical talents.
3 She thinks he's athletic.
4 She thinks he's amusing.

D 🔵 **Make it personal** Who are your favorite performers? If you were a performer, what would you like to be? Do your classmates agree?

My favorite actor is Wagner Moura.

I love soccer, so I'd like to be a famous soccer player.   *Really? You're good at telling jokes, so maybe you should be a comedian!*

2 Grammar May, might, could, must, can't + be

A ▶9.11 Listen to two people speculating about the blond man in the picture. Then match deductions 1–6 to reasons a–f.

Deduction
1 He's a celebrity.
2 He's an athlete.
3 He's not an athlete.
4 He's a dancer.
5 He's not a dancer.
6 He's a comedian.

Reason
a He's graceful.
b He's handsome.
c He's wearing a sport shirt.
d He's thin.
e He's making his date laugh.
f His legs are thin.

B ▶9.11 Listen again and notice the modal verb in each deduction, 1–6. Reconstruct the sentences. Listen again to check.
1 *Must. He must be a celebrity.*
2 _____
3 _____
4 _____
5 _____
6 _____

C Complete the grammar box.

⚠ **Common mistakes**
could / might / may
He ~~can~~ be tired.
Do you think they're
~~Can they be German?~~

> Modal verbs express different degrees of certainty.
>
> She must be tired – she just ran a marathon.   She might be tired – she was working all day.
> She can't be tired – she slept all day.
>
> Complete 1–3 with *must, could / may / might, can't / must not.*
> If you feel: 1 very sure, use _____.
>   2 unsure, use _____.
>   3 something is definitely not true, use _____.
>
> To ask for a deduction, *must* and *can't* are rarely used. Ask: *Do you think …?*
> Do you think it will rain tomorrow? It might – there are a lot of gray clouds today.

➜ Grammar 9C p. 154

D ▶9.11 Listen again and mark the stress in 1–6 in **2B**. Practice in pairs, saying the sentences with the same stress and intonation.

🎵 *I could be brown, I could be blue, I could be violet sky, I could be hurtful, I could be purple, I could be anything you like*

9.4

E ▶9.12 In pairs. What do you think the items in photos 1–4 are? Listen for more clues. Compare with other pairs. How many pairs got all four correct first time?

> Number 1 might be a kiwi, because of the color.

> No, it can't be a kiwi, because of the texture. It could be a …

F 🟢 **Make it personal** Make a conclusion about situations 1–5. Try to find someone with the same conclusions. Who has the most matches?
1 You see a handsome man eating alone in a restaurant.
2 Jorge, a good student, has suddenly missed a lot of classes.
3 An old friend doesn't answer your messages.
4 You see a couple holding hands and laughing.
5 One of your neighbors has 14 cats, 10 dogs, and 6 rabbits.

> What conclusion do you have for situation 1? He must be waiting for someone.

> My conclusion is that he might be away from home on a business trip.

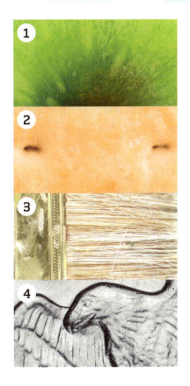

3 Reading

A Why do people jump to conclusions? Choose the option you think is most likely to be true. Then read quickly to check.
1 Because we know we are right.
2 Because experience makes us sure.
3 Because it satisfies the brain.
4 Because it reduces anxiety.

Why we jump to conclusions

You call and text your friend to invite her to a special concert and she doesn't respond. You immediately conclude, "She must be mad, for some reason." We've all done it before – something happens and you jump to a conclusion without any evidence. Psychologists argue that jumping to conclusions is common in many situations, but did you know that there is a reason why we do this? Thanks to what we now know about the brain, we understand why we make these as**sump**tions when we have no evidence.

Neu**ro**logists say that when we assume something that we don't know and it feels logical to us, our brain feels satisfied. We don't have to be right to feel satisfaction, we just need to believe we're right. In this case, certainty is more important than accuracy. Being sure gives us a feeling of satisfaction, although it also makes us feel anxious and sad. It is much healthier to live in uncertainty than to jump to a conclusion, but uncertainty doesn't come with the same feeling of satisfaction from the brain. 🤔

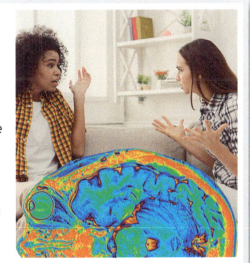

B ▶9.13 Listen, reread, and circle the best answers.
1 It is **normal** / **unusual** to make an assumption.
2 The science of the brain **can** / **cannot** explain why we make assumptions.
3 We **don't want to** / **want to** make sense of things.
4 It is **not necessary** / **necessary** to be completely correct to feel satisfaction.
5 It is better for us to be **sure** / **unsure** about something.

C 🟢 **Make it personal** **Oops, I did it again!** In pairs, share stories about times when you or someone you know jumped to the wrong conclusion. Who has the best example?

> Once I called my girlfriend and she didn't call me back for two days, so I thought she was angry about something, but she was actually in the hospital!

119

9.5 How do you get on with your siblings?

ID Skills Identifying reasons

A Where are you in the birth order in your family? First, in the middle, youngest, or are you an only child? Has this had an effect on your life and personality?

> *I'm an only child, so I like being by myself. And I guess I was spoiled as a child.*

B Read the article and match headings 1–6 to paragraphs a–e. There's one extra.

1 The baby of the family
2 The flexible ones
3 The self-sufficient ones
4 The effect of birth order
5 The bossy ones
6 The best of all

Birth order and you

a Your siblings, you love them, you hate them, you need them, you don't need them. Birth order, that is whether you are the oldest, the youngest, or in the middle in your family, can have an effect on your personality and your family dynamics. Are you similar to or completely different than your brothers and sisters? Birth order can help to explain why. According to Alfred Adler, an Austrian psychiatrist, birth order has a profound effect on how you see the world. Here are a few of the observations that Adler makes.

b First-born children are natural leaders – they are more responsible and mature and are more accustomed to adult company. They are often more intelligent than their later born siblings and they can be aggressive, because they are used to being in charge. They like being alone.

c Middle children, on the other hand, are often the opposite of first-born children. They feel they don't have any particular role in their family, so their friends are often more important to them than their family. They are good at negotiating and sociable, and people see them as adaptable and relaxed. At the same time, they often keep secrets and don't open up much about their emotions.

d As for the youngest in the family, they tend to be friendly and sociable. They like to be with other people and are often charming. They like to be the center of attention. They are not good at being alone and they get bored easily, but they have a lot of self-confidence and are not afraid to take risks. They tend to be more

irresponsible, because they know that someone will always help them if they have any kind of problem.

e What about if you are an only child? Well, it seems that one of the main issues for only children is that they have to work harder to make friends, because they don't immediately have them in the family. They are often more independent and are used to spending time alone and entertaining themselves.

C ▶ 9.14 Listen, reread, and complete the chart. Find the number of adjectives indicated in each column in the text in **B**.

First born (3+)	Middle children (3)	Youngest children (3+)	Only children (1)

D ▶ 9.15 Listen and note Michael and David's birth order. What's the matter with Michael?

> *I'd tell Michael to buy a new car with credit!*

E ▶ 9.15 Listen again. In pairs, what would you say to Michael, David, and Jane?

F 🔵 Make it personal Form groups by birth order. Do you agree with what the article says about your position? Then form mixed groups and compare. Any surprises?

> *I agree that the oldest child is the most intelligent!*   *Are you the oldest child?*   *Yes, of course!*

9.5 Is there something I can help with?

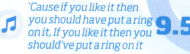

🎵 *'Cause if you like it then you should have put a ring on it, If you like it then you should've put a ring on it* 9.5

ID in Action Giving advice

A ▶9.16 Match problems 1–5 to suggestions a–f. There's one extra. Listen to check.

1 I've lost my phone.
2 My boyfriend works on weekends.
3 I have a headache.
4 I'm bored at my job.
5 I'm failing math.

a Go home and lie down.
b Look in your room.
c Get a new one.
d Work harder.
e Talk to him.
f Why don't you run away?

> **Common mistakes**
>
>   'd
> You/better listen.
>
> My mom made me ~~to~~ clean my room.
>
>   I were
> If I'm you, I'd go to the party.
>
> The subjunctive is easy in English because it doesn't have new verb forms. You only notice it in expressions like *If I were you, I'd ...* Increasingly, people now also say *If I was you, I'd ...*

B ▶9.16 Listen again and complete dialogues 1–5. Do each of **A**'s lines sound like suggestions or orders?

1 A: _____ go upstairs and look in your room?
   B: That's a good _____.
2 A: If I _____ you, I'd _____ to him and explain that it's not fair.
   B: _____ for the suggestion, but you don't know my boyfriend.
3 A: You _____ go home and lie down. You _____ be at a party.
   B: You're _____.
4 A: _____ looking for a new job?
   B: _____ for the tip.
5 A: You _____ start working harder or you won't get into college.
   B: I _____.

C In pairs, think of suggestions for Noah, Harper, or Claudia. Find a new partner who chose a different person and role-play both situations.

I have a cold and a headache, but I have an important meeting with my boss later.

Noah

If I were you, I'd cancel the meeting.

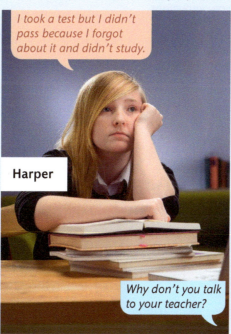

I took a test but I didn't pass because I forgot about it and didn't study.

Harper

Why don't you talk to your teacher?

I've got a promotion in my company's Canadian office, but my boyfriend Juan hasn't finished college.

Claudia

I'd find out how Juan feels.

D 🔵 **Make it personal** Think of real problems people have. In groups of four, role-play giving advice.

A: Explain your problem.   B, C, D: Give A advice.

My sister doesn't like her job because she has to work long hours and they don't pay her very well.

If I were your sister, I'd change my job!

Writing 9 Giving advice

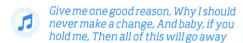

Give me one good reason, Why I should never make a change, And baby, if you hold me, Then all of this will go away

A Read Ben's post on an online advice forum and the two responses. Which response is from:
a   a friend of Ben's?
b   a professional counselor?

From: Ben

Can anyone help, please? I'm worried about my brother. His girlfriend broke up with him and now she's dating his best friend. He's lost his job at the restaurant where he was working, and I think he owes money to some of his friends. His school grades are going down too. What do you think I should do? I need some advice.

¹Dear Ben,

You're in a difficult situation, but here are a few ideas and suggestions for you. First of all, try not to panic. You need to stay calm. ²You have to talk to your brother. Why don't you invite him for lunch or coffee? If I were you, I'd tell him how worried I was about him. Then you should give him the opportunity to talk, and let him explain how he's feeling. Ask him if he understands why ³his girlfriend ended their relationship and let him know that you are there to support him. Try to make him see how important school is for his future, even if it's difficult to see that now. Maybe you could offer to help him with his school work. ⁴My advice is, ⁵don't lend him any money: this won't help him. He has to take responsibility for himself and you need to help him with this.

⁶With sincere good wishes,

Marlena Duncan

What's up, dude?

Sounds like yr bro is in a mess, sorry 2 hear bout that – stay cool and talk to him, man, like, ask him for a drink, etc, find out why his gf dumped him – IF he wants to talk about it ;-) best advice? – tell him youll help, not $$ so don't give him nada, call me if you need to talk, ok?

Hang in there man, you hear me?

Joe ☺

B Reread the responses. Who gives advice 1–8: Marlena (M), Joe (J), or both (B)?
1   Ben should stay calm and not panic.
2   He should arrange to meet his brother.
3   He needs to tell his brother he's worried about him.
4   He should find out why his brother's girlfriend left him.
5   He needs to be clear that he will help his brother.
6   He could help his brother with his school work.
7   He shouldn't give his brother money.
8   He should phone to talk more about his problem.

C Match the highlighted expressions in Marlena's response to the corresponding expressions in Joe's.

D Read **Write it right!** then rewrite 1–4 in the opposite style.

✓ Write it right!

To give advice, use a style appropriate to the subject.

	Formal style	Informal style
Start / End	Dear X; With best wishes / Sincerely	Hi / What's up?; Bye
Sentences	complete sentences	can be incomplete sentences
Directness	less direct: *If I were you, I'd share your worries with him.*	more direct: *Tell him you're worried!*
Idioms, slang, abbreviations, emoticons	do not use	OK to use
Punctuation	use capital letters, periods, and commas correctly	use fewer capitals, commas, and OK to use dashes

1   v sorry 2 hear bout yr prob
2   First, you need to talk to your brother before it is too late.
3   best advice? – stay cool, man & dump her, ok? understand?
4   If I were you, I'd try to persuade your friend to discuss the situation.

E **Make it personal** Read the problem and choose to write a formal or informal reply in 80–150 words.

From: Alicia K

Help!

My brother and sister are in the middle of a big fight and I'm caught between them. My brother has started dating my sister's best friend, and my sister is really angry. He's 22 and my sister's friend is only 17. My brother and sister are not speaking, but they call me every day and ask me to do something. What do you think I should do?

With thanks, Alicia

Before	Think of five suggestions and the order you want to say them.
While	Use features of the style you have chosen. Vary the expressions you use to give advice. Refer to the tips in **Write it right!**
After	Exchange responses with a classmate. Is your advice similar?

122

9 Green-eyed monsters

1 Before watching

A Match 1–10 to definitions a–j.

1. a **back**bone
2. a beast
3. a chicken
4. dumb
5. faults
6. fear
7. ignore
8. jealous
9. a knight in shining **ar**mor
10. surrounded by

a. spine, **spi**nal column
b. stupid
c. take no notice of
d. a scary animal
e. a person (usually a man) who helps another (usually a woman)
f. envious, green-eyed
g. a **cow**ard
h. be afraid of
i. on all sides
j. **de**fects

B In pairs, with sound off. **A:** Watch up to 0:35 and tell B what you see. **B:** Don't watch! Listen to A. Guess what they actually say. Then change roles.

> **A:** August's in the café, and he's unhappy. He's on his computer, talking to somebody.

> **B:** I think Daniel says, "Look at Paolo and Andrea."

2 While watching

A Watch up to 2:21. True (T) or False (F)?

1. Rory wants to challenge Paolo too.
2. Daniel says he's too nice to be so negative.
3. Daniel tells them to be nice to their friend Paolo.
4. Rory's pleased about how he's feeling.
5. Daniel warns Rory **jea**lousy is changing him.
6. August admits he's jealous too.
7. Rory de**nies** being jealous.
8. August decides to do something to challenge Paolo.

ID Café

B Who says 1–10, August (A), Rory (R), or Daniel (D)? Watch to check.

1. But you're all just making excuses.
2. I know my faults.
3. That guy is serious competition. In everything.
4. If you really want something, you will do whatever it takes.
5. No more excuses. Use your personality.
6. Dude, you're only physically strong! You have no courage.
7. She only pays attention to me when she wants something.
8. Both of you, grow some backbone.
9. Why didn't Lucy ask me to be her star?
10. Um, I gotta work on my writing.

C 🙂 **Make it personal** Have you (or people close to you) ever been really jealous? What or who of? Did it work out OK in the end?

> Yes, me! I was jealous of all my friends who had the first iPhone. In the end, I did some jobs for neighbors and made enough money to buy one.

3 After watching

A Check the advice Daniel gives August and Rory.

- [ ] Stop making excuses.
- [ ] Join the competition.
- [ ] If you really want something, do whatever it takes.
- [ ] Don't be like Steve Jobs.
- [ ] Use your genius brain!
- [ ] If you want to build muscles, go to the gym.
- [ ] Get some confidence.
- [ ] Grow some backbone.
- [ ] Stop using Paolo as an excuse.

B Complete 1–9 with these expressions.

a knight in shining armor	Chicken! Tell me the truth	
Grow some backbone	I bet	Join the club
Mind if I join you	one of the worst	
Tell me if I'm crazy, but	You're all heart	

1. _____! Get more confidence and don't be afraid.
2. He's like _____. He'll help anyone in trouble.
3. _____? I'm on a break.
4. _____. You're a great person!
5. _____ doesn't that girl look just like Liv Tyler?
6. **A:** I'm so tired from that long flight! **B:** _____, so am I.
7. _____ I'm smarter and a better journalist.
8. This is probably _____ feelings in the world
9. _____. Have you ever asked her out again?

C 🙂 **Make it personal** Role-play! In groups, create a role-play using as many expressions from **B** as possible. Perform it for the class.

> Tell me if I'm crazy but … isn't that Zac Efron talking to our teacher?

> No way. You're kidding!

123

10

10.1 Do you often feel stressed?

Institute For
MEDITATION & RELAXATION

Stressed out? Not again!

What's the biggest stressor for you in your daily life?
- [ ] poor diet
- [ ] multitasking
- [ ] financial problems
- [ ] pressure to succeed
- [ ] deadlines
- [ ] caring for a child
- [ ] a lack of sleep
- [ ] a lack of exercise
- [ ] peer pressure

1 Vocabulary Causes and symptoms of stress

A ▶10.1 Match the causes of stress to photos a–h. There's one extra cause. Then find six /k/ and five /ʃ/ sounds in the survey. Listen to check.

B ▶10.2 Listen to the survey. Number the photos in **A** in the order you hear them, 1–8.

C ▶10.2 Listen again and write the number of the speaker who:
- [ ] has no energy in the evenings.
- [ ] has to finish a piece of work today.
- [ ] gets sick when she's stressed out.
- [ ] never has any time off.
- [ ] makes the problem worse by worrying.
- [ ] has to pass a lot of exams.
- [ ] uses credit to buy things.
- [ ] has to do many things at the same time.

124

D Read examples 1–5, then match 1–3 below to uses a–c. Which of the examples are true for you?

🎵 *Wish we could turn back time, to the good old days, When our momma sang us to sleep, but now we're stressed out*

10.1

1 I'm under**paid**. = I don't earn enough money.
2 I'm over**worked**. = I have too much work.
3 I over**slept** this morning. = I didn't wake up when I was supposed to.
4 I under**achieved** in the test. = I didn't do as well as I could have.
5 I show a **lack of** interest in my studies. = I'm not motivated enough at school.

1 under-   a goes before a noun and means "not enough"
2 over-   b combines with a verb and means "not enough"
3 (a) lack of c combines with a verb and means "too much"

⚠️ **Common mistakes**

I have ^a lack of money at the moment.
I feel depressed when I don't get ~~sufficient~~ exercise.
        enough

E Complete 1–6 with *under-*, *over-*, or *lack of*. Then, in pairs, ask and answer the questions. Any big differences?

1 Is your diet very healthy or is there a _____ fresh fruit and vegetables?
2 Is the salary for teachers fair or are they _____ paid?
3 Do you know anyone who often _____ spends and then has a _____ money the following month?
4 Are you generally calm or do you sometimes _____ react?
5 When was the last time you _____ slept and woke up late?
6 Do you feel you've _____ achieved at anything in your life, when you could have done better?

I'm happy enough with my diet. I rarely overeat.

F 🎧 **Make it personal** Which problems in **A** have you / your friends had? In groups, choose the four most serious problems. Compare your list with another group and try to persuade them that your list is better.

For me, number 1 is financial problems, because if you have problems with money, you'll have other problems too.

Yes, but if you don't sleep enough, you'll get sick, so that's the most serious problem.

② Listening

A ▶ 10.3 Which of the 12 options do you think are good ways to relieve stress? Listen. Which three does the woman do? Why doesn't she do the others?

B ▶ 10.3 Listen again. True (T) or False (F)?
1 She's taking a yoga class.
2 She wakes him up in the middle of the night.
3 She has one cup of tea when she's stressed.
4 She discusses her deadlines with her boss.
5 She plans to take a class to help with her stress level.

C What would you do if you were: a) the woman? b) the man?

If I was her, I certainly wouldn't …

D 🎧 **Make it personal** How do you cope with stress? List six things you do. Find someone whose list is the same or almost the same.

I usually stay up all night if I have an exam. I drink coffee and energy drinks all night. After the exam, I sleep for a day!

I play loud music and dance for 10 minutes.

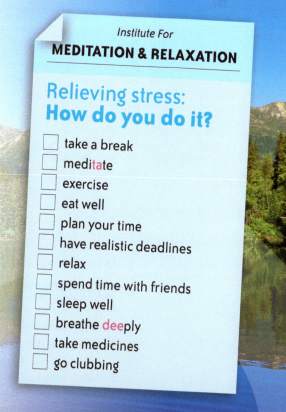

Institute For
MEDITATION & RELAXATION

Relieving stress: How do you do it?

☐ take a break
☐ medi**ta**te
☐ exercise
☐ eat well
☐ plan your time
☐ have realistic deadlines
☐ relax
☐ spend time with friends
☐ sleep well
☐ breathe **dee**ply
☐ take medicines
☐ go clubbing

125

10.2 Would you like to change anything in your life?

1 Vocabulary Lifestyle changes

A What lifestyle changes do the people in pictures 1 and 2 need to make in their lives? Use these ideas plus your own.

drink less soda   eat better   eat less salt   exercise more   get a new job
get more sleep   lose weight   organize and plan time   spend less time online
spend more time with friends / family   watch less TV   work from home   work less

> It looks like the woman should watch less TV.

> Yeah, and look at the bags under her eyes. She needs to …

B Read and match testimonials a and b to the pictures. Circle and share all the clues you found.

Do you need to "turn your life around"?

a I had a terrific day today, thanks to you. I went to bed early last night, so got up early and went to the gym for an hour, then had an omelet for breakfast back at home. Much better than the donut I usually eat at the office! Got to work on time and made a plan of what I needed to do all day. I also had a chat with my boss about my schedule and she agreed to let me work from home two days a week. Result! I finished everything I had to do today and then shared a home-cooked dinner with my family. I'm back on track and finally taking control of my life. Thank you!
By MyVeryBest

b Man! What a day! Started my new job today – seems like it's gonna be fun. I talked to a guy who travels a lot for work – that's exactly what I want to do. Was so busy that I didn't even have time to look at my phone! When I finally got home I had a late dinner with my sister. We had lasagne which was delicious (it was my nephew who cooked it!) – and I only watched TV for an hour! Wow! I feel so much better. Thank you – it's all thanks to the "Turn Your Life Around" seminar.
By BeginAgain

C ▶10.4 Listen, reread, and check the lifestyle changes in **A** that each person made.

D **Make it personal** Choose two lifestyle changes in **A** or your own ideas. In groups, find out about each other's changes by asking and answering 1–3. Which change do most people want to make? Whose change is the most unusual?
1. What are the advantages / disadvantages of making the change?
2. How easy / difficult is it to make the change?
3. What will happen if you do / don't succeed?

> First, I want to stop buying things wrapped in plastic because it's better for the environment. But it's difficult to do because so many products are sold in plastic.

2 Grammar Relative pronouns: *that* & *who*

🎵 *You know I'm the one who put you up there, Name in the sky, Does it ever get lonely? Thinking you could live without me*

10.2

A ▶10.5 Listen and number the photos in the order Patrick describes them, 1–6.

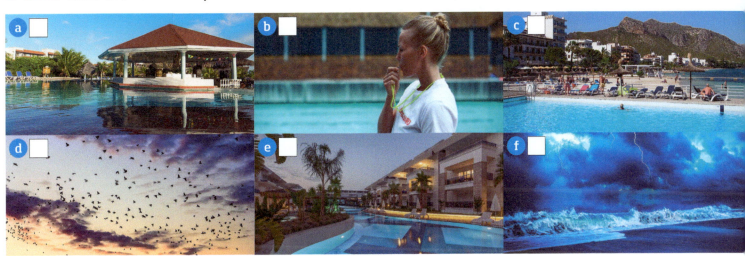

B ▶10.5 Listen again and complete 1–5 by adding the missing words. Then match 1–5 to five of the photos. What might he say about the sixth photo?

1. This is the hotel _____ was on the website.
2. You can see the swimming pool _____ was right outside our room.
3. This is the lifeguard _____ told us to get out of the water.
4. This is the bar _____ was next to the pool.
5. These are some of the birds _____ were flying around outside.

He might say, "This is the …"

C Read the examples in the grammar box and complete the rules. Does your language make a similar distinction?

> Use **relative pronouns** to join two clauses.
> *This is my brother **who** lives in Paris. This is my brother **that** lives in Paris.*
> *He's the man **who** sold me my car. He's the man **that** sold me my car.*
> *There's the café **that** sells the delicious French pastries.*
> *She's the lady I met yesterday.* (*lady* is the object of the clause).
> But *She's the lady who (that) lives next door.* (*lady* is the subject of the clause).
>
> 1 Use _____ and _____ for people. Use _____ for things.
> 2 You **can / can't** omit the relative pronoun when it refers to the object of the clause..
>
> ➜ **Grammar 10A** p. 156

⚠️ **Common mistakes**

~~*This is the computer what I bought today.*~~ *that*

D Complete 1–6 with *that* or *who*. Ask your classmates the questions and try to be the first to find positive answers to all of them!

1. Do you know someone _____ speaks three languages?
2. Do you have any friends _____ speak really good English?
3. Have you been to a place near here _____ sells good coffee and snacks?
4. Was there a star _____ you used to idolize when you were young?
5. What's the food _____ you most enjoy eating?
6. Is there anyone in your family _____ has had an accident recently?

Do you know someone who speaks three langauges?

No, but maybe you should ask Milton. I know he speaks Quechua.

E 🔵 **Make it personal** Let me introduce … In pairs, take turns showing photos. Identify and explain the main people / things in them. Ask follow-up questions too. Share any unusual stories or interesting information with the class.

This is a selfie that my sister Jane sent me. She's the one who studies in L.A.

Cool. When did she go there?

10.3 What's your attitude to money?

1 Reading

A In pairs, use this photo from a documentary movie, the lesson title, and the song line on p. 129 to guess what the documentary is about.

> It could be about an old woman who decides to go on an expensive vacation.

B Read the review and choose the best title. In pairs, share what you remember.

| The Influence of Money | Living without Money | A Weird Woman |

_____ tells the amazing story of Heidemarie Schwermer, a German psychotherapist who decided to start living a very different kind of life in 1996. That year, she left her apartment and gave away all of her things except a suitcase full of clothes. This was a decision that changed her life dramatically. She had no possessions, no place to live, and no way to buy the things she needed. The documentary followed Heidemarie in her day-to-day life and showed what it was like to live an alternative lifestyle.

Heidemarie was constantly on the move, meeting new people, and staying with old and new friends for a few nights. In addition to showing the daily problems she faced, the movie explores Heidemarie's philosophy and why she chose to live this way. We see that it wasn't easy for her to have no money in a society where everything is based on money. People often had strong opinions about how she lived. Some called her a "parasite" while others saw her as an "inspiration."

She managed to survive like this for 20 years, until she died in Kassel, Germany. She lived a very independent life and traveled all around Germany, and also often visited Austria, Switzerland, and Italy. She told people about her experiences and tried to convey the message that a simpler way of life was possible. This is a fascinating documentary for people who are interested in the themes of materialism and consumerism, and how money influences our way of thinking and living.

C ▶10.6 Listen and reread. True (T) or False (F)? Correct the false ones.

1 Heidemarie abandoned everything she owned.
2 She kept some money for emergencies.
3 She sometimes stayed with people she didn't know well.
4 It wasn't too difficult for her to live with no money.
5 She traveled to three continents.
6 The reviewer thinks people of all ages will be interested in the movie.

> I'd like to see it, because I want to know how she lived without money.

D 🎤 **Make it personal** Would you like to see this documentary? Why (not)? Is Heidemarie a parasite or an inspiration? Do you know any similar stories?

> I don't think she's a parasite because …

2 Vocabulary Money

A ▶10.7 Complete the dialogue between two students with the correct form of these verbs. Listen to check and add the two extra words you hear in each line.

| afford | cost | earn | pay for | save | spend | waste | win |

Amy: I need a new phone, but I can't _____ one.
Mark: Why don't you enter the raffle? It's only $20 and the first prize is a new iPhone. You might _____.
Amy: That's too much! I don't _____ much money at my job and I have to ____ all my school books. I don't want to _____ my money on raffle tickets.
Mark: Just trying to help! I know that it _____ a lot being a student nowadays. Come on! Let's go out and get a pizza. I just found $20 – let's _____ it!
Amy: You should _____ the money! … Or give it to me!

B Give two pieces of advice to Amy. What would you do if you found $20?

> She should definitely buy a raffle ticket.   I don't think so. That's a waste of money.
> I'd buy some games and have hours of fun!

⚠ Common mistakes

If I get another job, I can ~~win~~ *earn* more money.

I have 50 dollars, but I won't spend ~~them already~~ *it yet*.

128

C **Make it personal** In groups, do the questionnaire. Find the people who are most similar to / different than you.

🎵 Money, it's a crime, Share it fairly but don't take a slice of my pie, Money, so they say, Is the root of all evil today 10.3

What's Your Attitude To MONEY?

1 When you have extra money, do you spend it or save it?
2 Have you ever won anything in a raffle?
3 Do you think gambling is a good idea or a waste of money?
4 Is it better to earn money or to win money?
5 If there's something you want to buy but can't afford, do you buy it on credit or save for it?
6 Do you usually try to bargain when you buy things?
7 Have you ever found any money in the street? Did you keep it?
8 Do you agree with the song that money "is the root of all evil today"?

I'm not very lucky. I never win anything.   *I won a laptop once.*

③ Listening

A ▶10.8 ▶ What's a "freegan"? Listen to / Watch part one of the video and circle the correct answer.

A "freegan" is a person who:
1 likes to steal expensive things.
2 tries not to buy things.
3 doesn't care about the environment.

B ▶10.8 ▶ Listen / Watch again and number these words / phrases in the order you hear them, 1–6.
☐ alternative living strategies   ☐ freeganism
☐ anti-consumerist lifestyle   ☐ limited participation
☐ conventional economy   ☐ minimal consumption of resources

C ▶10.9 ▶ Listen to / Watch part two. Circle the correct options in 1–4.
1 She **often** / **rarely** takes furniture from **stores** / **the trash**.
2 She **works** / **lives** in **New York** / **Mexico** City.
3 She **has** / **hasn't** got **a little** / **a lot** of furniture in her house that's come from the street.
4 People from **the city** / **other towns** think recycling is a **good** / **bad** idea.

D ▶10.10 ▶ Listen to / Watch part three and check the items she'll take.
things for her bed ☐   furniture ☐
things that need some cleaning ☐   lost property ☐

E **Make it personal** How much do you recycle? In pairs, ask and answer 1–3 with reasons and follow-up questions.
1 What do you throw in the trash that others recycle?
2 How far would you go yourself? Which of these items have you bought or would you buy second hand?
   bedding   soft / wooden furniture   paintings
   clothes   fresh fruit and vegetables   toys
   jewelry   packaged food   electrical items
3 Are there more and more second-hand and charity shops in your city? Do you use them?

🔥 **Common mistakes**
I've started to buy some ~~items of second hand~~. *second hand items*

I'd never take anything out of someone's garbage, but if it's on the street, maybe.

Have you ever found anything useful?

10.4 How often do you post on social media?

1 Listening

A Do you ever have reunions with your old school or work friends? How often do you meet and what do you usually do?

> *I still see my friends from middle school.*
> *How often do you get together?*
> *Once or twice a year. We usually go out for a meal.*

B ▶10.11 Dictation. Listen to a message and write as much of it as you can. Check in pairs, then listen again. Did you get it all?

C Identify all the verb tenses in the message. Do you think your English grammar is getting better?

D 🔵 Make it personal In groups. Are reunions, family get-togethers, or surprise parties usually a good idea? Can they ever go wrong? Give examples.

> *I think reunions are usually a terrible idea. I don't want to see people from my past!*
> *But it's great seeing old friends, and remembering funny stories.*

2 Grammar Asking questions: review

A ▶10.12 Listen to the conversation and complete the chart. Is Kyle going to go to the reunion? Why (not)?

Name:	Kyle	Nicki	Mindy
Status:			
Children:			

B ▶10.12 Add an auxiliary or main verb and order the words in 1–6 to make questions from the conversation. Listen again to check. In pairs, ask and answer, plus follow-up questions.

1 last see / we / each other / when / ?
2 yet / married / you / ?
3 have / you / kids / any / ?
4 high school / still see / how many / from / you / people / ?
5 restaurant / it / which / at / ?
6 often / the / how / reunions / ?

⚠ Common mistakes

~~How much people were there?~~ *many*
~~How often you eat pizza?~~ *do*
~~Where you went?~~ *did go*
~~You like pop music?~~ *Do you*
~~How many years do you live here?~~ *long have you lived*

C Complete the grammar box. Which patterns do you find the easiest?

1 Put examples a–f in the correct places in the chart.

a Where did you go on vacation?
b How was the flight?
c Are you tired?
d How tall are you?
e Did you see that car?
f How many times have you been to France?

To make:	Yes / No questions	Wh- (subject) questions	How + adj / adv questions
Verb *be*:	1 Invert S and V	2 Q + *be* + S	3 *How* + adj / adv + *be* + S
Example:	c Are you tired?	_____	_____
Other verbs:	4 Use an A	5 Q + A + S	6 *How* + adj / adv + A
Example:	_____		

2 *What* or *which*? Read the examples and complete the rules.

Which apple would you like? The red one or the green one? The red one, please.
What fruit do you like? I like apple, pineapple, and watermelon.

Use _____ to ask a general question.
Use _____ to ask about a restricted group.

➡ Grammar 10B p.156

D 🔊 **Make it personal** Complete and answer 1–6. Compare in small groups. Ask follow-up questions too. Who has the best attitude?

🎵 *How deep is your love?, Is it like the ocean?, What devotion are you?, How deep is your love?, Is it like Nirvana?, Hit me harder again, How deep is your love?*

10.4

Language learning is more than just coming to class …

1 _____ did you register for this English class?
   early   on time   late

2 _____ have you missed this semester?
   never   once or twice   more than twice

3 _____ you enjoyed taking English this year?
   yes   more or less   no

4 _____ did you practice English outside of class?
   never   sometimes   often

5 _____ you going to take English again?
   definitely   maybe   no

6 _____ English do you know now?
   more than before   same as before   less than before

I think Lina has the best attitude. She registered for class early and she hasn't missed any classes at all.

③ Pronunciation *How* + adj / adv question stress

A Match these words to emojis a–g. Are you an emoji user?

| people | see | home | Facebook |
| time | English | happy | |

I love them. I use a lot.

B ▶10.13 Listen to Mickey's messages. Which word has the main stress in each *How* question?

C In pairs, practice the questions using the correct stress. Then share your answers.

D 👤 **Make it personal** In pairs, imagine you're long-lost friends who have just found each other on social media. Create a chat and include emojis. Then act out the best part of your chat as a conversation.

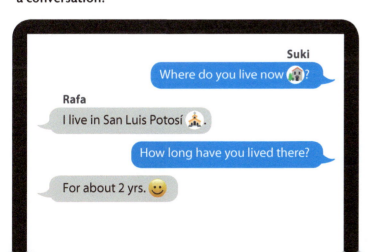

Mickey
Hey! I'm so 😊 to 👁 you! What's new?

Mickey
How much 🕐 do you spend studying or working?

Mickey
How often do you check f?

Mickey
How long have you lived in your current 🏠?

Mickey
How long ago did you start learning 🇺🇸?

Mickey
How many 👨‍👩‍👧 have you met online?

⚠️ **Common mistakes**
~~How big~~
What size is your apartment?
~~How far (away)~~
At what distance is it?

10.5 Do you enjoy reading in English?

Skills Identifying reasons

A What's different when you read in your language compared to reading in English? Answer in pairs.

> It's hard for me to read for long in English.

> True. I don't read many long texts anyway. I usually just read short things on my phone.

B Read the article as fast as you comfortably can. How long did you need to read 196 words? In pairs, compare what you remember, then complete the chart.

How to be a better reader
By Dr. Samuel Marshall

The key is to read faster. Here's why it's important. The average reading speed of a child in elementary school is around 200 words per minute (wpm). For adults, it's about 250–300 wpm. Contestants at the World Championship speed reading competitions can reach 1,000–1,200 wpm!

To be an excellent reader, a goal of 500-800 wpm is ideal. This will allow you to read a lot of information in a short time and still understand most of what you are reading. Reading in a second language is different, because, of course, you won't immediately understand a lot of the words that you read. This means that you don't understand what you read, you read slower, and so you don't enjoy reading, which then means you don't read much. It's a vicious circle, one which makes it difficult to improve your reading speed, because you need to practice more to read faster and you also need to read faster to understand more. Many second language readers read at 100 wpm or less. You really need to read at a speed of at least 200 wpm.

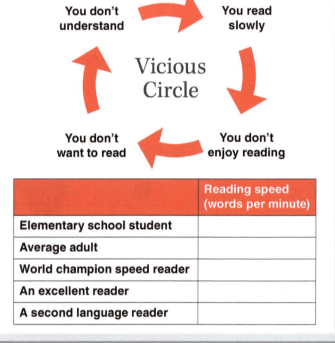

	Reading speed (words per minute)
Elementary school student	
Average adult	
World champion speed reader	
An excellent reader	
A second language reader	

Here are a few tips to help you to read in English.

1. Try to read things you're interested in and already know something about. If you don't enjoy reading, you won't do it.
2. Read something in your language and then try to read it in English.
3. Make sure longer texts aren't too difficult. If you don't understand more than about eight words per paragraph, choose another text before you get frustrated.
4. Use English subtitles when you watch movies in English. This helps your listening, pronunciation, and spelling.

C Do you enjoy reading in a) your first language? b) English? Why (not)? If not, is the reason the vicious circle in B?

> I like catching up with the news online in my language, but when I read it in English there's a lot I don't understand, so I get frustrated quickly.

D Read tips 1–4 in one minute. Do you do any of these things?

E ▶10.14 Listen and complete Dr. Marshall's other tips, 1–4. Which have you tried?

1. Give yourself _____ minute to read an article. Get as far as you can. Do this _____ times, and try to read _____ each time.
2. Read the same _____-word article as many times as you can in _____ minutes.
3. Read at the same speed as your class. Read an article of _____ words in only _____ seconds.
4. Use an alarm to help you. If you want to read at _____ words per minute, the alarm will go off every _____. See where you are in the text.

F ⬤ **Make it personal** Find a text of about 400 words. Read it using one of the tips in **E**. Compare in groups. Did it help you to read faster?

> I read something I'm interested in but the first time I only read half of it in a minute.

10.5 How would you describe your best friend? 10.5

ID in Action Describing and identifying

A ▶10.15 Listen and circle the items that are referred to in each photo.

B ▶10.15 Study **Common mistakes** and circle the best options in 1–3. Listen to check.

1. A: Pass me my phone, please.
   B: Sure. Which **phone** / **one** is it? The black **phone** / **one**?
   A: No, the silver **phone** / **one**.
   B: This **phone** / **one**?
   A: No, mine is the silver **phone** / **one** in a white case.
2. A: Oh look, there's Rich.
   B: Who's Rich?
   A: You know. He's the guy **who** / **which** Jody's dating.
   B: Oh yeah. Which **guy** / **one** is he? The guy **with** / **without** glasses?
   A: Yeah, the one **with** / **without** a beard. The one **who's** / **which is** wearing a hat.
3. A: Have you seen my glasses?
   B: Are they the **glasses** / **ones** on the table?
   A: No, those are **his** / **Jake's**. Mine are the big **glasses** / **ones**.
   B: There are two big **pairs** / **glasses**.
   A: Well, mine are the black **pairs** / **ones**.

Common mistakes

Which sweater do you want? The black. → one

I don't like the grays. → gray ones

Which book is the your book? → one is

That is the mine.

What lovely flowers! Do you like the reds? → red ones

C In pairs, take turns describing one of these people without saying their name. Your partner guesses who it is.

She's the one with curly hair.
Is it Judy?
No, the younger one.
Is it Maria?
Yes.

Ray   Judy   Sam   Carlos   Vicky   Martin   Maria

D In groups, put all your personal items (phones, keys, books, pens …) on a table and mix them up. Describe which one is yours until everybody knows whose everything is.

Mine is the one in the embarrassing gold case.   *Mine are the ones with a red key ring.*

E 🎤 **Make it personal** In pairs, take turns showing photos with at least two people in each. Answer questions about the people until your partner can identify each one.

Are they the same age?   *No, Louise is a year older.*   *Is Louise the one with red hair?*   *No, that's Allie.*

You say I'm crazy, 'Cause you don't think I know what you've done, But when you call me baby, I know I'm not the only one

Writing 10 A narrative

 Finally it has happened to me right in front of my face, My feelings can't describe it, Finally it has happened to me right in front of my face, And I just cannot hide it

My sister Ella and I were going on vacation on the same day, but traveling to different places at different times. Surprisingly, we had both been very organized and had packed our bags the night before and put our travel documents on the kitchen table.

I left the house first, at 7:30. I had allowed plenty of time to get to the airport, but there was little traffic and I arrived very early, just after 8:00. <u>Until then</u>, everything was going well. But then I checked my travel documents and the awful truth hit me. Stupidly, I had picked up my sister's passport instead of my own! <u>As soon as</u> I realized, I called my sister, but her phone went straight to voicemail. <u>For the next 10 minutes</u>, I kept phoning but she didn't answer. <u>Eventually</u>, I decided there was no option but to drive home. Luckily, there was just enough time before my flight.

I had just arrived home when my phone rang. It was my sister and she had my passport. Unfortunately, she was now at the airport, looking for me! She had realized the mistake a few minutes after I left. Obviously, if I had her passport, neither of us could go on vacation. So she had jumped in her car and driven straight to the airport. She arrived <u>just before</u> I got back home again!

<u>In the end</u>, we met up in the airport car park. I caught my flight with a few minutes to spare. But since then, I've always checked my passport before I leave home!

A Read Tom's story and number the events 1–9 in the order they occurred.
- ☐ Tom arrived at the airport.
- ☐ Ella phoned Tom.
- ☐ Tom and Ella left their passports on the table.
- ☐ Tom tried to phone Ella.
- ☐ Ella drove to the airport.
- ☐ Tom met Ella and got his passport back.
- ☐ Ella realized Tom had the wrong passport.
- ☐ Tom picked up the wrong passport.
- ☐ Tom drove home.

B Match time expressions 1–6 to the <u>underlined</u> expressions in **A**.
1 For a short while
2 Finally
3 After some time
4 Right after
5 So far
6 A little earlier than

C Study **Write it right!**, then find five comment adverbs in the text in **A**.

✓ **Write it right!**

In a narrative, you can use comment adverbs to show the reader your attitude or feelings. These include: *clearly, fortunately, hopefully, luckily, obviously, stupidly, surprisingly, unbelievably, unfortunately*.

D Replace the words in *italics* with one of the comment adverbs from **A**.
1 *Like an idiot*, I left my keys at work so couldn't get into my apartment.
2 *It was really lucky that* my neighbor had some extra keys.
3 *As everyone knows and understands*, you can't travel without a passport.
4 *Although I didn't expect it at all*, I got an A in my last project.
5 *I'm very sorry to say that* I can't come to your party – I'll be away on vacation.

E 🔵 **Make it personal** Think of an unusual or lucky story that happened to you or someone you know. Write a narrative in 150–200 words.

Before	Look back at the time expressions in **B** and comment adverbs in **C**. Think about the key moments in your story in the order you want to tell them.
While	Use a variety of past tense forms and time expressions to explain what happened and when. Include comment adverbs to show your attitude or feelings.
After	Exchange narratives with another student. Ask two follow-up questions about their story.

134

10 The dog days of August

1 Before watching

A In pairs, look back at the ID Café lesson titles and photos and remember all you can. Who are your favorite / least favorite characters? Why? How do you think ID Café is going to end?

B Match 1–8 to definitions a–h.
1 improved   a disorganized, untidy
2 a joke   b better
3 a makeover   c a complete change of look
4 a mess   d a financial prize, usually academic
5 a scholarship   e intelligent or well-dressed
6 to share   f have complete confidence in
7 smart   g the opposite of *serious*
8 to trust   h each having an equal part

C Guess how August is feeling and why.

2 While watching

A In pairs. **A:** Watch but cover your ears. **B:** Listen but cover your eyes, up to 1:58. Compare what you understood.

B Now both listen and watch to check. What else did you pick up? How will Lucy react?

C Watch up to 3:05. True (T) or False (F)?
1 Lucy thinks a tomato has hit his apartment.
2 The house is a mess because Rory's away.
3 Andrea describes August as a disaster.
4 August's mess is self-inflicted.
5 The $35,000 scholarship decision is this afternoon.

D Try to complete the extracts. Watch again to check. Guess what they decide to do.
Andrea: Lucy. Boy, am I _____ you're here.
Lucy: What happened here? It's like a _____ came through here …
Andrea: This is what _____ when Daniel's not here.
Lucy: Who could _____ like this? Not me.
Andrea: Me either. Here is our _____.
Lucy: Is this a _____? What has he done to himself?
Andrea: Yeah. I asked that too. My brother, he's _____ about an interview.

E Watch from 3:10 to 3:32. In pairs, role-play a dialogue for what Andrea and Lucy are thinking.

What do you think of his sweater?   *I don't like it … He looks like my dad!*

F Listen from 3:48 to the end. Number the words in the order you hear them, 1–10. How does Lucy feel about herself? Will August get the scholarship?

artificial   hand   passion
confidence   improved   special
the first step   intelligence
foundation   makeover

3 After watching

A Circle the correct options and complete with the correct form of *-self*.
1 August **has / hasn't** spilled food on _____self.
2 He **does / doesn't** know how to take care of _____self.
3 Andrea can't get him organized by _____self.
4 August has a really **high / low** opinion of _____self.
5 Andrea and Lucy give _____**selves / August** a drum roll as he walks in.
6 Lucy is extremely **fond of / doubtful about** _____self.
7 They encourage August to believe **in / on** _____self.

B Complete 1–8 with these words and phrases.

a little	almost	as smart as	first	for success
more	real	so	whatever	

1 He looked _____ cute.
2 I could _____ date him myself.
3 To do well in that interview, you have to dress _____.
4 You needed a _____ change, August, but this is just the _____ step.
5 You need to have _____ confidence in yourself!
6 Why not look _____ you are?
7 You just needed _____ something special. You know?
8 Artificial automatic intelligence people, or _____ you call them.

C 🎤 **Make it personal** In groups of three, answer 1–4. Any surprises?
1 Are you generally tidy / untidy / good at taking care of yourself? Have you ever lived alone? Did (or would) that change anything?
2 Do you dress / behave very differently at home compared to when you're out? Do your clothes affect how you feel?
3 Would you say you're generally self-confident?
4 Do you like your English-speaking self?

I rarely look in a mirror, except when I'm about to go out.

I do get shy if I have to speak in public or in front of a camera.

135

R5 Grammar and vocabulary

A **Picture dictionary.** Cover the words on these pages and use the pictures to remember:

page	
112	11 wedding words
114	5 relationship words and expressions
118	10 types of performers
119	4 mystery objects
124	8 causes of stress
126	13 lifestyle changes
127	descriptions of 6 vacation photos
155	8 pairs of picture words in lines 5 and 6 of the consonants chart

B In pairs, decide which adjective combinations apply to photos 1–3. Do you agree on each?

The teacher is … bored / interested

The students are … boring / interesting

C 🔵 **Make it personal** In groups, give at least two answers to each option in 1–3.
1 What makes a teacher interesting / boring?
2 When was the last time you were confused / terrified?
3 What do you find irritating / exhausting?

When teachers just talk about grammar, I think they're …

D 🔵 **Make it personal** In groups, make a conditional chain like the model. Use the sentence starters or your own ideas. Which group can make the longest chain?

If I lived in Germany, I'd speak German.

If I spoke German, I could get a better job.

If I got a better job, …

Sentence starters:
If I spoke English well …   If I were a superhero …
If I won the lottery …   If it were …

E ▶R5.1 In pairs, match 1–5 to a–e. Listen to check.
1 Look! They're holding hands.
2 Zara's very late.
3 What's in this package?
4 Who's that guy?
5 Look, the money's gone!

a It could be Kim's son. He looks like Kim.
b It can't be a pair of socks. It's too heavy.
c They must be dating now.
d There must be a thief in the room.
e She might be stuck on the bus.

F 🔵 **Make it personal** Complete 1–5, then compare in pairs. Do your answers reflect your attitude towards money?
1 A bank is a place …
2 A lottery is a thing …
3 Credit cards are things …
4 Shopping is an activity …
5 A financial advisor is a person …

For me a bank is a place you use to save money.

G In pairs, play *Describe it, don't say it!* A: Describe five words / phrases from this book. Use English, mime, drawings, sounds, or rhyme, but don't say the words. B: Listen and say the words / phrases A describes.

It's a phrase for someone who's really jealous!

H Correct the mistakes. Check your answers in units 9 and 10.

🔴 **Common mistakes**
1 At first, I wasn't interesting in the movie, but the final part was very excited. (2 mistakes)
2 If I would know John, I would talk to him. (1 mistake)
3 What would you do if you see your best friend with your ex-girlfriend? (1 mistake)
4 She can be hungry, because she didn't eat something today. (2 mistakes)
5 You better make your homework. (2 mistakes)
6 My boss made me to stay late in work. (2 mistakes)
7 That's the car who I bought the last week. (2 mistakes)
8 People which play sports have a lot of pression to win. (2 mistakes)
9 My brother wins a lot of money, but he loses it on ridiculous things. (2 mistakes)
10 Could you pass me my coat? No, not that, the blue. (2 mistakes)

Skills practice

R5

♪ *Last Christmas, I gave you my heart, But the very next day you gave it away. This year, to save me from tears, I'll give it to someone special.*

A Read the article about siblings. Are 1–5 True (T) or False (F)? Are sibling relationships good in your family?
1. Brothers and sisters fight more when they're children.
2. It's unusual for siblings to change their opinions of each other.
3. Rivalry always starts when the second child is born.
4. Parents don't like to see competition between their children.
5. The Jacksons had a better relationship when they were younger.

Sibling Rivalry

Do you get along with your brothers and sisters? Are they your best friends or do you never see them? It's really common for siblings to fight, especially when they're young. And don't be surprised if one minute you love your brother or sister and the next minute you can't stand that same sibling.

Competition between brothers and sisters can start before the second child arrives and it continues as children get older and they have to share toys, food, and, most importantly, attention from their parents. It can be hard for parents to watch, but it's very normal and, as children get older, the rivalry hopefully changes into a warm friendship – but not for everyone! Look at the Jacksons and Noel and Liam Gallagher. They used to make music together but now they fight all the time!

My sister's kids fight all the time!

B ▶R5.2 Listen to part one of a radio show. Complete with Carla (C), Dr. Brayman (DB), or Jack (J).
1. _____ is nervous.
2. _____ and _____ are in a relationship.
3. _____ calls all the time.
4. _____ asks for advice.
5. _____ gives advice.
6. _____ gets jealous easily.

C ▶R5.3 Guess the correct options you will hear in 1–6. Then listen to check. All correct? Do you agree with Dr. Brayman's advice?
1. **She** / **He** is starting to ignore **his** / **her** phone calls at work.
2. **She** / **He** is starting to have secrets and tell lies.
3. **She** / **He** is becoming more jealous.
4. **She** / **He** needs to talk to **him** / **her** and discuss **his** / **her** emotions.
5. **She** / **He** needs to make **her** / **his** partner feel more confident about their relationship.
6. Dr. Brayman thinks this **will** / **won't** change their situation quickly and **she** / **he** / **they** should talk to a counselor.

D In pairs, play *Problems!* Flip a coin. Heads = one space; tails = two spaces. Role-play each situation.

A: **Child.** You don't want to go to school.
B: **Parent.** Make your child go to school.

A: **Broken heart.** Your bf / gf broke up with you.
B: **Friend.** Support him / her and give advice.

A: **Student.** Your course is boring.
B: **Friend.** Give advice.

A: **Teenager.** You don't have any money. Ask for some.
B: **Friend.** Give / refuse money. Give advice.

A: **Lonely.** Your bf / gf travels all the time.
B: **Friend.** Listen and give advice.

A: **Nervous.** You have to speak at a friend's wedding.
B: **Friend.** Make suggestions.

A: **Husband.** You left your cell phone in a taxi.
B: **Wife.** Make a suggestion.

A: **Tired.** You can't sleep at night.
B: **Doctor.** Give some advice or some medicine.

E In groups, do the quiz then look back to check. Score two points for each correct answer. Which group got the most points?

How much do you remember?
1. Which U.S. state is visited in lesson 6.1?
2. What does Barbara Hartsfield collect in lesson 7.3?
3. What did Penny and Harry talk about in Unit 8?
4. What happened to the two people in lesson 9.2?
5. Who are BeginAgain and MyVeryBest in Unit 10?

I think the state in lesson 6.1 is …

F ▶R5.4 **Make it personal** **Question time!**
1. Listen to the 12 lesson titles in units 9 and 10.
2. In pairs, practice asking and answering. Use the book map on p. 2–3. Ask at least two follow-up questions. Can you have a short conversation about all the questions?

What do you think about marriage?

I don't think about it at all!

137

Grammar Unit 1

1A Review of present tenses and simple past

Simple present

Subject	+	
I / You / We / They	live	in Paris.
She / He	plays	volleyball.

	−	
I / You / We / They	do not / don't live	in Ecuador.
She / He	doesn't play	golf.

A	S	I (O)	Short answers + / −
Do	you	like sports?	Yes, I **do**. / No, I **don't**.
Does	he	live here?	Yes, he **does**. / No, he **doesn't**.

Q	A	S	I (O)
When	do	I / you / we / they	get up on weekdays?
Why	does	Sue	work at night?

Form: infinitive form for I / you / we / they. Add -s for he / she / it **except**:
- have / has (*She has a dog.*)
- verbs ending C + -y, change -y to -ies (*He often cries!*)
- verbs ending in -ch, -o, -sh, -ss, -x, add -es (*She watches TV then goes to bed.*)

Use:
- routines, habits, repeated actions
- facts
- scheduled events
- time phrases (*every morning, sometimes, etc.*)

Present continuous

Form: present of *be* + verb + *-ing*. See spelling rules for main verb in Grammar 2A p. 140.
- *I'm watching TV right now, so I'm not studying.*

Yes / No

Present of *be*	S	Verb + *-ing*	
Am	I		
Are / Aren't	you / we / they	listening	to the news?
Is / Isn't	she / he		

Wh-

	Present of *be*	S	Verb + *-ing*	
Who	am	I	talking	to?
Why	are	they	driving	fast?
When	is	it	arriving?	

Use:
- an action happening now: *I'm listening to the radio.*
- processes in progress: *I'm studying English (but not today!)*
- future plans / arrangements: *What are you doing after class? I'm going to the dentist.* NOT *I go to the dentist.*

Simple past

Form: the same for all persons. Most verbs are regular, and end *-ed*. Verbs ending *-e*, add *-d*. Verbs ending C + *-y*, change *-y* to *-ied*. (*We **studied** hard, but **didn't pass** the test.*)

Yes / No

A	S	I	O	Short answers
Did	they	go	to the concert?	Yes, they **did**. / No, they **didn't**.

Wh-

	A	S	I	O
Where	did	he	go	last weekend?

Subject

	Simple past	O
Who	wrote	the book?

Use: completed past events. *What happened to you last night?* NOT *What did happen to you last night?*

1B Future forms

will / won't

I'll go to the movies tonight. I have a ticket. (definite plan)
OK, I'll have a coffee. (unplanned decision)
It won't rain today. (prediction)

Will you do the dishes? Yes, I will.
Who will they invite to the party? They'll invite their friends.

Form: *will / won't* + infinitive.
Use: definite plans, unplanned decisions, predictions.

Going to

Use *be + going to* + infinitive for predictions and intentions.
I think she's going to win the race. (prediction)
They're going to bring their friend to the party. (intention)

Going to and present continuous as future

Use both *going to* and present continuous for fixed plans or arrangements. There's usually little difference in meaning.
He's going to go shopping. / He's going shopping.

1C should / shouldn't

He **should** eat healthy food. He **shouldn't** eat so many fries.
Should we take the train? Yes, you **should**.
Which one **should** we take? The first one.
Form: *should / shouldn't* + infinitive for all persons.
Use: advice, opinions, and suggestions.
For **questions**, use the ASI / QASI model.

Unit 1

1A

1 Circle the correct options in 1–5.
1. He's **studying / studies** every night for about two hours.
2. We **paid / pay** our credit card bill last week, so we **don't / didn't** worry about it this week.
3. I always **eat / ate** fast food when I was a teenager. I **loved / was loving** it but now I don't like it at all.
4. My neighbor **wants / is wanting** to take a vacation in the U.S., so **she needs / is needing** to get a visa.
5. At the moment, I'**m working / worked** in a music store. I **help / 'm helping** customers to find the music they **like / are liking**. It's more fun that I **imagine / imagined**.

2 Order the words in 1–6 to make questions.
1. to / did / on your last vacation / go / the beach / you / ?
2. usually / English / study / when / you / do / ?
3. English / why / you / learning / are / speak / to / ?
4. weekend / what / last / do / you / did / ?
5. with / you / now / who / living / are / ?
6. what / next / you / are / Saturday / doing / ?

3 🟢 **Make it personal** Write answers to 1–6 in **2** about you.

1B

1 Complete 1–5 with *'ll*, *will*, or *won't*.
1. Buy our new laptop and you _____ be disappointed!
2. That cashmere coat _____ probably still look great in 20 years.
3. Oh, no! I can't believe you _____ be able to come!
4. What _____ you do when you're in NYC next week?
5. I _____ see you when I get back from my trip.

2 Complete 1–5 with *'ll probably*, *'ll definitely*, or *won't*.
1. I _____ do my homework tonight. I'm too tired.
2. She _____ send you a postcard. She always writes to her friends.
3. They _____ join us at the Steak House Restaurant. They're vegetarians.
4. I think they _____ arrive on time. They're usually punctual.
5. He _____ win the Academy Award for Best Actor this year. He's obviously the best.

3 Circle the correct options in 1–5.
1. Your daughter's **going to be / is being** very rich when she's a movie star.
2. A: **Will you / Are you going to** help me with my homework, please? B: Of course!
3. A: What **will you do / are you doing** this evening? B: I **see / 'm seeing** Joe.
4. Do you think we **will win / are winning** the lottery?
5. My sister'**s coming / will come** home tonight. We're very excited! She **has / 's having** a party.

4 🟢 **Make it personal** What will happen in these photos? Read the prediction for photo 1, then write predictions for photos 2 and 3.

call friend / be on time   see banana peel / fall   buy girlfriend ring / get married

He's going to call his friend to say he won't be on time.

1C

1 Complete dialogues 1–3 with *should* or *shouldn't* and these verbs.

be   come   go   listen   spend   stay

1. A: I need a jacket for this wedding, but everything is too expensive.
   B: You _____ _____ too much. Look for special sales.
2. A: My friend loves live music. Where _____ she _____ ?
   B: She _____ _____ to the new club with me tonight!
3. A: You sound really sick. Maybe you _____ _____ in class this week.
   B: My doctor said I _____ _____ home, but I don't think I _____ .
   A: Maybe you _____ _____ to him!

2 🟢 **Make it personal** Give advice to the speakers in pictures 1–3. Use *should* or *need to*.

1 You need to call him on your cell phone.

1 *I don't know where my husband is!*
2 *The book is too high.*
3 *I'm sorry I'm late for class.*

139

Grammar Unit 2

2A Past continuous

S	Past of *be*	Verb + *-ing*
I / He / She	+ was − was not / wasn't	**driving** a truck.
You / We / They	+ were − were not / weren't	**surfing** the Internet.

Form: past of *be* + verb + *-ing*.

Verb + *-ing*	Spelling rules
go + *-ing* = going, see + *-ing* = seeing, study + *-ing* = studying	Most verbs, add *-ing*.
hope + *-ing* = hoping, share + *-ing* = sharing	Verbs ending *-e*, change *-e* to *-ing*.
die → dy + *-ing* = dying lie → ly + *-ing* = lying	Verbs ending *-ie*, change *-ie* to *-y* + *-ing*.
run → running sit → sitting	One-syllable verbs ending consonant-vowel-consonant (CVC), double the final C and add *-ing*.
be**gin** → beginning oc**cur** → occurring **listen** → listening al**low** → allowing en**joy** → enjoying **trav**el → traveling	Verbs with two or more syllables ending CVC, double the final C (except *w, x,* or *y*) when the last syllable is **stressed**.

Use: actions in progress at a particular time in the past.

Q	Past of *be*	S	Verb + *-ing*
What	were	you / we / they	**doing** when I called?
Where	was	I / he / she	**going** at 6 p.m?

State verbs

Some verbs that express "state" or "condition" do not appear in continuous forms, for example:

Thoughts: *agree, believe, forget, guess, know, remember, think, understand*
Emotions: *adore, hate, like, love, need, prefer, want*
Senses: *feel, hear, look, see, smell, taste, touch*
Possession: *belong, have, own*

- Our teacher **needs** a new cell phone.
- My grandmother doesn't **understand** English.
- I don't understand the difference. NOT *I'm not understanding the difference.*

Some verbs have both a "state" and an "active" meaning: *be, have, think.*

- He **has** brown eyes. / He **is having** a good time at the party.

It's increasingly common to hear state verbs in the continuous form:

- *I'm loving it!* or *You're looking really good today.*

Be careful with state verbs in the past.

- I didn't know you last year. NOT *I wasn't knowing you last year.*
- When I was young, I wanted to be rich. NOT *When I was young, I was wanting to be rich.*

2B Past continuous vs. simple past

- I was cooking dinner when the phone rang.
- The power went out while I was writing an email to my friend.
- While I was waiting at the bus stop, it began to rain.

Simple past	Spelling rules
We **played** tennis yesterday.	Most verbs, add *-ed*.
He **danced** a lot at the party yesterday.	Verbs ending in *-e*, add *-d*.
The car **stopped** before the accident.	Verbs ending CVC, double the final C and add *-ed*.
They **tried** to talk to you last Monday.	Verbs ending C + *-y*, change *-y* to *-ied*.
She **bought** some new shoes.	Some verbs are **irregular**. See list on p. 158–159.

Use simple past for an action that interrupts an action in progress (past continuous).

Use *when* or *while* to connect the actions. If *When / While* is at the beginning of the sentence, use a comma after the main clause.

- When I was shopping, I lost my keys.
- I lost my keys while I was shopping.

Q	Past of *be*	S 1st action	Verb + *-ing*	Linking word	S 2nd action	Past verb
What	were	you	doing	when	the phone	rang?
Where	was	he	going	when	it	happened?

He was playing hockey when he slipped on a banana peel.

140

Unit 2

2A

1 Complete 1–5 with the past continuous of these verbs.

do   go   look   talk   wait

1 What _____ your friends _____ last night?
2 Why _____ you _____ in my bag?
3 _____ he _____ about me?
4 How long _____ she _____ for a taxi?
5 Where _____ you _____ yesterday?

2 Simple past or past continuous? Correct the mistakes in 1–5.

1 What was you trying to do?
2 Did you sleep when I phoned you?
3 My sister was having 19 years when she went to college.
4 While she was at college, she was calling me every week.
5 It was rain at lunchtime yesterday so I ate in the office.

3 Circle the correct options in 1–7.

1 My grandmother **knew** / **was knowing** a lot about cars.
2 I **don't mind** / **'m not minding** doing the dishes.
3 What are you **think** / **thinking** about?
4 I **wasn't understanding** / **didn't understand** what you said.
5 I **agree** / **'m agreeing** with you.
6 My sister **is having** / **has** a new car.
7 I always **liked** / **was liking** swimming.

4 Complete 1–5 by adding the simple or continuous form of the verbs. Present or past?

1 Amy Winehouse a lot of tattoos. (**have**)
2 The milk bad so I threw it away. (**taste**)
3 I couldn't sleep because my neighbors a party. (**have**)
4 you your country will win the next World Cup? (**think**)
5 They pizza with too much pepperoni. (**not like**)

5 🎧 **Make it personal** Write four sentences about yourself using these time phrases.

last night   at 7 a.m. yesterday
this morning   yesterday afternoon

I was eating breakfast and checking Instagram at 7 a.m. yesterday.

2B

1 Complete 1–5 with the correct form of the verbs.

1 We _____ baseball in the park when it _____ raining. (**play, start**)
2 The other car _____ the back of my car when I _____ to work. (**hit, drive**)
3 I _____ you yesterday when you _____ in the mall. (**see, shop**)
4 When Ariana _____ home, we _____ in the kitchen to give her a surprise. (**arrive, hide**)
5 I _____ down the street when I _____ . (**walk, slip and fall**)

2 Order the words in 1–5 and add *was* or *were* to make sentences.

1 he / chicken / cooking / phone / rang / when / the / .
2 an / driving / they / when / earthquake / there / .
3 playing / computer / on / her / she / while / power / games / out / went / the / .
4 cycling / home / Sam / when / he / tire / got / flat / a / .
5 the Internet / funny / found / surfing / video / I / while / I / a / .

3 🎧 **Make it personal** Imagine what the people in photos 1–6 were doing when the power went out. Write six sentences.

1 He was making a date with his new girlfriend.

Grammar Unit 3

3A Present perfect 1: past experiences

S	A	Past participle
I / You / We / They	have / 've have not / haven't	**been** abroad. **done** the dishes.
He / She	has / 's has not / hasn't	**stayed** in a hotel recently. **traveled** a lot. **studied** English before. **worked** hard today.

Form: have / has + past participle. Past participles of regular verbs are the same as the simple past. See list of irregular past participles on p. 158–159.

Use: past experiences without a specific time. Use the simple past for a specific time in the past.

▸ On Monday morning, ask: *How was your weekend?* NOT *How has been your weekend?* (The weekend is finished.)

Yes / No ❓	Short answers ➕ / ➖
Have you (ever) **seen** a panda?	Yes, I **have**. / No, I **haven't**.
Have they (ever) **visited** Thailand?	Yes, they **have**. / No, they **haven't**.
Has he / she (ever) **tried** Peruvian food?	Yes, he / she **has**. / No, he / she **hasn't**.

For short answers, do **not** contract the **subject** with the **auxiliary**.

▸ Have you ever been to New York?
▸ Yes, I have. (NOT *Yes, I've.*) I went there in 2011, just before Christmas. It was great.
▸ No, I haven't, but I'd love to. I've always wanted to see Times Square.

Note: with the present perfect, *ever* means *in your whole life*.

3B Present perfect 2: completed actions

S	A	Participle + O
I / You / We / They	have / 've have not / haven't	**already finished** work. **eaten** lunch **yet**.
He / She	has / 's has not / hasn't	**checked** Facebook **already**. **just woken** up. **read** the news **yet**.

Use with:
▸ *already* for actions completed before now. Note that *already* has two possible positions.
▸ *yet* with sentences for actions that are expected to happen but are incomplete.
▸ *just* for recently completed actions.

Note: Present perfect is more common in British English. In American English, it's more common to use simple past for completed actions with *already*, *just*, and *recently*: *I just woke up*.

Yes / No ❓		
A	S	Past participle + O phrase
Have	I / you / we / they	**already finished** your work? **seen** the new Spider-Man movie **yet**?
Has	he / she / it	**eaten** breakfast **already**? **stopped** raining **yet**?

Use:
▸ *already* in questions when you expect a positive answer.
▸ *yet* in a question when you don't know if the answer will be *yes* or *no*.
▸ *Have you got 5G yet?* NOT *Have you yet got 5G?*

3C Present perfect 3: unfinished past

Use present perfect with *for* or *since* to talk about an action or state that **started in the past and continues now**:

▸ *for* + **time expression** for the duration of an action.
I've had a headache for about two days.
I haven't spoken to him for a long time.

Past — Duration = **for** — Now

▸ *since* + **time expression** for the point in time that an action started.
I've lived here since I was a little girl.
Marion has worked here since 1998.

Past — Point in time = **since** — Now

Duration	Point in time
for a long time	since yesterday
for many years	since 1984
for 10 weeks	since I left college

Wh- ❓

Q	A	S	Past participle
How long	have	I / you / we / they	**studied** here?
	has	he / she / it	**worked** here?

▸ *How long have you been here?* NOT *Since when are you here?*

142

Unit 3

3A

1 Look at Mark's souvenirs. Complete 1–8 with the past participles of the verbs.
1 Mark's _____ on the Panama Canal. (**sail**)
2 He's _____ to the U.S. several times. (**be**)
3 He's _____ the Statue of Liberty in New York. (**see**)
4 He's _____ in the Andes Mountains once. (**climb**)
5 He's _____ photos of Paris from the top of the Eiffel Tower. (**take**)
6 He's _____ the Iguazú Falls in Argentina and Brazil. (**visit**)
7 He's _____ all the way to China. (**travel**)
8 He's _____ a souvenir of a phone box in London. (**buy**)

2 🟢 **Make it personal** Change 1–8 in **1** so they are true for you. If you haven't had the experience, add *but I've* and include something similar you have done.

I haven't sailed on the Panama Canal, but I've sailed on a yacht.

3 Complete the dialogue with the verbs in the present perfect, ➕ or ➖.
A: _____ you ever _____ Chicago? (**visit**)
B: No, I _____ there. _____ you? (**be**)
A: Yes, I _____ . I really enjoyed it.
B: Does Chicago have that big skyscraper … uh, what's it called?
A: Yes, it does. Its name _____ recently _____ . It's now called the Willis Tower. (**change**)
B: Wow, you know a lot about it!
A: Yeah, it's a great place to visit. My brother lives there. I _____ with him and his family several times. (**stay**)

4 🟢 **Make it personal** Write five sentences about places you've been and what you did there.

I've been to Spain with my family. We visited my cousins in Madrid and went sightseeing.

3B

1 Order the words in 1–5 to make sentences.
1 he / abroad / three / has / times / been / .
2 yet / Jenny / learned / hasn't / to / drive / .
3 I / been / to / New York / business / on / several / have / times / .
4 paid / they / already / the / hotel / bill / have / .
5 haven't / spent / money / all / yet / our / we / .

2 Correct two mistakes in each of 1–5.
1 I have ever been to Italy. I've hear it's fantastic.
2 Have you never gone to a musical in a theater?
3 He have yet paid for his trip with his credit card.
4 They hasn't seen the *Mona Lisa* already, so they're going to the Louvre today.
5 Have you ever been in Miami? I've come back just. It's amazing!

3C

1 Complete 1–5 with the verbs in the present perfect, ➕ or ➖. Use contractions. Add *since* or *for* in the correct place in the sentences.
1 He _____ in the UK 10 months and he really loves it. (**live**)
2 They _____ on Baker Street the early 1990s. They moved a long time ago. (**live**)
3 I was a kid, I _____ always _____ staying in hotels. (**like**)
4 She _____ from that seat she sat down! (**move**)
5 Mr. Martin _____ that awful hairstyle the 1990s. (**have**)

2 Read Jackie's profile and correct nine mistakes.

My name is Jackie. I was born in Michigan and moved to California in 2009. I live in L.A. since then. I stay in San Francisco a few times, but I've ever lived there.

Since I was 25, I had the same apartment. I been there 14 years. I lived in San Diego for a few months, but I didn't like it. I never been back. My family lives in Los Angeles too since 2020, but I've only visit them a few times so far.

3 🟢 **Make it personal** Write a similar profile about yourself, saying where you and your family have lived, worked, or studied.

Grammar Unit 4

4A Used to and simple past

- I **used to** play a lot of sports, but I'm too busy now.
- My brother **used to** make fun of me when I was young.
- Did you **use to** watch a lot of cartoons?
- She didn't **use to** like fruit, but she loves it now.
- My family **used to** live in Chicago, but we moved to L.A. in 2019.

Note: Use to and used to have the same pronunciation: /juːstə/.

	S		A	Used to	I	
⊕	I / You / He / She /	–		**used to**	be	happier.
⊖	We / They		**didn't**	use to	like	swimming.

	Q	A	S	Used to	I	
❓	What	**did**	you / he / she / we / they /	use to	do go feel	in summer?

Form: used to + infinitive for all persons. Questions and negatives use the auxiliary did (not).

Use: past states that have ended and actions that happened regularly in the past but don't happen now.

- My dad used to ride a motorbike when he was younger. NOT ~~My dad was riding a motorbike when he was younger.~~
- I usually go to the gym before work. NOT ~~I'm used to go to the gym before work.~~

For short Yes / No answers, use:

- ⊕ Yes + subject + did.
- ⊖ No + subject + didn't.
- Did you use to live in Santiago? Yes, I did, but my boyfriend didn't.

Use **simple past** to talk about past activities and events at specific points in time.

- My uncle arrived a few minutes ago.
- Did you see the news yesterday?
- There was a storm last night.
- We saw a great movie last week.
- My sister was born in 2004.

4B Comparatives and superlatives, as … as

- Camping is **cheaper than** staying at a hotel.
- It's probably **the ugliest** building in Manhattan.
- That hotel is **the most expensive** in London.
- New York is **as** expensive **as** London.
- She's **as** beautiful **as** her mother.
- The UK is **not as** big **as** the U.S.

One-syllable adjectives

Most one-syllable adjectives, add -er / -est.
Adjectives ending **CVC**, double the final consonant and add -er / -est.

Adjective	Comparative	Superlative
rich	richer	the richest
big	bigger	the biggest
hot	hotter	the hottest

One- / two-syllable adjectives ending -y

Change -y to -ier / -iest.

Adjective	Comparative	Superlative
crazy	crazier	the craziest
easy	easier	the easiest
heavy	heavier	the heaviest

Adjectives with two or more syllables

Use more / the most.

Adjective	Comparative	Superlative
beautiful	more beautiful	the most beautiful
complicated	more complicated	the most complicated
exciting	more exciting	the most exciting
expensive	more expensive	the most expensive

The opposite of more … than is less … than, and the opposite of the most is the least.

- The subway is usually less crowded at night.
- Vatican City is the least populated city-state in the world. It has only about 800 residents.

Irregular adjectives

Adjective	Comparative	Superlative
good	better	the best
bad	worse	the worst
far	farther / further	the farthest / furthest

As … as

Use as … as for two things with similar qualities. It is very common in comparisons that use non-literal images.

- The wind is **as** cold **as** ice.
- It was the scariest movie we've ever seen! My little sister was **as** white **as** a sheet.
- That joke is **as** old **as** a dinosaur.

Use not as … as to criticize and talk about differences.

- His pizzas aren't **as** good **as** Mario's pizzas.
- The U.S. is **not as** populated **as** China.
- Vinyl is **not as** easy to take care of **as** CDs.
- Lionel isn't **as** tall **as** Cristiano. NOT ~~Lionel isn't so tall like Cristiano.~~

Unit 4

4A

1 Order the words in 1–5 and add *used to* or *use to* to make sentences or questions.
1. father / old / records / collect / my / .
2. your / you / did / play / friends / with / baseball / ?
3. a / a / I / horse / beautiful / have / I / child / was / when / .
4. like / he / math / when / high / was / in / didn't / he / school / .
5. cleaner / city / your / be / is / now / than / it / did / ?

2 Look at the pairs of pictures and complete 1–4 with the correct form of *used to* and a noun. Then match 1–4 to a–d.

1. They _____ eat a lot of unhealthy _____,
2. She _____ bite her _____,
3. He _____ have much _____.
4. He _____ get good _____,

a. but now she's getting a manicure!
b. but now he studies a lot more and is top of the class.
c. but they are much healthier now.
d. He has lots now, but he has no free time.

3 🟢 **Make it personal** Write one-sentence answers to 1–5.
1. Have you changed any bad habits?
2. What did you use to do for fun when you were a kid?
3. What kind of music did you use to listen to?
4. What were your favorite TV programs?
5. What kind of kids did you use to hang out with?

1 I used to eat too much salt.

4B

1 Complete 1–5 with one comparative / superlative and one *as … as*.
1. When I first moved here, the neighborhood was _____ (**quiet**) a mouse. But now it's _____ (**noisy**) than Delhi!
2. Wow, John's lost a lot of weight. He used to be the _____ (**heavy**) guy at work. Now he looks _____ (**good**) he did 10 years ago!
3. Tablets are not _____ (**small**) smartphones, but they are _____ (**good**) because you can read them easily.
4. My mom types _____ (**fast**) than most people, but she's not _____ (**good**) me at sending messages on her phone.
5. I don't go out _____ (**often**) I used to when I was _____ (**young**).

2 Correct the mistake in each of 1–5.
1. Instagram isn't popular as Facebook.
2. My brother is most interested in video games than I am.
3. We've thought about getting a dog that's not as big like our last one.
4. That was the most ugly haircut I've ever had in my life.
5. This new phone is more bad than my last one.

3 🟢 **Make it personal** Use 1–5 to make comparisons that are true for you.
1. soccer / basketball / volleyball
2. staying in / going out / traveling
3. Chinese food / Japanese food / Peruvian food
4. sunny weather / rainy weather / windy weather
5. playing video games / listening to music / watching YouTube videos

Volleyball isn't as exciting to watch as basketball. Soccer is the best game to play and watch.

145

Grammar Unit 5

5A Obligation and prohibition: *have (got) to / can't*

- We've **got to** take the test tomorrow. / We **have to** take the test tomorrow.
- You **have to** bring a pen to the test. / You'**ve got to** bring a pen to the test.
- You **don't have to** write in black, you can use blue. / You **haven't got to** write in black, you can use blue.
- I **can't** use a cell phone in the exam room.

Have (got) to

	S	A	Have (got) to	I	
+	I / You / We / They		have to / have got to		work tonight.
	He / She		has to / has got to		
−	I / You / We / They	don't / haven't	have to / got to		work tonight.
	He / She	doesn't / hasn't	have to / got to		
?	A	S	Have to	I	Short answers
	Do	I / you / we / they	have to	work tonight?	Yes, we **do**. / No, we **don't**.
	Does	he / she			Yes, she **does**. / No, she **doesn't**.
	A	S	Got to	I	Short answers
	Have	I / you / we / they	got to	work tonight?	Yes, I **have**. / No, I **haven't**.
	Has	he / she			Yes, she **has**. / No, she **hasn't**.

Use:
- **have (got) to** to express an obligation. **Have got to** is more common in speaking (*I've got to go now*) and is often pronounced *gotta* (*I've gotta go now / I gotta go now*).
- negative forms to express no obligation: you have a choice.

Note: *got to* is pronounced /gɑtə/, *have to* is /hæftə/, and *has to* is /hæztə/.

Can't

S	A	I
I / You / We / They / He / She	can't	smoke in this building.

Use: to express prohibition.

5B *too / enough, too much / too many*

- She's **too busy** to study.
- Your bag's going to break. There are **too many** things in it.
- Shhhh! You're making **too much** noise and I can't concentrate.
- Can you get that book for me? I'm **not tall enough**.
- I have 10 cousins. Including me, that's **enough people** for a soccer team.
- I like cooking, but I **don't** have **enough time**.

Too + noun or adjective means excessive.
Use **too many** with countable nouns (*too many cars*) and **too much** with uncountable nouns (*too much time*).
Enough means sufficient, **not enough** means insufficient.
Enough goes **after** adjectives, but **before** nouns.

"Table seven says the fish isn't cooked enough."

5C Zero and first conditional

Zero conditional

Conditional clause			Result clause		
If / When	S	Present verb		S	Present verb
If / When	it	**rains**	a lot,	the river	**floods**.
If / When	I	**don't sleep**	enough,	I	**get**	angry easily.

Use: for facts, generalizations, things that are always true.
If or *when* introduce the conditional clause. When the conditional clause comes first, use a comma to separate the clauses.

- If you don't ask for anything, you don't get anything.
- People sometimes quit when they don't succeed the first time.

First conditional

Conditional clause			Result clause		
If	S	Present verb		S	Will +/−	I
If	I / you / we / they	**don't get up**	now,	I / you / we / they /	**will**	miss	the bus.
If	he / she	**gets up**	late tomorrow,	he / she	**won't**	be	on time.

Use:
- specific events that are probable or certain and their future results.
- promises and warnings.

Use simple present in the conditional clause. Don't use a comma when the result clause comes first.

- If we see him tomorrow, we'll give him your message.
- I promise I won't tell anyone if you tell me a secret.

146

Unit 5

5A

1 Complete 1–5 with *got to*, *have / has to*, or *can't*.

1 You can leave to use the restroom, but you _____ return in five minutes. You _____ take your phone with you.
2 He's really _____ study harder! If he doesn't improve his grades, he _____ stay on the basketball team.
3 Do you _____ work on Saturday night, or can you come to my party?
4 Mom usually gets home by 6, but tonight she _____ stop at the grocery store first.
5 My brother works in a bar. He doesn't _____ wear a uniform, he can wear his own clothes, but he often ____ work late nights and weekends.

2 Correct the mistake in each of 1–5.

1 You don't got to go to the grocery store later. I've already done all the shopping.
2 I'm allergic to cheese and bread so I don't can eat pizza.
3 I can't come tomorrow. I've to go to the dentist.
4 Lena hasn't to work tomorrow so she can stay in bed.
5 It's important to be punctual. Everybody have to be on time for the test.

5B

1 Complete 1–5 with *too / enough / too much / too many*.

1 My sister has saved 20% of her salary and now she has _____ money to buy a car.
2 That math class is way _____ difficult for me and there is _____ homework. I'm dropping it!
3 Are you strong _____ to carry that bag? Do you want some help?
4 I didn't eat at the party. There were _____ people and there wasn't _____ food.
5 I used to live in the country, but the commute was _____ far and the salary wasn't high _____. So I quit my job and moved!

2 Match 1–6 to a–f.

1 My son is annoying. He wastes
2 They're going to be late. They haven't got
3 Her eyes hurt. She spends
4 We can't take this course
5 I couldn't study much
6 There wasn't enough time to walk

a too many hours working on the computer.
b because it's too advanced.
c too much time doing nothing.
d because there were too many people around.
e so we had to take a taxi.
f enough time to catch the bus.

3 🧑 Make it personal Write your ideas about 1–4 in complete sentences.

1 Name a profession that earns too much money.
2 Name a profession that doesn't earn enough money.
3 Name a car that is too expensive.
4 Name a food that is not tasty enough for you.

I think professional baseball players earn too much money. Some of them get more than 2 million dollars a month!

5C

1 Order the words in 1–5 to make sentences. Notice where there is a comma.

1 Do you love him?
/ know / him, / he / you / don't / won't / tell / if / .
2 His flight leaves very soon.
/ won't / he / board / if / doesn't / go / he / now, / .
3 Why don't you eat something?
/ you / you / regularly, / angry / get / eat / don't / if / .
4 Are you going on vacation?
/ need / go / you / States / a / the / visa / when / you / to / .
5 Are you doing Internet dating?
/ happy / meet / person, / nice / a / if / you'll / you / be / very / .

2 Correct two mistakes in each of 1–5.

1 We are going to the beach this weekend. If the water be too cold, we don't swim.
2 If is raining tomorrow, they cancel the soccer game.
3 I have a part-time job after school. If I gets home too late, I won't to do my homework.
4 If my roommate get up early, she always make coffee.
5 If I will pass the test next week, I will to get my driver's license.

3 🧑 Make it personal What will happen? Write a zero or first conditional sentence for at least five of these situations.

late for work
learn English well
miss the bus
wake up late
win the lottery
get married
feel hungry

When I'm late for work, my boss usually makes me stay later.

147

Grammar Unit 6

6A Verb + gerund (verb + -ing)

I don't feel like dancing.

Some verb phrases and verbs are followed by a gerund:
- I try to **avoid** driv**ing** in the rush hour.
- My friend always does funny things at school. I **can't help** laugh**ing** in class.
- Do you **enjoy** work**ing** here?
- My mom **keeps** los**ing** her glasses, she does it every day.

Verbs followed by a gerund			
adore	dislike	keep	recommend
allow	don't mind	mention	regret
advise	enjoy	mind	risk
avoid	feel like	miss	stop
can't help	finish	practice	suggest
can't stand	hate	propose	understand
consider	imagine	quit	

Go + gerund

Use *go* + gerund to talk about fun activities and hobbies:
- I go running every day.
- We went shopping at the mall last week.

Most verbs can also be used without *go* to mean the same:
- I run every day.
- We shopped at the mall last week.
- I went swimming yesterday. NOT ~~I go to swimming yesterday.~~

In the present perfect, the verb *be* can also be used for activities:
- I've gone / been camping many times.

Gerunds

Use the *-ing* form (gerund) after prepositions and as the subject of a sentence:
- I'm interested in snowboarding.
- Skiing is a popular winter sport.

6B Verb + infinitive / verb + gerund

Verb + infinitive

Some verbs are followed by the infinitive:
- Oh no! I forgot to lock the door!
- I really want to learn to drive.

Verbs followed by an infinitive			
agree	hope	offer	seem
ask	learn	plan	wait
decide	mean	promise	want
expect	need	refuse	wish
forget			

I CAN'T WAIT TO FIND A CLEAN CAR!

Verb + gerund or infinitive

Some verbs combine with a gerund or infinitive with little change in the meaning:
- She **started driving** when she was 17. / She **started to drive** when she was 17.
- He **continued talking** for hours. / He **continued to talk** for hours.

Verbs followed by a gerund or an infinitive			
begin	continue	like	prefer
	hate	love	start

Use the **infinitive** as the second verb if:
- the first verb is in the *-ing* form: I am **continuing to** learn new things every day.
- the second verb is a **state verb**: He's **starting to love** his new course.
- I'm beginning to understand English grammar! NOT ~~I'm beginning understanding English grammar!~~
- We're starting to feel hungry. NOT ~~We're starting to feeling hungry.~~

148

Unit 6

6A

1 Match 1–5 to a–e.
1 Jogging is
2 Smoking is not
3 I'm excited about
4 Karen's got a terrible cold. She keeps
5 Can I have your newspaper when you've finished

a starting college next year.
b reading it?
c coughing.
d permitted in this building.
e a good form of exercise.

2 Order the words in 1–5 to make sentences or questions.
1 a / sport / be / can / dangerous / diving / .
2 you / a / have / getting / new / considered / job / ?
3 watching / how / a / movie / about / ?
4 in / living / he / city / the / misses / really / .
5 doing / you / do / enjoy / what / relax / to / ?

6B

1 Complete 1–4 with the correct form of these verbs. There's one extra verb.

cook   cry   go   have   make   take

1 Marie suggested _____ to a restaurant, but Joel felt like _____ at home.
2 Can you imagine _____ a party on the moon? It would be a lot of fun!
3 My grandpa can't help _____ when he watches *Titanic*.
4 When you don't enjoy _____ a class, it's hard to do well.

2 Match photos a–f to 1–6. Then complete 1–6 with the correct form of the verbs.
1 She has just finished _____. (**eat**)
2 They have agreed _____ business. (**do**)
3 She is asking _____ home. (**go**)
4 She is practicing _____ first aid. (**give**)
5 He forgot _____ his coffee and left it on the car. (**pick up**)
6 They really enjoy _____ video games. (**play**)

3 Correct two mistakes in each of 1–5.
1 After drive all night, we had to stopping to sleep a little.
2 I really dislike to wash the dishes and never do if I can avoid to have to do it.
3 I recommend to go to Rome for your honeymoon. You can sightseeing in many romantic places.
4 Mike wants to learn cooking so he needs buy some books.
5 To be a teacher is a good job if you are interested in to help people.

4 Circle the correct options in 1–5.
1 I asked him not **to play** / **playing** his music so loud.
2 If she wants **to continue** / **continuing** her piano lessons, she'll need to study!
3 Would you mind **to help** / **helping** me with this computer program?
4 I never thought I'd quit **to smoke** / **smoking**, but I've finally done it!
5 He decided **to leave** / **leaving** class early and go home to rest.

5 🟢 **Make it personal** Complete 1–4 about yourself.
1 My friends like me because I enjoy _____.
2 I'm learning to _____ at the moment, because _____.
3 I usually avoid _____, because _____.
4 I prefer _____ to _____, because _____.

149

Grammar Unit 7

7A Pronouns: some-, any-, every-, no-

See **nothing**.   Hear **nothing**.   If you hear **something**, don't tell **anyone**.

- I put my keys **somewhere**. Where are they?
- There's **something** in the way she moves.
- I know **someone** that looks like you.
- Ask Julia. She knows **everything** about baseball.
- There was **no one** in the room when I got here.
- They don't know **anything** about physics.
- Do you have **anything** valuable in your bag?
- Does **anyone** want a drink?
- Is there **anywhere** to sit?

⊕ Verbs

	Unidentified	All in a group	− meaning	− & ?
For a **person**	someone	everyone	no one	anyone
	somebody	everybody	nobody	anybody
For a **thing**	something	everything	nothing	anything
For a **place**	somewhere	everywhere	nowhere	anywhere

- Almost everybody has a cell phone these days. NOT ~~Almost everybody have a cell phone these days.~~
- I didn't do anything fun on the weekend. NOT ~~I didn't do nothing fun on the weekend.~~

Use -*one* or -*body* to talk about people. The meaning is the same.

All the pronouns in this section use the singular form of the verb.

Note: *All* uses a plural verb:
- **All** the students in my class **are** Mexican. / **Everyone** in my class **is** Mexican.

7B *So* and *such*

- It's **so** hot! It's almost 40° C.
- I knew **so many** people at that party!
- There was **so much** traffic **that** I was late this morning.
- That's **such a** tragedy! I can't believe **that** happened.
- We had **such a** great time at your party **that** we didn't want to go.

Use:
- **so** to intensify adjectives and adverbs.
- **such** to intensify the characteristics of nouns.
- **so / such ... that** is often used to express a result.

"I've been so busy reading books on walking and running that I haven't had time to walk or run."

- We have such wonderful neighbors. NOT ~~We have so wonderful neighbors.~~

7C Passive voice: present and past

- These sweaters **are made** by hand.
- This fabulous dress **was designed** by Vera Wang.
- Thousands of shoes **are sold** every day in the U.S.

	S	V	O	Complement / agent of the passive
Active	J.K. Rowling	wrote	Harry Potter	in a café.
Passive	Harry Potter	was written		by J.K. Rowling in a café.
Active	Security guards	don't protect	this building	at night.
Passive	This building	isn't protected		by security guards at night.
Active	People	eat	a lot of pasta	in Italy.
Passive	A lot of pasta	is eaten		in Italy.

Form: be + past participle.

Use: when the object or event is more important than who did it.

When it's necessary to say who / what did the action, use *by*.

Four easy steps to transform an active voice into a passive:
- The **object** of the active voice becomes the subject of the passive.
- Use verb *be* in the same tense as the main verb of the active voice.
- Put the main verb in the past participle.
- If necessary, use *by* + the subject of the active voice to insert the **agent** of the passive.

Unit 7

7A

1 Complete 1–6 with *anyone, anything, someone, something, everyone, everything, no one,* or *nothing.*
1 Do you know _____ that lives in Chile?
2 _____ tastes better than chocolate. It's my favorite food.
3 I'll wait until _____ has stopped talking before I start.
4 Excuse me, can I ask you _____?
5 My new girlfriend and I want to go to a place where ____ knows us and we can be alone!
6 There was a power outage at work and _____ stopped working, even the lights. We couldn't see _____, until _____ found a flashlight.

2 Match 1–5 to a–e. Then add the correct verb to a–e.
1 I can't cook because there's
2 I don't have
3 It was a great party.
4 Someone phoned earlier,
5 Does anyone

a have a pencil I could _____?
b but they didn't _____ their name.
c nothing in the fridge. Let's _____ out to eat.
d anything to _____. I'm so bored.
e Everyone _____ they enjoyed it.

3 Correct one mistake in each of 1–5.
1 He didn't do nothing on Sunday. He just stayed at home.
2 Someone have taken my cell phone!
3 I left my window open in the storm! Now everything I have are totally wet.
4 I didn't tell someone your news. Your secret is safe.
5 At the airport, they ask, "Do you have something to declare?"

4 ⬤ Make it personal Write your ideas about 1–5 in complete sentences.
1 Name something you can't live without.
2 Name someone you love.
3 Name somewhere you go often.
4 Did you eat anything before class? What?
5 Did you go anywhere on your last vacation? Where?

7B

1 Complete 1–4 with *so* or *such*.
1 That movie is _____ fantastic! I've seen it twice.
2 My boss is _____ a difficult person; he's obsessed with punctuality and order. It can be _____ annoying.
3 I didn't know she could be _____ brave! She's _____ a hero.
4 Our tutor is _____ an exceptional speaker. That was the best lecture I've ever heard.

2 Add *so* or *such* to 1–5 and match to a–e.
1 Are you angry that
2 Vera did a good job that
3 Their singing was impressive that
4 Rosa and Jorge went to Canada. It was cold that
5 John was a good player that

a they couldn't feel their feet.
b they were asked to perform at the concert.
c his team gave him a special medal.
d you can't even talk to her about it?
e she got a promotion.

3 ⬤ Make it personal Complete 1–5 so they are true for you.
1 _____ is such a great movie!
2 _____ is such an inspiring person!
3 _____ makes such good food!
4 I'm so happy when _____.
5 I'm so sad when _____.

7C

1 Rewrite 1–5, passive to active or active to passive. Which three sound more natural in the passive?
1 The law prohibits smoking in this area.
2 People make a lot of things in China these days.
3 *Once Upon a Time in Hollywood* was written and directed by Quentin Tarantino.
4 Jennifer Lopez and Angelina Jolie wore these beautiful dresses.
5 People downloaded one million songs from iTunes in its first week.

2 Circle the correct options in 1–5.
1 Miguel de Cervantes is **knew** / **known** for his book *Don Quijote.* The book **is** / **was** published in 1612.
2 A lot of The Beatles' songs **was** / **were** recorded at Abbey Road studios in London. Most of them **was** / **were** written by Lennon and McCartney.
3 Hamburgers **is** / **are** usually **make** / **made** from meat, a bun, salad, and cheese.
4 Thousands of phones are **find** / **lost** every year, but only some of them are **return** / **returned** to their owners.
5 Millions of movies **was** / **were** downloaded last year, but most of them **wasn't** / **weren't** paid for.

3 ⬤ Make it personal How is a hamburger made? Write a delicious description!

First, the hamburger is put on the grill. Then the bun is cut in half …

151

Grammar Unit 8

8A Phrasal verbs

- The TV volume is really low. Can you **turn** it **up**?
- It's getting dark. Do you want me to **switch on** the light?
- When will you **give back** my bike?
- I'll **give** it **back** tomorrow.
- I just lost my glasses. Can you help me **look for** them?

Man: Turn up the volume! **Woman:** No! Turn it down!
Boy: Give it back! It's mine!

A phrasal verb is a combination of a **verb** + **particle** (preposition or adverb) that usually has a different meaning to the original verb. For example, *look* = focus your eyes in a particular direction; *look for* = try to find. Phrasal verbs are very common in **informal** fluent speech and writing.
Most phrasal verbs are separable (the object noun can go between the verb and the particle).

- She turned the light on. / She turned on the light.

A few are inseparable – the object can only go after the particle.

- Juan cared for his mother when she was sick.

To *find out* if a phrasal verb is inseparable, *look* it *up* in a dictionary.

8B Future forms 1: *will* and *going to* for predictions

- We probably **won't** be able to live on Mars. (prediction)
- I think there **will** probably be a lot of people at the concert. (prediction)
- I don't think it**'s going to be** hot tomorrow. (prediction)
- My sister**'s going to have** her baby very soon. (prediction based on evidence)

Will

	S	Modal	Adverb	I	O phrase
➕	He	will / 'll	definitely / probably	find	a job.
	S	Adverb	Modal	I	O phrase
➖	We	definitely / probably	will not / won't	get	a promotion.
	Modal	S	Adverb	I	O phrase
❓	Will	I	definitely	go	to Europe?

Going to

	S	Be	Adverb	(Not) going to	I	O phrase
➕ ➖	I	am / 'm	probably	going to / not going to	have	fun.
	We	are / 're				
	He	is / 's				
	Be	S	Adverb	Going to	I	O phrase
❓	Are	you	definitely	going to	live	on the moon?
	Is	she				

Use *going to* or *will* for predictions.
Going to is more common in spoken English and is usually pronounced *gonna*.
Use *going to* for predictions that are based on evidence.
Adverbs modify predictions: *possibly* → *probably* → *definitely / certainly*.

- It's 7:30. You're going to be late for school. (prediction based on evidence) And you're probably going to miss the first class too. (modification)

8C Future forms 2

- You need a volunteer? I**'ll do** it! (quick decision)
- The package **will arrive** by 2 p.m. (fact)
- You can tell us. We **won't** tell anyone else. (promise)
- They**'re going to visit** their uncle in Paris. (fixed plans)
- I**'m not going to** go to that party. (intention)
- Look at that cloud! It**'s going to** rain any minute! (prediction based on evidence)
- They**'re flying** tomorrow. (arrangement with the airline)
- She**'s working** this weekend. (arrangement with her company)
- The show **starts** at 7 p.m. (schedule)

Use:
- **will / won't** for statements of facts, quick decisions, promises, or predictions.
- **going to** for decided plans, intentions, and predictions based on evidence.
- **present continuous** for fixed plans, or arrangements with other people.
- **simple present** for scheduled events.

To differentiate **present continuous** for future from actions that are happening now, use a future time expression:
- I'm leaving. (now)
- I'm leaving in half an hour. (future)

152

Unit 8

8A

1 Complete 1–6 with these prepositions.

down   in (x 2)   off   on   out

1 Please switch _____ the lights when you leave.
2 Where can I plug _____ my cell phone? I need to charge it.
3 Can you turn the air conditioning _____ a little? It's really cold in here.
4 When you check in online for a flight, the company emails you the boarding pass so you can print it _____ at home.
5 Get _____ the car and I'll take you to the bus station.
6 It's getting cold. I'm going to put _____ a sweater.

2 Order the words in 1–5 to make sentences and questions.

1 horror / you / movies / are / into / watching / alone / ?
2 she / her / looking / glasses / for / is / reading / .
3 many / of / have / college / dropped / year / how / out / people / this / ?
4 money / did / put / much / the / vending / in / machine / he / how / ?
5 off / before / shoes / take / in / your / you / come / .

8B

1 Rewrite 1–6 as future predictions using the words in parentheses.

1 The party is a lot of fun. (**probably**)
   The party is probably going to be a lot of fun.
2 There are a lot more economic problems. (**definitely**)
3 We can take a vacation on Mars. (**in 2020**)
4 We don't have any fish in the oceans. (**probably / 100 years from now**)
5 NASA makes contact with an alien civilization. (**before 2050**)
6 We can't eradicate poverty before the end of this century. (**certainly**)

2 🟢 Make it personal Correct one mistake in each of 1–5. Do you agree with the statements?

1 We will can speak fluent English one day.
2 There won't probably be any homework today, so we'll have a free evening!
3 We definitely not going to find a cure for cancer soon.
4 Our country has the best soccer team and is definitely winning the next World Cup!
5 If I'm going to pass my exams, I'll be a teacher.

8C

1 Complete 1–6 with *will / won't* or *be + going to / not going to*.

1 _____ you _____ be back before dinner?
2 Sorry I didn't wash the dishes. I _____ do them tomorrow, I promise.
3 It's a long way to the airport and the bus is terrible. We _____ take you in our car.
4 I _____ go to school tomorrow because I have to go to the doctor.
5 I'm so sorry I hurt you. I _____ do it again.
6 A: What's that man doing on the bridge? Oh no! He _____ jump!
   B: Don't worry. It's a bungee-jumping platform.

2 Look at the ticket and circle the correct options in the dialogue.

A: Hey, Billy Sonic **plays** / **is playing** at The Arena this weekend, do you want to go?
B: I'd love to, but **I'm working** / **will work** on Saturday.
A: Really? What time **do you finish** / **are you finishing**?
B: **I'm going to finish** / **finish** at 5 p.m. What time's the show?
A: Uh, the doors **open** / **will open** at 7 p.m.
B: OK, cool. Can you get me a ticket and **I'm going to** / **I'll** pay you back?
A: No problem. It's going to **be** / **being** great!

3 🟢 Make it personal Write your answers to questions 1–4.

1 What are you doing this weekend?
2 When does your English course finish?
3 What will you do after that?
4 What are you going to do when you've learned enough English?

When I've learned enough English, I'm going to look for a job in California.

153

Grammar Unit 9

9A -ed and -ing adjectives

- Wow, that movie was **terrifying**!
- Janet has traveled a lot. She seems really **interesting**.
- We are going to be totally **exhausted** after our vacation!
- The analyst is **bored** with his patient's dreams.

Use:
- -ed or -ing adjectives after verbs such as *be, become, feel, get, look, seem*, etc.
- -ed adjectives to describe a feeling or a condition.
- -ing adjectives to describe what causes the feeling or condition.

The spelling rules are the same as for simple past (-ed) and continuous verbs (-ing). See Grammar 2A and 2B p. 140.

Use **intensifying adverbs** before a participle adjective to show the degree of feeling.

| very | really | extremely | absolutely / totally / completely |

Intensifying adverbs go before the main verb, auxiliary, or adjective they emphasize:
- Kim **absolutely** adores hip hop.
- Jo is **extremely** tired of working on Sundays.
- I don't **really** like bananas.
- Rob cooks **very** well.

Tiring is used to describe the thing that makes you feel tired.
- Your husband looks really tired. Is he OK? NOT *Your husband looks really tiring. Is he OK?*
- I've had such a tiring day at work that I'm going to bed. NOT *I've had such a tired day at work that I'm going to bed.*

9B Second conditional

- If I had wings, I would fly. (but I don't have wings = not real)
- If my father didn't have to work, he would play more golf. (but he has to work = not real)
- She would enjoy school more if she didn't have to study math. (but she has to study math = not real)
- If you won the lottery, what would you buy first? (but I don't think you will win = improbable)
- Would you be scared if an earthquake happened here now? (but I don't think it will happen = improbable)

Conditional clause			Result clause		
If / When	S	Past verb ⊕⊖	S	Would ⊕⊖	I
If	I / you / he / she / we / they	**were** taller,	I / you / he / she / we / they	would	play volleyball.
		didn't need money,		wouldn't	work.

Form: *if* + **past verb** + *would* + **infinitive**.
- If cell phones didn't exist, how would your life change? NOT ~~If cell phones wouldn't exist, how would your life change?~~

The **conditional** clause uses a past tense to talk about an imaginary, unreal, improbable, or impossible present or future event.

When the result clause comes first, don't use a comma.

Use *were* with all subjects in formal English. In informal English, people increasingly use *was* with the first and third persons singular: *If I was you, I'd tell him.*

We often use the phrase *If I were / was you, I'd ...* to give advice.

9C May / might / could / must / can't + be

- You've been on a plane for 15 hours. You **must** be tired! (certain that it is true)
- She went downtown, so she **might** be at the mall or she **could** be at the library. (uncertain)
- You **can't** be hungry. You just ate a big dinner! (certain that it isn't true)
- My dog is acting strangely. Do you think she's OK? (asking for speculation / deduction) She **may** be. But take her to the vet to check.

Use:
- modals (*can't / might / may / could / must*) to speculate or make deductions based on evidence, and to express degrees of certainty.
- **Do you think ...?** to ask for speculation or a deduction:
  Do you think Liverpool are going to win? They might!

Unit 9

9A

1 Correct one mistake in four of 1–6. Be careful! Two have no mistakes.

1. It's a totally depressing movie about a young family that loses everything.
2. I get exciting at Christmas – I love all the food and the decorations.
3. Jane was feeling very stress because she has a job interview tomorrow.
4. She's been to the spa and now she feels very relaxing.
5. They can't even think about cooking dinner – they're totally exhausted.
6. The baseball game was a little bored. Nothing happened for hours.

2 Complete 1–5 with the *-ed* or *-ing* form of the verbs.

1. I have a three-month-old cousin. I'm totally _____ how much she cries! (**amaze**)
2. That was the most _____ flight I have ever been on! (**terrify**)
3. When he finished the race, he was so _____ that he collapsed. (**tire**)
4. Do you turn red easily when you are _____ ? (**embarrass**)
5. She read my work and said it was _____. Is that good or bad? (**surprise**)

9B

1 Circle the correct options in 1–6, then match to a–f to make second conditional sentences.

1. If you **seen** / **saw** a crime,
2. If Ellen **had** / **was having** long hair,
3. If I found out my partner **was** / **is** cheating,
4. If you **could** / **was able to** time travel,
5. What would you **do** / **did**
6. If she **doesn't** / **didn't** want to go out with you,

a. would you visit the past or the future?
b. would you call the police?
c. she would look just like Alex Morgan.
d. she wouldn't and she'd make an excuse.
e. I'd dump him immediately.
f. if your parents told you not to marry someone you loved?

2 Use the prompts to make second conditional questions.

1. flight / what / if / you / do / miss / you / ?
   What would you do if you missed the flight?
2. how / away / you / win / the / give away / if / lottery / much / you / ?
3. if / emails / your / be cheating / you / partner's / think / if / you / read / ?
4. if / any / be / who / can / you / professional / if / you / sportsperson / you / be / ?
5. you / if / here / where / not / live / like / you / ?

3 🟢 **Make it personal** Write your answers to questions 1–5 in **2**.

9C

1 Correct two mistakes in each of 1–6. Be careful! Not all the mistakes are modals.

1. Jack isn't answering his phone. He can be in a meeting, or maybe he's leaving it at home.
2. You got a promotion! That's great news! You must to be such pleased!
3. Have you notice he's in really good shape? He must doing a lot of exercise!
4. I think that man look familiar. He can to be a famous actor.
5. Celia must be exhausting. She traveled all night and she was sit on the bus for hours.
6. Someone has took your wallet? Oh no! You could be really angry.

2 🟢 **Make it personal** Make at least two deductions about photos a–e using *must*, *could* / *might* / *may*, or *can't be*.

They could be tourists in Egypt. Or they might be guides who are showing tourists the pyramids.

Grammar Unit 10

10A Relative pronouns: *that* and *who*

- Tessa loves a guy **who** lives in a different city.
- These are the videos **that** you asked me to send you.
- Are those the people **that** used to work with you?

Sentence 1	Sentence 2	Relative clause
	S V O	
He's the actor.	I love him.	That's the actor **who** / **that** I love.
I live in a house.	It has two pools.	I live in a house **that** has two pools.

A relative pronoun refers to a noun mentioned previously.
Use relative pronouns to join two sentences or ideas.
The relative pronoun is optional when it refers to the object of a sentence.

- The city I love the most is Rome. / The city that I love the most is Rome.

One / ones

- Which are your **keys**? Are they the **ones** with the Mickey Mouse key ring?
- Which **one** is better for me? A **Mac** or a **PC**?
- "Where's your **car**?" "It's the old black **one** over there."
- "I've heard that **joke** before." "Yeah, the old **ones** are the best."
- "Have you read **Harry Potter**?" "Which **one**?"

Use: to avoid repeating singular and plural nouns.
Don't use one / ones after a **possessive** (*my, your, his, her, Julia's*):

- You do **your job**, and I'll do **mine**. NOT ~~You do your job, and I'll do the my one.~~

Don't use one / ones directly after a **number** or a **quantifier** (*some, many, a few*):

- When we're getting ready to go out, I only need **10 minutes** but my boyfriend needs **20**.
- "Can I have **some cookies**, please?" "Oh! Can I have **a few** too?"

10B Asking questions: review

- **How many** times have I told you not to do that?
- **How much** time do we have for the test?
- **How long** did you stay in New York?
- **How old** is your father?
- **How tall** are you?
- **How far (away)** is your house?
- **What** do you call this in English?
- **What** are you going to do this weekend?
- **What** should we do to stop climate change?
- **What's** glass made of?
- **Which** shoes do you like? The black ones or the red ones?
- **Who** did you go on vacation with?
- **Why** don't we go for a coffee?
- **Is** she working this weekend?
- **Do** you often eat hot peppers?
- **Don't** you like this cake? Come on! It's delicious!

Q	O	A	S	I	
How much	money	do	I	need?	
How many	friends	does	your brother	have	on Facebook?
How fast		can	you	run?	
How often		do	you	work out?	
Which	colors	does	your partner	like	best?
Where		will	you	go	after class?
What	music	would	you	choose	to hear?
Who		did	she	meet	last night?
Where		don't	they	want	to live?
What	food	doesn't	he	like?	
		Do	we	have	any money left?
		Doesn't	your city	have	a metro?

Use:

- **how much** for quantity + U nouns.
- **how many** for quantity + C nouns.
- **how + adj. / adv.** to ask about quantity or degree.
- **which** to ask about things when there is a limited choice.
- **what** for general questions.
- **who** to ask about people.
- only an auxiliary for *Yes / No* questions.
- negative **ASI** questions to confirm information you think you know or to show surprise.

"So, how far is the restroom?"

Unit 10

10A

1 Add *who* or *that* in the correct places in the dialogue. Which three pronouns are optional?

A: Hello, we'd like to check in. My name's Cristina and this is my husband, Clive.
B: Ah, hello! You're the people booked online. Welcome to Hotel Flamingo.
A: Thank you. Could you tell me a little about the area?
B: Sure! There are some great restaurants you'll love. There's one around the corner has live music every night. I think there's a musician plays traditional songs tonight. And here we are, this is your room.
A: Oh! Uh … this isn't the room we saw on the website.
B: No. I'm afraid the room you booked has a problem with the shower. But this room is even bigger and has the same view.

2 Combine the two sentences in 1–5 using *who* or *that*.
1 This is the gym. This gym was on the website.
2 She is a girl. I knew her in high school.
3 That is the taxi driver. I met him at the basketball game.
4 There are five books. You have to read the books this semester.
5 Do you know a club? A club has good music.

3 Rewrite five of these sentences to avoid repetition and use *one / ones* correctly. Be careful! One sentence has no mistakes.
1 "Mom, can I eat those apples?" "Which?"
2 My dad's looking for a new car, a car with seven seats.
3 Look! We've got two letters. This one is my one and that one is your one.
4 Those earrings are nice, but I like the big earrings better.
5 I have seven cousins. The young ones are still at school and the old ones are already working.
6 I like the Fast and Furious movies but some ones are better than others.

10B

1 Complete dialogues 1–5.
1 A: _____ was your computer?
   B: About $900. But it has a massive memory.
2 A: _____ people are coming to the reunion?
   B: About 30 I think. Nearly everyone.
3 A: _____ your best friend dating anyone?
   B: No, she _____. Do you want to ask her out?
4 A: _____ pie are you going to have?
   B: Not the chicken one. Can I have a vegetable one, please?
5 A: _____ have you been in the line?
   B: Over 20 minutes. It's taking a long time.

2 Correct the mistakes in 1–7. There are eight mistakes.
1 What are those ladies over there? They look like friends I knew in college.
2 How often you eat fast food?
3 How much time did you live in New Mexico before you moved to Boston?
4 Do he change his status on Facebook every hour? How often he tweets?
5 Has you met many interesting new people recently?
6 How much people do you stay in touch with every day?
7 What juice will you having? Orange or pineapple?

3 🟢 **Make it personal** Order the words in 1–6 to make questions. Write your answers to the questions.
1 often / newspaper / do / you / a / how / buy / ?
2 bus / the / take / school / how / does / long / ?
3 how / bags / are / your / heavy / ?
4 every day / do / coffee / how / you / much / drink / ?
5 center / is / city / it / to / far / how / the / ?
6 been / beach / year / times / you / many / have / to / the / how / this / ?

157

Verbs

Irregular verbs

Irregular verbs can be difficult to remember. Try remembering them in groups with similar sounds, conjugation patterns, or spellings.

Simple past and Past participle are the same

Base form	Simple past	Past participle
bring	brought /brɔt/	brought
buy	bought	bought
catch	caught /cɔt/	caught
fight	fought	fought
teach	taught	taught
think	thought	thought
feed	fed	fed
feel	felt	felt
keep	kept	kept
leave	left	left
mean	meant /mɛnt/	meant
meet	met	met
sleep	slept	slept
lay	laid	laid
pay	paid	paid
sell	sold	sold
tell	told	told
send	sent	sent
spend	spent	spent
stand	stood /stʊd/	stood
understand	understood	understood
lose	lost	lost
shoot	shot	shot
can	could	could
will	would	would
build	built /bɪlt/	built
find	found /faʊnd/	found
hang	hung	hung
have	had	had
hear	heard /hɜrd/	heard
hold	held	held
make	made	made
say	said /sɛd/	said
sit	sat	sat
swing	swung /swʌŋ/	swung
win	won /wʌn/	won

Base form and Past participle are the same

Base form	Simple past	Past participle
become	became	become
come	came	come
run	ran	run

No changes across the three forms

Base form	Simple past	Past participle
cost	cost	cost
cut	cut	cut
hit	hit	hit
let	let	let
put	put /pʊt/	put
quit	quit /kwɪt/	quit
set	set	set
split	split	split

Special cases

Base form	Simple past	Past participle
be	was / were	been
draw	drew /druː/	drawn /drɔn/
fly	flew /fluː/	flown /floʊn/
lie	lay	lain
read	read /rɛd/	read /rɛd/

Simple past + -en

Base form	Simple past	Past participle
beat	beat	beaten
bite	bit	bitten
break	broke	broken
choose	chose	chosen
forget	forgot	forgotten
freeze	froze	frozen
get	got	got / gotten
speak	spoke	spoken
steal	stole	stolen
wake	woke	woken

Verbs

Simple past + -en

Base form	Simple past	Past participle
beat	beat	beaten
bite	bit	bitten
break	broke	broken
choose	chose	chosen
forget	forgot	forgotten
freeze	froze	frozen
get	got	got / gotten
speak	spoke	spoken
steal	stole	stolen
wake	woke	woken

Base form + -en

Base form	Simple past	Past participle
drive	drove	driven /drɪvən/
eat	ate	eaten
fall	fell	fallen
give	gave	given
ride	rode	ridden /rɪdən/
see	saw /sɔ/	seen
shake	shook	shaken
take	took	taken
write	wrote	written /rɪtən/

Base form ending in *o* + -ne

Base form	Simple past	Past participle
do	did	done /dʌn/
go	went	gone /gɔn/

i - a - u

Base form	Simple past	Past participle
begin	began	begun
drink	drank	drunk
ring	rang	rung
sing	sang	sung
swim	swam	swum

ow - ew - own

Base form	Simple past	Past participle
blow	blew /blu:/	blown
grow	grew	grown
know	knew	known
throw	threw	thrown

ear - ore - orn

Base form	Simple past	Past participle
swear	swore	sworn
tear /tɛr/	tore	torn
wear	wore	worn

Sounds and usual spellings

S Difficult sounds for Spanish speakers
P Difficult sounds for Portuguese speakers

▶ To listen to these words and sounds, and to practice them, go to the pronunciation section on the Richmond Learning Platform.

Vowels

/iː/	three, tree, eat, receive, believe, key, B, C, D, E, G, P, T, V, Z	
/ɪ/	six, mix, it, fifty, fish, trip, lip, fix	
/ʊ/	book, cook, put, could, cook, woman	
/uː/	two, shoe, food, new, soup, true, suit, Q, U, W	
/ɛ/	pen, ten, heavy, then, again, men, F, L, M, N, S, X	
/ə/	bananas, pajamas, family, photography	
/ɜr/	shirt, skirt, work, turn, learn, verb	
/ɔr/	four, door, north, fourth	
/ɔ/	walk, saw, water, talk, author, law	
/æ/	man, fan, bad, apple	
/ʌ/	sun, run, cut, umbrella, country, love	
/ɑ/	hot, not, on, clock, fall, tall	
/ɑr/	car, star, far, start, party, artist, R	

Diphthongs

/eɪ/	plane, train, made, stay, they, A, H, J, K
/aɪ/	nine, wine, night, my, pie, buy, eyes, I, Y
/aʊ/	house, mouse, town, cloud
/ɔɪ/	toys, boys, oil, coin
/oʊ/	nose, rose, home, know, toe, road, O

160

Sounds and usual spellings

☐ Voiced
☐ Unvoiced

Consonants

/p/ pig, pie, open, top, apple
/b/ bike, bird, describe, able, club, rabbit
/m/ medal, monster, name, summer
/w/ web, watch, where, square, one
/f/ fish, feet, off, phone, enough
/v/ vet, van, five, have, video
/θ/ teeth, thief, thank, nothing, mouth
/ð/ mother, father, the, other
/t/ truck, taxi, hot, stop, attractive
/d/ dog, dress, made, adore, sad, middle
/n/ net, nurse, tennis, one, sign, know
/l/ lion, lips, long, all, old

/s/ snake, skate, kiss, city, science
/z/ zoo, zebra, size, jazz, lose
/ʃ/ shark, shorts, action, special, session, chef
/ʒ/ television, treasure, usual
/k/ cat, cake, back, quick
/g/ goal, girl, leg, guess, exist
/ŋ/ king, ring, single, bank
/h/ hand, hat, unhappy, who
/tʃ/ chair, cheese, kitchen, future, question
/dʒ/ jeans, jump, generous, bridge
/r/ red, rock, ride, married, write
/j/ yellow, yacht, university

161

Audio script

Unit 1

◉1.2 Notice unstressed *and* = /ən/, *for* = /fə/, *to* = /tə/, but /tu/ before a vowel.

RH = radio host

RH Hi, and welcome to "Life in 10 Seconds"! Last week, we asked you, our listeners, to call in and, in only 10 seconds, tell us your number one priority in life. Listen to what you said:

1 Hi! Uh ... well, your health is the most important thing in your life. Definitely. It's my top priority. I'm planning to live to be 100. Or 120 – why not?!

2 I like to feel comfortable about money. I grew up poor, and my parents were always worried about how to pay the bills, but, you know, I went to college and now I have a good job and earn enough money to feel secure.

3 I live for today! I want to enjoy every day of my life. Fun is the most important thing for me. Oh, and baseball of course: Let's go Giants!

4 My job defines who I am. I want a good career and I'm very ambitious. This means that I work hard, but hard work is good for you.

5 I never stop studying. In fact, I'm taking a class in neuroscience at the moment. Continuing to learn is the best thing we can do. It's good for you and it keeps you young.

6 Without love, what else is there? It's the most important thing in the world. I always need to have a partner. Love is all we have in life ... and um ...

7 What's the point in having work and money if you have no free time? Time to enjoy things is more important than money. Much more. You don't need a lot of money to have a good time.

8 People are more important than things. My friends and family are the most important thing for me. Oh, and my dog too! Hello, baby! Who's a good girl?

9 You know, I don't want to live in a world without art and music. Culture is so important for me – I need to have art, and literature, and movies, and music and ...

10 I live for exercise! I need to look good and I want to stay in shape. I'm running at the gym now! And then I'm ...

◉1.3 Notice unstressed *to* = /tə/, *but* = /bət/, *a* /ə/, and *the* /thə/.

1

C Hi! I'm Casey Murray and I'm 22 years old. I finished high school, but I didn't go to college. I'm a security guard, but my job isn't very interesting. My hobbies are playing video games and I love shopping! I never have the money to do all the things I want to do. I have to work every day in a boring job because I need to pay my bills, but I

really want to be a singer. I love to sing and dance and I want to be a professional singer. Singing is my passion, but I'm not singing at the moment because of my job.

2

R My name's Ricardo Sutton, and I'm a 28-year-old attorney from Canada. I finished grad school two years ago, and I have a good job that I really like. I love travel and languages (I speak Spanish, French, and Japanese), but I work really long hours and I don't have much vacation time. I'm also taking a class, so I'm always too tired to go to the gym – I'm exhausted after work, and I work on weekends, too, so, I'm out of shape. Yup, I really need to exercise more because I'm desperate to get in shape.

◉1.6 Notice /u/, /ʊ/, and /eɪ/ and their different spellings.

A I'm listening to my brother's band. They sound great! They practice every Friday and I come every week. They're going to be famous one day.

B Do you really think so? I can hear them and I think they sound like they need to practice more than once a week!

2

C That's a nice jacket. It looks really cool.

D Thanks, I bought it on sale last week – it wasn't expensive. I looked at it for a long time before I bought it. I don't really like the color – it's not a color I usually wear.

C It looks good on you.

D Thanks.

3

E This chewing gum is delicious. It tastes awesome!

F I don't like chewing gum.

E I do, and I like unusual flavors like this one: bacon!

F Bacon chewing gum! That's weird.

4

G What is on those pizza slices? They smell awful!

H It says here, it's the chef's secret recipe.

G Hmm ... I think maybe we should go somewhere else.

H Yeah, I think you're right – let's get out of here.

5

I I don't like this sweater. It feels rough. I don't like wearing it!

J But it's warm, and it's cold outside, so you need to wear it!

I No!!

◉1.7 Notice the connections.

1

M1 What do you think about those singers?

W1 They sound_awful. Let's get_out of here!

2

W2 How about going to the beach?

M2 That sounds_awesome. Yeah, I really need a vacation.

3

M3 What do you think about these phones?

W3 Hmm ... They look_old. What_about those over there?

4

W4 This movie looks good. Shall we go see_it?

W5 It looks_awful. I hate romantic movies.

5

M4 Do you like this perfume?

W6 Uh-huh. It smells_amazing.

6

M5 Dinner's ready – want some meatballs?

B & G Thanks, Dad. Mmm. They smell_ awesome.

7

M6 I really like this sweater. Do you?

M7 Yes! It feels_expensive.

8

W7 What do you think_of these gloves?

W8 Well, They feel extra_soft, but ... umm ... how much are they?

9

M8 Do you like the sandwich

W9 Mmmm ... It tastes_amazing!

10

M9 What do you think_of these cookies?

M10 They taste old. Where did_you get them?

◉1.9 Notice dark /l/ and normal /l/.

1

W = waiter   C = customer

W I'll take your order now.

C Great, thanks. I'd like the fish.

W Good choice! You'll enjoy it.

C Mmm! This fish is good. It's really tender and juicy.

2

A What time will you be at the party tomorrow?

B About 8. What about you?

A I'll definitely be there by 9. Hey! Listen to this! You'll love it. It's so cool.

B Yeah, wow, this is amazing! It's fantastic! I'll download it now.

3

A Your mother will love this perfume.

B Hmm ... really? It smells ... um ... interesting. Unusual. No, she won't like it. She doesn't like fruity smells. I'll try another one, please.

A OK ... what about this one?

4

A I'm looking for a painting as a gift for my wife on our wedding anniversary.

B I suggest this wonderful new painting by Henrietta Jonquil.

A Ah yes. My wife will love this. It's a beautiful painting. Awesome!

B Yes, and it's only 25,000 dollars.

A Hmm ... I'll take this postcard of it.

B That's 2 dollars. Will you need a bag?

A Yes, I will.

Audio script

5

A This blanket feels so soft. It's 100% wool.

B It looks nice and warm. But my kids won't like it. They're allergic to wool.

A Oh, well, the synthetic blankets are over here.

◉1.11 Notice /k/, /aʊ/, and /ɔ/.

M Where is everyone? Why's nobody at our party?

W Well, Fran called – she has a headache.

M Hmmm ... What about Lenny?

W He texted. He has the flu.

M And Gaby?

W She has a stomachache.

M Really? What about Helen and Marcos?

W Helen has a cold ... and Marcos has a cough.

M They're both sick? And I suppose Jenny is too?

W Yes ... Jenny has a fever ...

M What about Brad? He's really healthy.

W Oh, he just texted. Sorry, guys. I have a really bad toothache. I'm in bed.

M I can't believe it! Are all our friends are sick?

W Hmmm ... This seems strange. Is there another party tonight?

M I think you're right! They're all at another party ... and we're not invited!

◉1.12 Notice /h/.

1

M = mom   D = daughter

M What's the matter?

D Oooh ... I have a headache.

M You should take a painkiller and you shouldn't go to the party.

D I guess you're right.

2

D = doctor   M = man

D How are you feeling?

M I have a cough and a fever and I ache all over.

D You have the flu. So, you should stay in bed and rest. Drink plenty of water, but you shouldn't eat anything. Don't eat until the fever goes down.

M OK, doctor, thanks. I'm not hungry anyway.

3

W = woman   M = man

W Are you OK?

M Ow ... I have a toothache.

W Aaah! You should see a dentist as soon as possible. You shouldn't eat or drink anything hot or cold.

4

W = woman   M = man

W How are you?

M Ugh ... I feel awful. I have a cold.

W You shouldn't go out. You should drink a lot of warm fluids and you should stay warm. I'll make you some soup.

M Thanks.

◉1.14 Notice /aɪ/ and /ɪ/.

This is Lori, with my advice for the Unhappy Wife whose father-in-law comes in and out of their house, borrows things, and gives them no privacy.

Dear Unhappy Wife,

This is a very delicate situation, but you should take your father-in-law out to dinner and tell him that you have a problem. You shouldn't be mean, but you should be very clear that what he is doing is making you unhappy.

If he ignores you and continues to come to the house and borrow things, maybe you should change the locks on the doors.

I hope this helps. That's all for now. See you next week.

◉1.16 Notice the intonation in offers and responses.

1

A That looks heavy. Do you need a hand? ↗

B Thank you. That's very kind of you. ↘

2

A I can't do this problem.

B Do you want me to help you? ↗

A Yes, please! I have a test tomorrow and I don't understand it. ↘

B OK, let's see.

3

A What are you doing? ↘

B I'm painting the kitchen. ↘

A Can I help you? I love painting. ↗ ↘

B Umm ... I think I can do it myself, but thanks for the offer. ↘

4

A How's the art project coming along? ↘

B It's OK, but I can't get the colors right. ↘

A Would you like me to help you? I'm good with this software. ↗ ↘

B Thanks, Dad, but I have to do it myself.

A OK, no worries.

Unit 2

◉2.1 Notice the spelling of /iː/ and /ɪ/.

RP = radio presenter

RP So, we asked six listeners the question: How do you usually get your news? Here's what they said.

1 I still read the newspaper every day. I, uh, don't like reading on a computer screen – I like to hold the paper in my hand and turn the pages. Sometimes I just scan the headlines, to, you know, get an idea of big developments.

2 I get all my news on social media, I guess. When there's anything big happening, I hear about it there. I don't need to make a special effort to go and find out – it's right there.

3 Hmm ... I guess I usually watch news on the TV. I always watch in the morning when I'm getting ready for school. I don't have to waste time reading, I can just listen and watch. Also

we often watch the news on TV when we're eating at home. We sometimes have some very interesting discussions!

4 On the radio. I listen all day. I wake up to the radio, listen to the news in bed, and then listen in the car. I love radio because you can listen when you drive to work. I even listen when I'm working out.

5 I work from home – I'm a web designer, so I'm online all day long and I have my favorite websites that I use for news. I often check the headlines. I never watch TV, but I watch a lot of TV shows online.

6 On a mobile device, so I can check the news on the move. I'm lucky, I have a smart phone and an iPad, and usually check my news apps when I'm commuting to work. And doing it this way, there's no destruction of trees and there's no trash.

◉2.2 Notice the connections.

1 And today will be sunny with temperatures_ up to_25_degrees in some areas. Tonight we can expect_some_rain, and it will start cloudy in the morning and stay that way for most of the day tomorrow, so it will be a little colder.

2 This week's box_office_hit is *Miracle Men* starring Ben Gardner. It's_just_been_ announced that Gardner will be in a_new_ movie with Michelle Warren coming_out in the fall.

3 The latest news we have is that all the main highways into the city are clear just_now, but there_is heavy congestion in_the_downtown area and you_are_recommended to stay_ away, if possible.

4 In baseball_news, the Cardinals have_ reached the final of the_World_Series, where they_will_face Texas. The Cardinals beat Arizona 5–2 tonight.

5 The World Summit_on_climate_change has come to_an_end after only_eight_days with no_real_agreement reached between world leaders from over_50_nations.

6 All_over_the_country today there were protests about the rising_price_of_food. The government is considering reducing_the_tax on fruits_and_vegetables.

7 When a local_news_team went to visit_ grandmother, Maria Braun, to ask questions_ about_her_daughter they got more than they expected. Maria_chased_the_reporters with a baseball_bat and called_the_police. The reporters got_no_answers to their questions about her daughter, who is suspected_of_ hacking into local government_computers.

◉2.3 Notice /wəz/, /wɔr/, and the spellings of /tʃ/.

D = Dad   A = Allie   M = Mike

D Hello, Allie! It's Dad. What were you doing when I called last night? You didn't pick up.

A Sorry, Dad. Uh, what time was that?

163

D It was about 8 o'clock.

A Oh, yeah, I was watching a fantastic nature show about the jungle. I really didn't hear the phone. Did you see the show?

D No, I didn't. What about Mike? I called him too.

A He was making dinner at 8. His famous burgers – you know what he's like – they have to be perfect.

D Hmph! And the twins? I called them too.

A They were playing video games – and anyway, they never answer their phones.

D They couldn't stop playing to talk to their grandfather?! Nobody answered the phone. Nobody wanted to talk to me!

A Don't be silly, Dad – we honestly didn't hear our phones – and you have to send a text message if you want to talk to the twins.

D OK – I just wanted to check ...

A But how are you, anyway?

D Fine ... well, it was good talking to you. Bye, dear.

A But we haven't even had a chance to ... Bye, Dad.

M What did your dad want?

A I don't know. He just wanted to say hello, I think!

⊙2.6 Notice the pronunciation of *sh* and *tch*.

1

M1 What did you watch on TV last night?

W1 Oh, I watched a great show about the animals and plants that live in rainforests in southeast Asia.

M1 Sounds interesting! I love shows about nature.

2

M2 I was watching a cooking competition for young people last night.

W2 Oh yeah – what did they have to cook?

M2 They had to use ingredients they hadn't seen before, and cook a dish in 45 minutes!

W2 Huh! No pressure then!

3

M3 So, was the show interesting?

W3 Yeah, lots of scientists were giving examples of how the weather has changed and why this is happening. And then they predicted what might happen in the future.

M3 Mmm. That's scary to think about.

4

W4 Did you see that movie last night? It was awesome. A woman turns into a superhero and rescues people and, um ... then she ....

M4 Hmm. Sounds awful to me. Not my type of movie.

5

W5 I love comedy – I was watching a great new series about an Australian family last night. It was really funny. A girl wanted to impress her new boyfriend by baking him a cake – but she couldn't get the secret recipe and it was a disaster!

M5 I saw that too! It was hilarious! And I loved it when Brendon ...

6

A What were you just watching?

B It was a crime show. The detectives started out looking for some missing diamonds and ended up discovering major crime at an offshore bank.

A Not again! All those shows are the same.

⊙2.7 Notice pronunciation of *oo* and *ou* spellings.

P = presenter   R = reporter

P Tonight on *What on Earth is Happening?*, we have stories from different parts of the world about recent extreme weather events. We'll be visiting nine different countries – here's a taste of what's to come. From Bangladesh:

R1 It's been raining and raining for hours and now there's a terrible flood in our town.

P And from London:

R2 It hasn't rained much this year, so there's going to be a drought. Get ready for a dry summer.

P And the latest from Argentina:

R3 The moon passed between the Earth and the sun and there was a total solar eclipse. Everything went dark in the middle of the day! It was really weird, but cool at the same time!

P And in Florida today:

R4 Hurricane Minnie hit today: the wind was so strong that it broke windows. It was a huge hurricane with wind speeds of up to 130 mph.

P Meanwhile in South Africa:

R5 There was a massive rainbow because the sun was shining when it was raining in the National Park. There was even a double rainbow. So beautiful!

P And in Chile:

R6 There was a magnitude 5.0 earthquake yesterday. Some buildings were damaged, but luckily nobody was badly hurt. The earth shook for about 15 seconds.

P While in Indonesia:

R7 There was a tsunami warning so everyone made it to safety. The waves were 20 feet high, so there was damage along the coastal areas.

P And in Mexico:

R8 There were huge thunderstorms overnight that left many homes without power. Lightning struck trees in the area causing power lines to fail.

P And in Greece ...

R9 There were strong winds and the fire is still out of control. Homes are in danger, but firefighters are battling the flames ...

P So there's been extreme weather all around the world. Now let's hear the stories behind these headlines. Let's turn first to Bangladesh ...

⊙2.8 Notice **sentence stress** and the intonation in questions.

J = Jack   M = Mel

J Hi, Mel, are you **OK**? ↗

M Yes, but we've got **no electricity**. There's a **power outage**.

J On **no**, not **again**! What were you **doing** when the **outage happened**? ↘

M I was **cooking dinner** when suddenly the **lights went out**!

J Did you **finish making dinner**? ↗

M Yes, but it **didn't taste very good** because I **couldn't see** very well!

J What was **Jamie doing**? ↘

M The lights went out while he was **watching TV**, but now he's okay, doing his **homework on his laptop**.

J That's good! So **what did you** do when the lights went out? ↘

M I **found a flashlight** and some **candles**, so it's very romantic here!

J That's nice. I'll be **home soon** ... I just **have to** ...

M Oh no! I **have to go**. I need to **charge my phone**, it's about to die.

J Umm ... **how** are you **going to charge** it? ↘

M **Plug it in**, of course ... doh!

⊙2.10 Notice /dʒ/, /ng/, and two spellings of /n/.

N = Narrator   J = Jane   D = Dad

N Jane was chatting online when her phone rang. It was her boyfriend, Jake.

J Hi, Jake, how are you?

N He was calling to make plans for the weekend. But Jane's mom came in and looked at the computer screen while Jane was talking on the phone. She was reading Jane's emails when Jane got off the phone. She was very, very unhappy and told her mom that the messages were private.

J Stop that! Never read my messages! Go away!

N Jane's mom went downstairs. Her parents were talking when Jane went downstairs later.

D Hmm, yes. I agree.

N They were discussing Jane and the online messages.

⊙2.13 Notice the sentence stress.

A So, I was **cycling to school** when suddenly I **got a flat**!

B Oh, **no**!

A Yeah, so I **walked to school**.

B Uh-**huh**?

A So I was late for **class** and everyone was **taking a test** when I **got there**.

B That's **awful**! And then what happened?

A Well, I **started doing the test**, but I didn't have **enough time to finish**.

B That's **terrible**!

A So, of course, I **didn't pass** the test, but the **teacher said** I could do it **again next week**.

B **Phew**! **That's** good.

Audio script

Review 1

▶R1.1 Notice the sentence stress and intonation.

1 What were you **doing** at 6 p.m. **last night**? ↘

2 What did you **do** yesterday **evening**? ↘

3 Who did you **work with** in the **last activity**? ↘

4 What were you **doing** when class **started**? ↘

Unit 3

▶3.3 Notice the intonation ↗ ↘ of the questions.

P = Paula   H = Harry

P   So, how's Cathy, anyway? ↘

H   Fine, fine. Have you seen her photos? ↗

P   Yep, you showed them to me – last week and then again yesterday.

H   … and she's seen photos of me, too.

P   And she still liked you after you showed them to her? ↗

H   Yeah, she likes me. Anyway, she, uh, she says she wants to meet me.

P   Oh, finally! I mean, you've known each other for a year, right? That's a long time. So, when is she coming to the States? ↗ ↘

H   Uh … she's not. She wants me to go to Australia … like, next month.

P   That's great. I've been to Australia twice.

H   Oh yeah? Did you go on business? ↗ ↗

P   Uh huh. Zero fun. Just work, work, work. How about you? ↗

H   Nope. Never been there.

P   So … Have you started packing? ↗

H   Hmm …

P   What? ↘

H   Well …

▶3.4 Notice /d/, /t/, and /ɪd/ for -ed endings.

P = Paula   H = Harry

P   So … Have you started packing?

H   Hmm …

P   What?

H   Well … The thing is … I don't know if I'm actually going.

P   How come? I mean, you want to meet Cathy, right?

H   I do, I really do. It would be amazing to meet in person.

P   So …?

H   You see … The thing is … I'm, uh …

P   What?

H   I'm afraid to fly. There. I've said it.

P   Hmm … Like a phobia or something?

H   Yeah.

P   But, uh, have you ever traveled by plane?

H   Once. Mom took me to Disneyland when I was five … I cried all the way there. No, seriously, I was terrified. And all the other

passengers were shocked, of course. They thought Mom was killing me or something.

P   Dude, I had no idea … So what are you gonna do?

▶3.5 Notice how the /h/ sound in *her* almost disappears in fast speech.

P = Paula   H = Harry

P   … Dude, I had no idea … So what are you gonna do?

H   I don't know.

P   Well, easy … Tell her to come to New York. Problem solved.

H   Nope, can't do that.

P   Why not?

H   She lost her job and doesn't have much money, you know … and she really wants me to meet her parents.

P   Well, then tell her you're afraid to fly.

H   No way! I'm too embarrassed to admit I'm scared to fly.

P   Hmm … Have you ever tried therapy? Maybe it can help you get …

H   Twice. It didn't work. I really don't know what to do.

P   Hey, I have an idea. Why don't …

▶3.8 Notice the long pauses // and the short pauses /.

L = Lisa   M = Meg

Day 1

L   Wow … // this place has changed … // a lot.

M   Have you stayed here before?

L   Oh yeah. / A few years ago. // But now … // I mean, / what kind of hotel is this? // Look at these walls / and this carpet … Oh my God! A mouse!

M   Where? Where?

L   There! There! / Oh, it's gone, / thank God. // Meg, / listen, / we've got to get out of here.

M   But … // we've only just arrived!

L   Yeah, but we haven't checked in yet. And more important – we haven't paid yet. // I tell you what, / let's stay at the hotel near the station.

M   Wait a second. // How much money are we talking about?

L   Well, / I guess it's a little more expensive, but …

M   Lisa, / I can only spend $50 a night. I've already told you like five times.

L   Well, / no, / not really. // You spent a lot of money shopping for clothes yesterday, so I didn't think money was a problem.

M   Well, / it is, actually.

Day 2

L   I'm going to the National Gallery today. // Julie's been there / and she says it's fantastic. // What are you going to do?

M   Well, // I haven't been to the West End yet / and I really want to go. // We could meet up for coffee at around three o'clock. // What do you think?

L   Yeah, but / look … // the weather has changed. // It's really cloudy now, / a perfect day to go to the National Gallery.

M   Well, // I really don't want to see old paintings today. // Sorry.

L   Well, // if you're sure. // I'll see you at three / and then I can tell you all about the Gallery.

Day 3

L   Oh! / That was a loooong day. // I'm exhausted. / Goodnight, Meg.

M   Lisa, / I just want to read a little before I go to bed.

L   Oh // Meg …

M   I'm reading *101 Things To Do Before You Die*. // It's a book with lots of suggestions of cool, / exciting things to do, // things that can change your life! Have you read it?

L   Uh … // No, I haven't. / And I'm really, really tired.

M   I started it when we got on the plane / and I've already read the first 20 ideas. // It's fascinating.

L   Look, Meg. / We woke up really early this morning, / I'm exhausted / and I can't sleep with the lights on. // Sorry.

M   OK, / OK, / sorry, Lisa. // I'll read downstairs in the lobby, then. // Good night.

▶3.10 Notice the stress in the auxiliary verbs.

M   Hey, Lisa, have a look at this list!

L   What is it?

M   It's a kind of bucket list at the back of the book I'm reading.

L   Oh, yeah, I remember - *101 Things To Do Before You Die*. So … let's see. Oh look! Visit London! We've both done that so, yup, obviously, we've both been abroad too.

M   Yeah. And there are lots more cool ideas here too. Look at these ones – see? I've never swum with dolphins, uh, or ridden an animal. I'd love to ride a camel or an elephant.

L   Oh, I've already done that. I used to ride horses when I was a girl. But I haven't swum with dolphins yet!

M   And look at this one – learn to dance. Ah! I've never learned to dance, because, uh, I have two left feet.

L   Oh! I can't dance either, I want to learn tango.

M   Me too! Daradaradara …

L   OK, so what else have you done?

M   Hmm. Well, I've made lots of birthday cakes … oh and I've just fallen in love.

L   No way! With who?

M   With London.

L   Ha ha, very funny.

M   Sorry! Uh … I've been a DJ a few times, so that's another one, and, uh … I've already tried extreme sports.

L   Yeah?

M   I went snowboarding in Colorado last year.

L   Nice!

165

M Yeah, awesome! But you know what, I've never done volunteer work, or planted a tree, or donated blood. Oh my god, I'm so selfish!
L Look at this one – have a child. Have you had a child yet?
M Lisa! Of course I haven't!

⊙ 3.12 Notice /t/, /d/, and /ɪd/ for -ed endings.

I = interviewer   R = Rita   T = Tina

1
I ... really true, isn't it? So, Rita, how long did you live in Barcelona?
R I lived there for, uh, seven months ...
I Did you have a job?
R Yep. I worked as an au pair for four months.
I How was the experience?
R Well, when I first looked at Raul and Ricardo, I thought ...
I Who?
R The twins.
I Oh, OK.
R So, when I first saw them, I said to myself: "I'm going to get on the next plane and get back home now." But after a while ... well, I fell in love with the boys ... and I realized that I was born to be around kids. Period. So that's how I decided to be a teacher, not a lawyer.
I Oh, so you wanted to study law?
R Well, Mom and Dad insisted for a long time – they really wanted me to be a lawyer. But now they don't talk about it anymore. Thank God. So what I really ...

2
I ... absolutely right. So, Tina, how long have you been in the UK?
T Uh, I've been in the UK since September, so ... yeah, that's six months ... But I arrived in Scotland six weeks ago.
I How do you like it?
T Honestly?
I Uhhuh.
T I hate it. Life sucks here. Yeah, I thought it was going to get better when I got a job, but ...
I Oh, so you're working?
T Yeah, I got a job at Tesco and ...
I What's that?
T Oh, a big grocery store. Or supermarket as they call them here.
I How long have you worked there?
T Three weeks. The longest weeks of my life.
I Have you made any friends?
T No, not yet. But my cousin's just come to visit, I haven't seen her for a long time, so that will be great!

⊙ 3.14 Notice the intonation in the questions and expressions of surprise.

B = Barry   L = Linda   M = Miguel

1
B ... exactly, and that's when I wrote my very first song.
L What? ↘ Wait a second. ↘ Did I hear you say that you wrote a song, Barry? ↗

B Uh huh. I called it "The Moon and the Stars." Grandma still cries when she hears it.
L Wow! ↘ Really? ↗ How old were you at the time? ↘
B Uh, about nine, I guess. I learned how to play the piano when I was four, so ...
L You're kidding me! ↘ When you were four? ↘ Wow. ↘ You've never told me that.
B Really? ↗ I thought you knew. Anyway, when I got into college, I had to ...

2
L ... much, much better when I was a child. These days, there's nothing good on – absolutely nothing.
M What? ↘ What do you mean nothing? ↘
L Well, maybe one or two shows, but they're either late at night or on cable.
M Hmm ... I don't agree ... I think the late night news is good and some of the documentaries ... come on ... they're just fantastic.
L Oh, come on, fantastic? ↗ Well, I don't agree, Miguel. I think they're just stupid. That's why I don't let the kids watch TV at home.
M But, uh, then you let them spend hours on the Internet, right? ↗
L Well, not hours, but ... You know, I have no problem with them being on their phones.
M No way! ↘ But that makes no sense, Linda. You see ...

Unit 4

⊙ 4.4

1 Notice /z/ and the three spellings of /s/.

M = Michael   G = Gloria (Mom)   D = Dad

M Mom. Can I have these?
G What? Headphones? What's wrong with yours?
M They're really big and uncomfortable. I want wireless ones, Mom! Please!
G No, honey, those are too expensive.
M But, Mom, come on. All my friends have these wireless headphones! It's not fair! You promised, remember? You said that if I helped you with the housework, you'd buy what I wanted.
G Michael, I know, but we're talking about three hundred dollar headphones here, not just a toy! That's a lot of money. Listen, I can get you these wireless earbuds instead. How about that?
M My life is awful! I hate my life ...
D Oh dear ... Gloria, rule number 1: if you make a promise to a kid, you can never, ever break it.
G I know, especially a kid like Michael.
D Look ... It's important to make children do the dishes, make the bed, and help around the house ... I get that ... But promising a gift in return? Bad idea.

2 Notice the intonation ↗ ↘.

F = Freddy   S = Susan   B = Brenda (Mom)
P = Phil (Dad)]

F Hey, Susan. Wanna play? ↗
S I can't leave the house. I have homework to do – a lot of it! ↘
F We can watch a couple TV shows and then we can go to McDonald's. ↘
S No, I have a big test next week and I need to get an A plus this time. ↘
F Well, will you die if you get a B? ↗
S Yeah! Duh! ↘
B Susan, close those books now and go have some fun. ↘
S But, Mom! I haven't finished ... ↘
B Susan, you're a smart kid. You should know that children who do a lot of homework every day don't necessarily do well in exams ... ↘
S But, Mom ... there's nothing healthy to eat at McDonald's! I haven't had any vegetables today! Please, let me stay home. ↘
B Susan, it's not a request– it's an order. Go out and have fun! ↘
P Brenda, I'm a little worried about our daughter.
B Me too. Where did we go wrong, Phil? ↘
P Well, once I read somewhere that young parents usually make more mistakes with their children. Guess they're right. Are we awful parents, Brenda? ↘ ↗
B No, of course not. But we could do better. How about if we ... ↘

⊙ 4.7 Notice /ð/ (voiced) and /θ/ (unvoiced).

J = Julia   D = Dad

J Oh, I miss those days. Life was so much easier.
D What do you mean? Do you miss school? I thought you hated that place!
J Well, yes, but I was just a kid, you know, and that's what kids do, right, Dad? They hate school, they sit at the back of the class, they...
D Hmm ... your brother likes school.
J Well, Danny's a nerd, so of course he does. Uh ... Dad, there's something, uh, there's something I've never told you, you know ...
D Oh yeah? What?
J Remember that time you and Mom thought I was sick?
D You used to be sick all the time, Julia – at least until you were 12. You used to eat everything you found! One day you ate bird food, remember?
J No, I mean that time you took me to the hospital ...
D Oh, your leg. Of course. Your mother and I almost went crazy that day.
J Well, I was sort of ... lying.

166

Audio script

○ 4.8 Notice pronunciation and spelling of the final /l/ and /m/ sounds.

D = Dad   J = Julia

D   What do you mean? We saw it! Your left leg was dead.

J   No, it wasn't, Dad. I was lying.

D   Lying? What do you mean lying?

J   Look, I really didn't want to go to school, Dad. We had a big test and, uh..., well, I was afraid to get a bad grade. I'm sorry.

D   But ... Julia, we took you to the hospital! Why didn't you tell us?

J   Look, I'm sorry. I really am. I didn't use to do it all the time. I never lied about the serious stuff. I swear.

D   Wow ... five hours at the hospital ... for nothing! I can't believe you did something like that. We were so worried. Unbelievable ...

○ 4.9 Notice /iː/ and /ɛ/.

To some people, vinyl records bring back memories of growing up in the 1960s and 70s when rock and roll was king. Back then, music lovers listened to Elvis Presley and The Beatles on black disks spinning on a turntable.
Today's younger generation didn't grow up with records. So for them, vinyl is cool.
Jack Lowenstein came to Crooked Beat Records in Washington, DC. and told us "I prefer to buy vinyl records over CDs." Sarah Griffith is into vinyl too. "More recently I've started buying more, you know, like old punk records and stuff."
In the early 2000s people turned away from CDs and started to download music online. Then vinyl made a comeback. Today, people buy more CDs and vinyl records than they buy music downloads. But the real story is music streaming. Streaming has revolutionized the music industry and more people stream music than download or buy either CDs or vinyl. In our next episode we look at the music streaming revolution.

○ 4.16 Notice the /d/ sounds and silent d endings.

R = Roy   B = Brenda   A = animal shelter assistant

R   Oooooh, they all look so adorable!

B   Yeah, right, Roy, adorable ...

R   Uh, excuse me, Miss... Hi... We, uh, we have a four year-old daughter and we'd like her to have a pet. She's an only child, so we want a pet that can keep her company ...

A   No brothers or sisters? Oh yeah, you should definitely get her a pet.

B   Like a bird ... or a goldfish, right?

R   Brenda, we've talked about that – goldfish are not as interactive as dogs. End of discussion.

B   But goldfish are quieter than dogs.

R   You see, we both work all day and, uh, we live in a small apartment. What would you recommend?

A   Have you considered getting a cat?

R   Well, to be honest, we were kind of thinking of a dog. We, uh ... prefer dogs.

B   Roy, YOU like dogs. I'd do anything to stay pet free. They're a lot of work!

R   Come on, Brenda, it's not as bad as it looks!

○ 4.17 Notice the weak forms in comparatives.

B   Roy, you like dogs. I'd do anything to stay pet free. They're a lot of work.

R   Come on, Brenda, it's not as bad as it looks!

A   Well, cats are not as good with kids, I know, but, well, they're independent animals, which is great if you're both busy and...

B   Hmm... and they're much quieter than dogs too.

R   But you see, we want Lynn to walk the dog, take it to the park, teach it how to sit... stuff like that.

A   Well, why don't you get a dog that's easy to train? You know, like a poodle or a Lab.

B   Like a what?

A   A Labrador – come here, let me show you.

R   Oh, he looks adorable! Come here, little doggy! Now who's the cutest dog in the world?

B   Does he bark a lot?

A   Well, yes, but not as much as a poodle.

B   I don't like noisy animals, you know. My life's stressful enough, thank you very much.

A   Hmm ... in that case, have you thought about getting a house rabbit? You won't hear a sound, I promise.

B   Hey, wait a second ... That's a great idea.

R   Yeah ... Why not? Rabbits are cute, small and quiet. Can you show us?

Review 2

○ R2.1 Notice the connections.

1   I've been_to Australia twice.
2   But ... we've_only just_arrived!
3   Yeah, but look ... the weather_has changed.
4   I lived and worked_as_an au pair in Barcelona for nine months.
5   Digital songs don't sound as_good_as LPs.
6   She used_to follow strangers around the house and make weird noises.

○ R2.2 Notice the sentence stress.

1   Oh, **we** used to **fight** over the remote control **every single day**. There were **three TVs** at home, but we **all** wanted to **watch the big** one in the living room. Good old days.

2   I **swear**! It **never was**. I mean, what was I **supposed to do** if the **dog** liked to **paint itself purple** and daddy's **car used to like driving itself**? I had **nothing** to do with **any of that**!

3   That's what **grandpa** used to say **every night** before **my sister and I went to bed**. **Every single night**. Oh, how I miss him.

4   **Of course not**! I was just **trying to push him away using my foot**. There was **no violence**, of course! I mean, he was **my brother**, **come on**!

Unit 5

○ 5.1 Notice the connections.

Welcome to Marlbury College! We hope you'll enjoy your visit. My name is Karen Crawford. First of_all, let me present some_of our classes. In picture one, we see a biology class. Slide two shows_a geography class. Number three shows_ some_of our history students and number four shows psychology students. Photo five is_a philosophy class and in six some_of our foreign languages students are doing a role-play. Slide seven is_a sociology class and number eight is_a chemistry class in our new chemistry lab. It's wonderful! Then slide nine shows_some_of our politics students having a very serious debate ...

○ 5.3 Notice the intonation of the questions ↗ ↘, /g/, and /dʒ/ sounds

Here at Marlbury College we have something for everyone! We offer degree programs at bachelor's and master's level. Call us today for a catalog! Are you interested in a new profession? ↗ We have vocational Certificate and Diploma programs in everything from cooking to banking.
Is it difficult for you to come to class? ↗ Don't worry! We offer a lot of our courses online – so you can study any time you want. Do you work all day and want to take classes in the evening? ↗ We can help you there too. We have a large choice of classes in the evenings, including French, Chinese and ESL classes. All this and more is available at our attractive campus with our high-tech modern facilities.
Call Marlbury today and find the best class for you. Not sure where to begin? ↗ Come to one of our free classes that are open to the public. You can meet our great teachers, and administrators, and get more information about Marlbury College.

○ 5.5 Notice intonation in the instructions.

T = teacher   S = student

1

T   OK – this is your final examination. You have ONE HOUR. Answer three out of five questions. You should spend about 20 minutes on each question. Remember, this is an exam, so there should be silence and no communication between any of you. You can start now.

2

T   OK! Let's do an exercise to practice the words. Look on page 18. Complete these sentences with an appropriate word from the list below. Then listen to check.

167

3

T So this is a group work activity. In a group of four, discuss the movie extract that we watched and find two things that you liked about it and two things you didn't like. OK?

S1 But what if we didn't like anything about it?

T You need to find two things in your group that you liked, so ask the other people in your group.

4

T Search online for a song line that you like featuring the words "used to." Bring a recording of it to the next class.

5

T In your journal, write or record an audio about how you felt about class today. What were the things you understood? Write a question that you have for next class.

S2 How much do we have to write?

T As much as you want, but at least one paragraph.

6

T We're going to do a pair work activity. In pairs. Talk about your plans for the weekend. Ask your partner what she or he is going to do. Then answer your partner's questions.

S3 I don't have a partner.

T Work with Loni and Michelle.

7

T This is your presentation for next week. Use PowerPoint to present your family to the class. Prepare at least four pages. For Monday morning, please.

S4 Monday! No way! We need more time! That's too soon! There's not enough time.

T That gives you a whole week. That's more than enough!

8

T So for this month's project we look at houses. We'll look at the construction of houses in different parts of the world and we'll consider the materials used and why. Yes, Mike?

S5 Are we working in teams?

T For some parts you'll be in teams and for some parts you'll be on your own.

9

T OK. Take out a piece of paper, we're going to have a quick test. You have two minutes to write the past tense of these verbs. Then hand your answers to me.

10

T All right, then. So, we've finished reading the book now and I want you to write a one-paragraph summary of the last chapter of the book.

S6 For when?

T Next class.

○5.6 Notice pronunciation of *have to* and *got to*.

M = Mark   C = Candy

M Wow! This class is going to be hard. Ms. Cosby says we can't miss even one session.

C That's not so bad! So we've got to come to every class – that's good.

M And we have to write a paper for next week.

C It's OK. It's just two pages.

M But I hate writing papers.

C You've got to write papers whenever you take a class.

M I guess so. And the teacher said we can't arrive late!

C Of course not, that's good! That will make you come on time.

M But what if I don't feel like coming?

C Come on, Mark! It's not that bad. And she also said we don't have to take notes, because all the handouts and the slides are available online.

M Hmm, I guess you're right! That should be easy!

○5.7 Notice the linking between two vowel sounds.

M = Mark   C = Candy   MM = Mrs. McCormack

M What are you doing tonight?

C I've got to study, because I have a test tomorrow.

M Another one! That's too bad! Do you have to study_on Saturday too?

C Uh, I don't have to study_on Saturday, but I want to, because I really need to get good grades this time. Why?

M Well, I wanted to invite you to_a party on Saturday. Should be_a good one!

C Oh! Well, my mom gets worried, so_I can't stay_out later than 12, but I could go for a while. But you'll have to_ask my mom, and persuade her.

M OK, pass me_over. Hello, Mrs. McCormack. This is Mark.

MM Hello, Mark. Busy studying?

M Yes, you know_me! Er, can Candy come to_a party with me_on Saturday?

MM Sure, but she has to be home by 12, please. I really worry if she stays out too late.

M Not a problem, Mrs. McCormack. I can't drive my dad's car after 11, so_I have to be home by then anyway.

○5.9 Notice the sentence stress and weak forms.

1

There were **too** many **exams. Awful.** My **grades** were **never** good enough. Or I just **failed too** many **times. Waste** of **time. Awful. Bye, bye!**

2

Well, **basically** I spent **too** much **time**, uh …, having **fun.** You **know**, too **busy** with **friends, concerts**, all the **parties.** I just **didn't** have **enough** time to **study!** So, I just **quit.**

3

It was **too** hard to choose a **major.** I did **psychology** – **hated** it – started **again. Philosophy**, hated **that**, and, **then**, **well**, there were **too** many **choices**, so I **quit.** And uh, got a **job.** And then **another** job. I **guess** I'm not **decisive** enough. But **then**, maybe I **am** … Oh, I don't know.

4

It wasn't **interesting** enough and I, uh, just stopped **enjoying** it. **Totally. Every** morning, I wanted to do **anything, an-y-thing**, except go to school. **Man**, just **thinking** about school was **too** depressing. **Miserable. Enough** was **enough.** So, uh, **boom!** Time to say **goodbye** and **fly.**

○5.10 Notice the phrases for agreeing.

W = woman   M = man

M I'm reading an article about the top reasons why people quit school or their job.

W Oh yeah? That's interesting. I bet reason number 1 for leaving jobs is money.

M Yep. It says "The number 1 reason why people leave their job is money, money, money."

W Sure, I mean, if employees are unhappy with their pay, they leave – if they can find another job.

M Well, I mean, uh …, we all want more if we can get it.

W And the second reason is …?

M Uh … uh … they'd like better benefits, like health insurance and pensions.

W Sounds right to me. Number 3?

M They feel they don't have a good relationship with their boss.

W Yeah, I hated my last boss – he lied all the time.

M Yuk. And the fourth reason is …?

W The stress of too much work?

M Uh-huh, their workload is too heavy. And …

W And number 5 must be that they don't like the place where they work.

M Yup, good job!

W I guess 'cos it doesn't have good facilities.

M Or it's dirty …

W Yeah, stuff like that. What about dropping out of college? Is that for financial reasons too?

M No, it says the first reason is that they don't have enough self-discipline to go to class every day. And to keep up with assignments and homework.

W Right! So, if students miss a lot of classes, they drop out of school. Well, no surprises there!

M Number 2 is when they feel too isolated or homesick away from their family and friends.

W can see that – I felt like that in college.

M Money is only number 3! When they don't have enough money to continue studying.

W So that's pretty different from work, then?

M Yeah, interesting, and 4 is … personal reasons. They have too many personal problems like breaking up with a partner or needing to care for a sick relative.

W That's terrible when that happens.

M Really. And the final one is …?

Audio script

W Wrong choice?

M Yup, when they find they chose the wrong thing to study, and, uh, feel they're not interested in what they're studying.

W Oh, yeah! I know people like that!

M Me too. Remember John ...

○5.14 Notice intonation in the questions.

Z = Zack   V = Vicky

Z Oh hi, Vicky. How's it going? ↘

V Oh hi, Zack. Everything's fine.

Z Uh ... Vicky? Did you see that email I sent out yesterday? ↗ ↗

V What about? ↘ You kind of send out a lot of emails!

Z The staff meeting we're having on Friday.

V Oh, yeah, I saw it and programmed it into my calendar, so it will remind me. It's at 11 a.m., right? ↗

Z That's right.

V And it's in the conference room, right? ↗

Z That's right. I also said I wanted ideas for the agenda. I don't have anything from you.

V That's weird. I posted my ideas on the team chat app as soon as I read your email.

Z Oh ... you posted them on the team chat app? ↗
– of course you did - uh ... OK ... I'll check that now. Um ... Thanks.

V Sure, Zack.

○5.15 Notice the intonation.

a

W = woman   M = man

W1 Watch out! If you're not careful, you'll fall in.

M1 If you help me get in, I'll row the boat.

b

D = Dad   M = Mom

D Whatever you do, don't eat that ice cream. If you do, you'll have to go to your room!

M If you eat all your dinner, I'll give you some ice cream.

c

D = Dad   M = Mom

D If you finish your homework, I'll take you out to the movies.

M I won't buy you a new bike if you don't get good grades. You'd better do your homework.

d

W = woman

W4 If you stay late, I'll give you the day off tomorrow. But be careful! If you don't improve your work, you'll be fired.

Unit 6

○6.1 Notice /ʤ/, /g/, and /ng/.

Welcome to fabulous Florida, the Sunshine State! It's the perfect place for all kinds of exciting outdoor activities. You can go hiking, fishing, or camping, and you can go diving or climbing. We have thousands of square miles of beautiful parks and countryside for you to explore. Or, if you prefer indoor activities, why not go bowling, go clubbing, or work out at one of our many great gyms? If you like exercising and enjoy sunny weather at the same time, you can even work out on our lovely beaches. And at the end of a fantastic day ... just hang out with your friends or the friendly locals! That's Florida – the Sunshine State.

○6.2 Notice pronunciation and spellings of /f/, /v/, and /b/.

R = Rosie   B = Ben

R Oh hi Ben! We just got back. It was such a great vacation!

B I bet! I'd love to go to Florida. Did you stay just in Miami?

R No. Martin and I went camping in the Everglades National Park. That was amazing.

B That's, uh ... interesting. How did it go?

R Well ... we were having a great time for the first few days. We went fishing and hiking.

B Did you catch anything? A cold maybe?

R No! But it was relaxing. And we saw alligators!

B Wow! Really?

R Yes. Then we went diving and saw more animals. We saw dolphins and a manatee and turtles.

B What's a manatee?

R Like a really big, fat, slow dolphin. Beautiful.

B Sounds like you had a great time!

R Yeah, we did – at first!

B What happened?

R Well, it's the rainy season and, uh, three days before the end of our vacation, it rained really hard, and our tent flooded and everything got wet.

B Oh no! That's why I never go camping!

R Yeah! At first we didn't know what to do – it was awful! Like, we were cold and our clothes and all our things were wet. But then we decided to stay the last two nights at a hotel in Miami and it was just fantastic. Totally.

B Right, so what did you do?

R Oh, we went bowling and we went clubbing. It was cool!

B Sounds like you had a really ... varied vacation.

R We sure did! Overall, it was great, but our tent is ruined forever!

○6.5 Notice /θ/ and /ð/.

W = woman   M = man

W My boyfriend Charlie did a triathlon the other day.

M Oh yeah?

W Yeah, but it was kind of extreme. Even more challenging than a standard triathlon! First he ran five kilometers along a beach.

M Uh-huh.

W Then he climbed up a rope, over a wall, and down the other side ... before running through fire.

M He what?

W Yeah, really! Then he jumped into the river and swam around an island, under a bridge, and past the stadium.

M Whoa!

W Then, he got out of the river and cycled 15 kilometers towards the finish.

M 15 kilometers!

W And after finally running across the finish line, he collapsed!

M I'm not surprised!

○6.6 Notice /aɪ/ and /iː/.

M = Martin   J = Jo

M Hey, do you want to go surfing this weekend? We could go to the beach and stay at that nice hotel.

J Hmm ... not really, I don't feel like getting hot and tired, and I don't really enjoy surfing.

M But, but I thought you did! Well, we could go swimming instead? They have a lovely pool at the hotel.

J I hate swimming – it's worse than surfing – it's so boring!

M I really miss going to the beach. I don't remember the last time we went.

J I have to say that I don't miss the beach, sorry, Martin. I like to stay cool – I'd rather stay inside. Do you want to go bowling this weekend? I adore bowling. You can stay inside and you don't get hot when you're bowling.

M You keep asking me that! You know I can't stand bowling. You know, I just don't get it. When I met you, you started swimming and surfing with me and you loved it!

R I suppose I did, but I guess I've changed. Right now I can't imagine getting onto a surfboard. Umm ... what about the movies? Let's go to the movies. We both enjoy doing that.

M OK – I guess so, but let's go surfing soon.

R Uh ... maybe.

○6.9 Notice the schwa /ə/.

A = adult   C = child

C So, you need a ball?

A Yeah, and two big goals.

C Right.

A And, um, you pass the ball from one player to another.

C Ooh, is it soccer?

A No, sorry. You pass the ball with your hands.

C OK.

A Yeah, and you have to put the ball down over the line to score.

C Oh! Is it American football?

A No, no, you don't wear a helmet. But it's similar. Um, you can kick the ball too.

C I see ... I think.

A It's popular in Australia, New Zealand, Argentina, South Africa, Europe, and, uh ...

C Got it! I know, It's ...

169

Review 3

○R3.2 Notice /æ/.

PS = pool supervisor   C = child

1 PS   Hey! You can't run in here.
2 PS   Hey! You can't dive in the pool. No diving!
3 PS   Sorry. You can't have food and drink in here.
4 PS   The showers are over there. You have to take a shower before you swim.
5 PS   How old are you?
  C   I'm six.
  PS   I'm sorry, children have to swim with adults. Where's your mom?

○R3.3 Notice pronunciation and spelling of /s/ and /z/.

Hi, my name's Clara Bush and I'm 22 years old. I'm from Phoenix, Arizona, but, uh, I'm living and studying in Mexico City for the summer. I really need to learn Spanish fast as I'm majoring in Spanish and have my final exams as soon as I get back, uh, at the end of August.

○R3.4 Notice *to* /tə/, *at* /ət/, and *of* = /əv/.

I absolutely adore, uh, traveling, I always have, and so when I turned 21 I decided, uh, to go and live in Mexico, um, to study Spanish. At first my parents didn't want me to leave the States, but in the end they agreed, uh, to pay for my studies here in Mexico City. Anyway, so now I'm here and it's great 'cos I can practice, uh, speaking every day, and I think my Spanish is really improving, and I hope, uh, to pass my final exam in two months. I kind of miss, uh, going to the mall with my friends back home, and of course my family, but I know I'll see them again soon. When I have finished, uh, studying here, I think I'm going to travel down south and maybe see some temples before I go home.

○R3.6 Notice /w/.

M = man   W = woman

W   Would you like to get into a crocodile tank with just a two-inch thick plastic cage around you?
M   What? Of course not, I'm not crazy! Why?
W   I think it sounds amazing! It's totally safe.
M   What are you talking about?
W   In Australia, you can get in a plastic tank and then you're lowered into the water.
M   And what's in the water?
W   Saltwater crocodiles!
M   That's ridiculous!
W   It's not. I think it sounds cool.
M   When did you start wanting to do ridiculous things?
W   It's not ridiculous – it would be fun. It's only for about 15 minutes.
M   That 15 minutes would seem like a lifetime!
W   And you get really close to the animals. They swim really close to you and you have a 360° view of them as they swim around you.

M   And try to eat you, I suppose!
W   But they can't get through the plastic! And the organizers photograph you and film you as you do it.

Unit 7

○7.1 Notice pronunciation of the -d endings, /d/ or /ɪd/, and their spelling.

Tune in to the Classic Movie Channel – we have something for everyone this week – here's the best of the week. For horror fans we have *Hereditary* – be prepared to be scared! If a drama is more to your taste we have *Boyhood*, or if you're in the mood for a comedy there's *Bridesmaids*. For all the family we have the adventure movie *The Hunger Games*, and for fantasy fans there are the *Fantastic Beasts* movies. If you like animated movies, don't miss *Inside Out*, or if you feel like watching a documentary, we have *Senna* – don't miss it!

○7.2 Notice /s/ and /z/ endings.

J = Jack   K = Kelly

J   OK, Kelly, you go stand in line for the tickets, I'll buy the popcorn.
K   I already bought the tickets online – we don't need to stand in line.
J   Cool, but we need to for popcorn.
K   Uh huh. ... Oh, no, the movie's about to start!
J   OK, well you buy the sodas – there's no one waiting – and I'll stand in line and get the popcorn.
K   OK, I'll go into the theater after I've bought the sodas, and you join me when you've got the popcorn.
J   OK – make sure you get us good seats.
K   I already chose the seats online, Jack, after I bought them! When was the last time you went to the movies?
J   Oh, yeah, I forgot you could do that. What movie are we seeing again?
K   I've told you five times, it's a classic horror movie called *Hereditary*.
J   But I don't like horror movies!
K   It's too late, Jack! I'll see you inside – in the dark .... Wooooooo

○7.6 Notice the schwa /ə/.

M = Male presenter   W = Female presenter

M   ... Welcome back to "You must be joking!," the radio show about the unusual things we all do. This week, we're looking at unusual collections ... Next up on our top 10 list ... Number 5 ... Barbara Hartsfield from Georgia in the U.S. Barbara collects miniature chairs.
W   What? You mean little chairs?
M   Yes, little chairs. Barbara is such a huge miniature chair fan that she has her own museum with thousands of little chairs.
W   Wow! That's funny.
M   Yep. There are little chairs at the museum inside bottles, chairs made from toothpicks,

chair earrings, everything is in the shape of a chair!
W   Wow! Such a lot of little chairs! I'd like to see that.
M   Well, that's nothing compared to number 4 on our top 10 ... Percival R. Lugue from the Philippines.
W   ... and ... what does he collect?
M   Fast food restaurant toys.
W   What, those little toys that come with meals for kids?
M   That's right. Well, Percival is so careful with his toys that he has over 15,000 of them.
W   That's so sweet!
M   Yep. Apparently, he is trying to collect all the fast food toys that exist in the world!
W   That's a lot of fast food!
M   So wait till you hear about the next collection in our top 10. Number 3 ... This one is a man called David Morgan from the UK. The man's such a passionate traffic cone fan that he has a collection of over 500.
W   You mean traffic cones that you see on the street?
M   Yes, that's right.
W   So, does he steal them?
M   Nope – he says he would never consider stealing one as they are so important for safety.
W   Wow! People really collect unusual things, don't they!
M   You betcha! After our commercial break, we're gonna ...

○7.7 Notice /b/, /v/ and /w/.

M   Welcome back ... You're listening to "You must be joking!" This week, we're looking at the unusual things that people collect. So, back to our top 10 countdown ... Number 2 ... Rainer Weichert from Germany enjoys bringing home a souvenir from all of his trips.
W   So? Everyone likes to do that.
M   Yes, but he doesn't bring a T-shirt or a key chain back he brings a "do not disturb" sign.
W   You mean, those signs you put on your hotel door?
M   Uh-huh.
W   Wow! Hard to believe there are such strange collections out there! Do not disturb signs? There are so many better souvenirs!
M   Yeah, I know! Really interesting, huh? Ready for number 1?
W   Yeah. Can't wait.
M   Our number 1 unusual collector is Nancy Hoffman from Maine in the U.S. She collects umbrella sleeves.
W   You mean the cover for an umbrella? Not the umbrellas?
M   No, just the sleeves. She likes them so much that she has collected them from 50 countries in the world.
W   And how many does she have?
M   Over 750.

170

Audio script

W Oh, my goodness! That's such a strange thing to collect. I suppose some of them are pretty, but …

▶ 7.9

1 three hundred billion / one hundred and six point nine billion / seventy-three point nine billion / fifty-three point two billion
2 seventy-one thousand six hundred
3 twenty-four percent
4 eight hundred and fifty
5 thirty-five percent
6 eighty-seven percent

▶ 7.12 Notice the short pauses and longer pauses.

B = Bruce   J = Judy

B … so why did I audition? I don't know. I was, uh, out of work, so I had all the time in the world to spend hours and hours camped outside the auditorium. Anyway, the big day arrived and I got there around 5, 5:30 a.m. – and Wow! it was such a huge place! Really huge! There were, what, 10,000 people standing in line. It was raining torrentially and they only let us in at 9! Can you believe those guys? Where was I? Oh, yeah, well, in the end, they only selected 200 people to audition in front of the show's producers. If your voice was good enough, you'd then advance to the next round and finally sing in front of the celebrity judges … You know, the bad, cruel guys. I made it to the top 200, but during my audition there was something wrong with the audio and I didn't get to sing in front of the TV judges … Actually, few people get that far – only 40, usually. Yeah, just 40. This was such a disappointment! I'd always wanted to meet the judges, you know. Guess I'll try again next year. Oh, by the way, my name's Bruce and I'm from New Jersey.

J … So my name's Judy Jackson, and I'm from Dallas. So, uh, I've always been interested in real estate and I have a blog about buying and selling houses – it's quite popular, with about 750 visits a day. Anyway, one day, someone from ABC – or was it NBC? – found my blog on the Internet and sent me an email asking me if I wanted to be considered for the show. You can imagine my surprise … I was chosen to be on TV! Yes, me! She said they were looking for interesting families. "Why me?," I thought. "I have such a conventional family!" Well, my immediate reaction was to say no, of course. Why on earth would I want to have someone watch me and my family fighting over buying a new house? But then I read somewhere that families were paid $20,000 to appear on the show … and, you know, at the time, Mark was unemployed, so I thought it over for a week or so and – surprise, surprise – in the end, I said yes. So I gave the woman a call and left a message … and again … and again … I called her at least 15 times. Guess what, all my calls were

ignored! All of them! Anyway, two months later – ironically – my family had to move house because of work, but we were never on the show.

Unit 8

▶ 8.3 Notice the connections.

D1 = smart alarm and coffee maker
W1 = woman

D1 It's time to wake up. Would you like me to let you sleep a little longer?
W1 Yes!
D1 Are you sure? You do have a very busy day.
W1 I'll get_up in five minutes.
D1 I'm going to turn on the coffee maker.
W1 OK, … no, wait! Don't turn_on the coffee maker! It's broken! Oh no! … What_a mess!

2
M1 = man   D2 = Jack, housework robot

M1 Jack! Wash the dishes.
D2 I'm sorry, I can't. You forgot to charge me this morning. I'm running on economy mode so I can save enough battery power to make the beds.
M1 No problem. Let me plug_you in.
D2 Thank you. Oh, that feels nice …

3
D3 = smart temperature control device
W2 = woman]

D3 It's way too cold in here. This is not good for your body. I'm going to turn up the thermostat.
W2 No way! I like it when_it's cool.
D3 Turning up the thermostat in 3, 2, 1 second.
W2 Hey, what_are you doing? Please, turn the thermostat down! Turn it down!

4
C = car computer   M = Michael

C Please, look at the face detection device … I'm sorry. I can't recognize you.
M What do_you mean?
C I can't recognize your face. Please, look straight into the face sensor … I'm sorry. I still can't recognize you.
M Oh no! Not again. You know what, I'm going_to switch_you off.
C Michael, you know you can't switch me off. You need to answer a few security questions.

▶ 8.4 Notice the intonation in questions ↗ ↘.

C = computer   M = Michael

C May I ask you a few security questions? ↗
M Yes, I suppose so!
C What's your full name? ↘
M Michael Jay Huff.
C How do you spell "Huff"? ↘
M H-U-F-F.
C Correct. Are you American? ↗
M No, I'm from Canada.
C When were you born? ↘
M October 5.

C Correct.
M This is unbelievable.
C How long have you had this vehicle? ↘
M What? ↘
C How long have you had this vehicle? ↘
M Since June.
C Information mismatch.
M June, July, who cares? ↘ Just start the car. Please.
C Did you say July? ↗
M Yes.
C Correct. Did you use this car on Tuesday? ↗
M Yeah.
C What were you wearing? ↘
M I can't remember what I was wearing. A white T-shirt, I think.
C Try again.
M Come on! Why are you doing this to me? ↘

▶ 8.9

1   Notice the /t/ and silent t.

S = Sue   B = Bob

S Guess what! I just bought a new car.
B Really? That's cool. I, uh, I'm going to try to sell mine in October or November. It's got over 80 thousand miles on it, I think – time to get a new one.
S Wow, that's a lot. Anyway, it's a brand new Prius and I was looking at …
B A Prius? No way! My Dad drives a Prius, too, you know …
S Really? That's a coincidence. I …
B Yeah, must be his third or fourth … You know what? I'll call him right now and tell him. He'll like that you're getting the same car as him. I have to …

2   Notice /t/ and /h/.

R = Regis   A = Ann

R Hey, wanna have lunch on Friday?
A I can't. I'm seeing the doctor on Friday.
R Oh yeah? Anything serious?
A No, just my annual check-up.
R That's good. You know it's important to always go to the doctor, don't you? I have a friend, she works long hours, gets no exercise and has such a bad diet, and I tell her "living like this, you're going to make yourself ill". So as I've told you before, you have to look after your health and get regular health checks.
A Regis! You know I have a health check every year!!
R Yeah, um … I'm going to get a check-up too. Maybe I've been working too hard and not looking after myself. You know, I really don't think you do enough exercise, you should …

3   Notice /g/ and /j/.

S = Sally   Y = Yuko

S Hi, Yuko! Just saw your tweet. Calling to wish you a safe trip.
Y Thanks. The plane leaves at two and I haven't started packing yet.
S Oh, don't worry. You still have about five or six hours …

171

Y I'm really excited. I'd like to know if all the stuff we see in movies …

S … is true? Oh, you bet it is … By the way, there's this great little restaurant on the corner of Broadway and 47th or 48th that you simply must try. Seriously, you've got to go there. I think it's called La Pasta … La Pasta something … Google it.

Y What about the Guggenheim? Teri says …

S Oh, there are some great museums. The last time I was there I went to the Museum of Modern Art and it was fabulous …

⊙8.12

J = Joe   C = coach

1 Notice the sentence stress and unstressed auxiliary verbs.

C1 Of course. **Joe**, what **can I help** you **with**?

J It's about **my career** … You see, I've worked at the **same company** for five, no, **six years now** and it feels like … well, it feels like I'm getting **nowhere**, you know what I mean? So, I guess **my question to you is** … Will I ever **get a promotion**?

C1 Don't worry, this is a very **common problem**. We'll need to talk more about why you feel like this. If you've been **there six years**, you **might get a promotion soon**, but I think you also need to **consider your future** with the company.

J Yes, I've thought about that too. I've been **there so long**.

C1 There's a good chance that **you'll decide** it's **time to move on**.

J I think that's a good idea!

C1 Well, I can help you **make that transition** too …

2 Notice the spelling of /e/ and /iː/.

J I just feel so tired all the time.

C2 Hmmm … tell me more about this. How's your sleep?

J Uh, not that great – sometimes I find it difficult to go to sleep, and I'm always tired when I wake up in the morning.

C2 That's not so good. Are you looking at a screen before bed?

J Well, yes, I always check my messages in bed.

C2 Well, if you put your phone away at least two hours before bedtime, you'll find that you sleep better.

J You think so?

C2 Absolutely.

J Thanks, I'll try that … and what about my headaches …?

C2 Well, possibly your headaches will stop as well if you stop looking at your phone before bed, but there may be other reasons …Tell me more about your headaches …

3 Notice pronunciation and spelling of /l/ and the -ls ending /lz/.

C5 So, how can I can help you, Joe?

J Um, well, you see, I've been seeing Emma for over a year now and I really like her …

no, I love her, but I'm not sure she feels the same. Sometimes I can't sleep because I'm frightened she's going to leave me.

C5 I see. And why are you frightened about that, Joe? Has she given you any reason to feel like this?

J Not really, no, but my last two girlfriends left me and I don't understand why.

C5 All right. The first thing you have to do is talk to Emma and tell her how you feel. Communication is essential in a relationship.

J Do you really think that will help?

C5 For sure. If you don't talk to Emma, you won't find out how she feels.

J But I'm not good at talking to people … and what if she says something I don't want to hear? How about I tell her I love her on Facebook? Is that a good idea?

C5 Probably not, Joe. You have to be brave and learn to say how you feel.

Review 4

⊙R4.1 Notice /d/ and /t/ endings.

… mostly cloudy during the day. So, if you've just tuned in, here are the answers to today's music quiz. Are you ready?
Number 1: "Imagine" was written by John Lennon in 1971, but it was only released four years later, in 1975. Pretty easy, wasn't it?
Number 2 may surprise you, but nearly 1.5 billion smartphones are sold around the globe every year – that's a lot of phones. Yep, you heard it right: 1.5 billion. How 'bout that?
Third question … Beyonce's first solo album was called *Dangerously in Love*. It was released in 2003 and went to number 1 in several different countries.
Question 4 … Amy Winehouse was only 27 when she was found dead in her apartment in London. Interestingly, singers Janis Joplin, Jim Morrison, and Kurt Cobain also died at age 27. And finally, here's our last question … American singer Ariana Grande is considered to be one of the world's best vocalists. Her albums have sold millions around the world.

⊙R4.2 Notice the sentence stress.

1

A … **hurry up**. We're going to **be late**. The movie starts **at nine**. **Oh no**! Your **battery's** almost **dead**.

B Is it? Uh oh – 2%. I'll **plug it in** – don't worry.

A **Where**?

B **In the car. Let's go.**

2

C I'm going **to bed**.

D But it's **only 8:30**!

C I know, but I'm going to **get up at 5 a.m.**

D **Why**?

C I have to **finish a project** and my **laptop is at the repair shop**, so I'm **going to school early**.

D **Seriously**? **5 a.m**?

3

E … Anyway, then **she told me** that I should …

F What?

E **She told me** that I should **look for another job** and …

F Look **for what**?

E Bill, why **do you always** have to have your music **so loud when I'm talking**?

F Oh, alright, I'll turn it down.

E Thank you. That's **much better**.

4

G … that's really **exciting**! I've never been there. Oh, you'll have a **wonderful time**.

H Yeah, we're **really excited**. The plane **leaves at ten**. I'm counting the minutes.

G What if I **need to speak to you**? You know, about the project … You're going to leave **your cell phone on**, right?

H Well, **actually, no**. I'm going to **turn it off** and only turn it **back on when I'm back home**.

G Really? But can I **call the hotel at least**?

⊙R4.3 Notice /ð/ and /θ/.

1 … and for the fourth consecutive month, unemployment has increased by 13.7%, twice as much as the same period last year. A spokesman for the …

2 … the governor's chances of reelection. Now, on to local news. A three hour power outage left the state of Michigan in the dark last night. 248 cities were affected and there are …

3 … won last night's Emmy for best actor. Pineapple is in trouble with their latest tablet – the pTab. Over the past two weeks, there have been numerous reports of pTabs exploding and catching fire. Apparently, two thirds of all pTabs produced in May were considered defective. A spokesman for Pineapple has …

4 … the largest in history. A small town in Brazil has also made history this week, as new evidence emerges that some of its inhabitants were contacted by extraterrestrials on April 12. The town, with a population of only 40,540, was visited by UFOs in the past and according to a local TV station …

Unit 9

⊙9.2 Notice /iː/ and /ɪ/.

WP = wedding planner   M = Michaela

WP OK, Michaela. Here's how it's going to work.

M Um, I don't want anything very fancy, just …

WP How long was your engagement?

M Er, three years.

WP Then you need something fancy. We'll have invitations like this – black with gold letters.

M Hmm – we actually just wanted plain white.

WP Then we'll have the wedding ceremony at your home and – we'll keep it small, just 200 guests.

M 200?! But that's not very small. We want the ceremony at the beach.

172

Audio script

WP 200 is small, sweetie. Then we'll have the reception in a fantastic big restaurant that I know, for say 500 people.

M But we can't afford that! You know, we're thinking, like about 50 guests in a small restaurant for the reception.

WP OK, just 400 guests at the reception then. And then your dress – I see it something like this: white and very feminine.

M Uh, I was thinking of something more simple, just a nice dress – blue or green.

WP ... and let's see ... about ten bridesmaids all carrying mountains of flowers.

M Ten! No, I just want my sister and my niece.

WP ... and the groom in white also – a white suit – and you'll both have huge gold rings – it's going to be fabulous!

M Um ... Andy hates wearing a suit and we want to have silver rings.

WP Details, details! We'll worry about that later ... And then the honeymoon on a remote island ... a big ecological tour.

M Well ... erm... that's not really what we had in mind ... we probably won't have time for a honeymoon until next year – and then we just want to go to a nice resort.

○9.7 Notice the connections.

M = man W = woman

M Hey, Sarah.

W Hi, Max. What's_new?

M Not much – you?

W I'm waiting for Tony. Have you seen him?

M Umm ... no.

W He's_always late these days and he never answers my calls.

M He's probably really busy_at work.

W Yeah, that must be it. I saw him with_a woman from work earlier. They were probably talking about work.

M Uh ... there's_something I want to ask you, Sarah.

W What is it? What's_up?

○9.8 Notice the silent letters.

M = man W = woman

M Uh ... Sarah, what would you do if Tony cheated on you?

W Well, it depends. If I saw him with another person, I'd confront him. We've been dating for a year, so I think I know him.

M Uh huh. What if a friend told you, what would you do?

W Mmm. ... If I didn't know for sure, I'd ask Tony first.

M Would you follow him, if you thought he liked someone else?

W No, I wouldn't. I'd trust him to tell me the truth, if he wanted to date someone else.

M I see ...

W Why? Is there something you want to tell me? You're his best friend.

M No ... I was just wondering.

○9.10 Notice the schwa /ə/.

M = man W = woman

M Would you like to be famous?

W I'm not sure. Uh, yes, I guess I'd like to be some kind of performer.

M And if you could be any kind of performer, what would you be?

W Hmm ... I don't know, maybe an actor or a singer? Or a musician?

M Really? But you don't play any instruments and you can't sing!

W Don't be so sure – I might have hidden talents!

M Hmm. They must be well hidden! I see you as an athlete or a dancer. You're so sporty.

W Uh, you think so? Really? I might be a good gymnast or a skater, something like that.

M Yeah, I can see that. Well, uh, um, I'd like to be a comedian or a magician.

W No way! What about a clown?

M Ha ha ha ha! What! What are you saying?

W Just that you're always falling over and you really make me laugh!

○9.15 Notice the sentence stress and schwa /ə/.

J = Jane M = Michael

J What's the matter, Michael?

M Uh ... nothing.

J Come on – I know you pretty well, what's wrong?

M Well, it's dumb really. You know my brother, David?

J Of course. He's your only brother and he's a doctor, right?

M Yeah, that's right. And I'm a teacher.

J So what about David?

M Well, he's just got a promotion and he's bought a new car.

J That's great!

M Yeah, it is, except that I can't help feeling jealous. I want a new car and I can't afford one, because my job doesn't pay as well as his!

J I see ... Is he older or younger than you?

M He's younger – I should be the one who makes more money and who buys a new car first!

J It's perfectly natural for you to feel jealous of your brother, especially because you're older than him, but really, is it that important?

M I suppose it's just a car.

J Yes, and think about all the stress he has in his job and the long hours he works.

M You're right – I never wanted to be a doctor.

J You see! You like your job, right? And you have a really nice life.

M That's true.

J Come on – let's go for a walk!

M If I had a new car, I'd take you out somewhere really nice.

J You don't need a new car.

○9.16 Notice sentence stress and weak forms.

S = son Mo = Mom W = woman M = man
D = daughter F = father

1

S I've lost my phone.

Mo Why don't you go upstairs and look in your room?

S That's a good idea. I was using it there earlier.

2

W1 I'm so fed up with my boyfriend. He always works on weekends.

M1 If I were you, I'd talk to him and explain that it's not fair.

W1 Thanks for the suggestion, but, uh, you don't know my boyfriend. I'm not sure that's the best thing to do.

3

M2 I have a really bad headache.

W2 You should go home and lie down. You shouldn't be at a party.

M2 You're right. I'm going home.

4

M3 I'm trying really hard, but, man, my job is so boring.

W3 What about looking for a new job? My brother has a restaurant and he might have a job.

M3 Hey! Thanks for the tip – I'd like to work in a restaurant.

5

D I'm failing math class.

F You'd better start working harder or you won't get into college.

D Yeah, I guess so.

Unit 10

○10.1 Notice /v/, /b/ and *have to* = /hæftə/.

Int = Interviewer

Int Hello! I'm conducting a survey for the Institute for Meditation and Relaxation. Do you have time to answer a question for me? What's the biggest stressor for you in your daily life?

1

W1 Hmm ... Well, in general, I would say that I always have so much work – my boss always gives me deadlines – I have to start and finish things with very little time. In fact, I have to do a report by the end of today, so, sorry, I have to go.

2

M1 My kids – I have two children – I love them, don't get me wrong, but it's just so hard caring for them all the time. I never get a break! Melissa! Stop that!

173

3

W2 It would have to be school – there's so much pressure to succeed – we have exams all the time and I need to do well to get into grad school.

4

M2 Uh … well, I never seem to have enough money. I have a job, but I'm overworked and underpaid, and I'm in school too, and by the end of the month I have no money and I have to pay for things with my credit card – it's just a vicious circle.

5

W3 Food and eating is the biggest problem for me – I don't have time to eat well and so I eat fast, easy food and this is a really poor diet – I don't eat well when I'm stressed, then I get sick.

6

M3 Definitely lack of sleep – when I don't sleep well, I get worried about not sleeping and that stops me from sleeping and then I get more stressed. Then, when I do sleep, I oversleep! I'm late for class … I have to go!

7

W4 I really need to exercise every day to get energy, but I'm always so tired when I get home at night that I just fall in front of the TV because I have no energy, so lack of exercise is my biggest problem.

8

M4 OK, great, thanks, talk to you later, bye … So, I try to do so many things at the same time, I'm answering the phone and writing emails and reading reports all at the same time. Multitasking is really stressful! Excuse me … This is John Maley.

▶10.5 Notice /m/, /n/ and /ng/.

P = Patrick   M = Molly

P Look! This is the hotel that was on the website.

M Wow! It's right on the beach. Cool. Is that where you stayed?

P No, when we got there they said it wasn't ready yet. So we stayed in this hotel, which was 30 minutes from the beach!

M Oh! Was the hotel nice at least?

P Yeah, it was great. You can see the swimming pool that was right outside our room.

M It looks awesome!

P And this is the lifeguard who told us to get out of the water because there was a storm coming.

M Wow! That was exciting.

P Yeah, there was thunder and lightning for about half an hour and lots of rain. This is the bar that was next to the pool. We watched the storm from there.

M That sounds like fun.

P Yeah. Look – these are some of the birds that were flying around outside.

M You sure do take a lot of photos!

P I know! Do you want to see some more?

M Um … Oh, wow, look at the time! I've gotta go! Maybe you can show me later.

▶10.9 Notice spelling and pronunciation of /g/, /dʒ/ and /z/.

Part of the lifestyle involves salvaging discarded food, clothing, and furniture from stores or other people's garbage! I happen to participate in one part of freeganism quite often: the part where you salvage furniture from the trash. Now I live in New York City, where I think it's pretty common to pick up trashed furniture or electronics, because people here just leave that stuff on the sidewalk for you to grab. And when you're on your way home and you walk by a perfectly good piece of furniture that you can use, why not just scoop it up and schlep it back to your abode? A huge percentage of the furniture in my house is actually from other people's trash. Recently I told that to some people who don't live in New York and they were like, "ewww", disgusted by it. While they understand the saving money, recycling side of it, they couldn't get past the other side of it. The "Someone-else-who-could-have-bedbugs-or-disgusting-hygiene-owned-that" side of it.

▶10.10 Notice /s/ and /z/.

There are some things I won't pick up – bedding, anything with a fabric covering, or just furniture that looks too dirty, but generally, if it looks like it works and it just needs a little cleaning – that crap is mine and I'm psyched! So how about you? What would you take out of the garbage and bring to your home, if anything? Is there a freegan in you? This week let's talk about that.

▶10.11 Notice /r/ and the intonation.

Hi, it's Nicki Mitchell and I was in the class of 2004. I was looking at my old school photos and I realized that we haven't had a reunion for ages. There are some people I haven't seen for years and we used to have a lot of fun together – remember? Do you know what happened to Kyle Rodriguez? I'd like to find him and I know you two were friends. Anyway, the reunion's going to be at Pete's Pizza on Friday night. I'll put this info on Facebook too, so please reply there if you can come. Can't wait to see you, bye!

▶10.12 Notice intonation in exclamations and questions.

K = Kyle   N = Nicki

K Hi, Nicki! Great to see you. When did we last see each other? ↘

N Around 10 years ago – when we finished high school. It was so cool to find you on Facebook and awesome that you could meet me. How are you? ↘

K Good – how about you? ↘ Are you married yet? ↗

N Yeah, married with two kids. Jason is five and Scott is three. Um … I married Rick Respini.

K No way! ↘ That's uh … wonderful.

N Do you have any kids? ↗

K Yes, my wife Jessie and I had twins last year.

N That's awesome! ↘

K Yeah … so how many people do you still see from high school? ↘

N Oh, around 50 maybe. We're having the next reunion in a pizza restaurant downtown.

K Oh yeah? ↘ Which restaurant is it at? ↘

N Pete's Pizza – they do great food. Do you want to come? ↗

K Yeah, I love their pizza! How often are the reunions? ↘

N Around every six months or so. The last one was a lot of fun. Your ex, Mindy, was there.

K Really? ↘

N Yeah, did you know she divorced her husband? ↗

K No! That's sad. Did they have kids? ↗

N No, no kids, but I don't know much about it. But you can find out all about it at the reunion.

▶10.13 Notice the **sentence stress**.

1 Hey! I'm **so happy** to **see you**! What's **new**?
2 How **much time** do you **spend studying or working**?
3 How **often** do you **check Facebook**?
4 How **long** have you **lived in your current house**?
5 How **long ago** did you **start learning English**?
6 How **many people** have you **met online**?

Review 5

▶R5.2 Notice /æ/ and /ɔr/.

P = presenter   C = Carla   B = Dr. Brayman

P Now for our next caller. Carla, you're through to Dr. Brayman.

C Hello, Dr. Brayman.

B Hi, Carla. What's your question?

C It's kind of hard to talk about …

B Don't worry, that's why you called. And that's why I'm here. Relax, really, it's fine.

C Thanks, Doctor. Well, OK, my question is about jealousy. My partner, Jack, calls me all the time to find out where I am and what I'm doing.

▶R5.3 Notice /ou/ and /ɔr/.

B = Dr. Brayman   C = Carla   P = presenter

B Well, Carla – this is a difficult problem. If a jealous partner calls all the time, the natural thing to do is not answer the phone calls. You know, just ignore them.

C Yes, yes, that's exactly what I'm doing.

B And then you start to grow apart and have secrets from each other. Have you found that happening?

C Yes, totally! I mean, sometimes, he calls me every hour, even when I'm at work! I don't

Audio script

answer the phone, or I sometimes tell him that I left my phone at home – anything so that I don't have to answer his calls.

B And I understand that, but this makes Jack more jealous and he calls you even more ... and so you have to find other ways not to take his calls and the problem becomes worse, not better.

C That's right, so what would you do Dr. Brayman?

B The best way to deal with a jealous partner is to talk about where the jealousy is coming from. Your partner may feel jealous because he's afraid of losing you. Try talking to him about his fears and worries. Tell him how you feel about him. Tell him that his jealousy is having a negative effect on your relationship.

C I see, so you think I should talk to him instead of ignoring his phone calls?

B Yes, but remember that he's not going to change from one day to the next. A problem like this could take months or even years to resolve, so you also need to decide if you want to take this time. If your partner agreed, I would recommend that you both go and talk to an expert.

C Yeah, maybe he would go to a counselor. I'll try it. Thanks, Dr. Brayman.

B Good luck, Carla.

P And our next caller is on line two ...

℞ Richmond

58 St Aldates
Oxford
OX1 1ST
United Kingdom

ISBN: 978-84-668-2557-3
Fourth reprint: 2022
CP: 896058

Publishing Director: Deborah Tricker
Publisher: Luke Baxter
Media Publisher: Luke Baxter
Content Developers: Paul Seligson, Neil Wood
Managing Editor: Laura Miranda
Editor: Hilary McGlynn
Proofreaders: Angela Castro, Nicola Gooch, Diyan Leake
Design Manager: Lorna Heaslip
Cover Design: Lorna Heaslip
Design & Layout: John Fletcher Design
Photo Researchers: Victoria Gaunt, Emily Taylor (Bobtail Media)
Audio Production: John Marshall Media Inc.
ID Café **Production:** Mannic Media

We would like to thank all those who have given their kind permission to reproduce material for this book:

Illustrators: Leo Teixeira, Amanda Savoini, Fabiane Eugenio, Odair Faléco, Talita Guedes

Photos: ALAMY STOCK PHOTO/AF archive, Aflo Co Ltd, Andrea Spinelli, CJG – Technology, Art Directors & TRIP, Caia image, Chris Howes/Wild Places Photography, Cultura RM, David Moody, Everett Collection Inc, Hero Images Inc, Jit Lim, Justin Kase zfivez, LJSphotography, Mircea Costina, Myron Standret, Nikolaj Kondratenko, Noriko Cooper, Panther Media GmbH, Peregrine, PhotoAlto, RooM the Agency, Science Photo Library, SIRIOH Co LTD, Sueddeutsche Zeitung Photo, Tetra Images, World History Archive, Zoonar GmbH; CARTOONSTOCK/ Alexei Talimonov, Mark Lynch; DESIGN GRAPHIC; DIAMEDIA/ Martin Poole/Moodboard; DINNERINTHESKY.COM; GETTY IMAGES SALES SPAIN/Abel Mitjà Varela, Adam Burn, Adam Taylor, adamkaz, AFP, akinshin, apomares, alenkadr, alexey_boldin, Andrea Spinelli, andresr, Antonio_Diaz, Archive Photos Creative, Ayumi Mason, Bambu Productions, Bertrand Rindoff Petroff, Betsie Van der Meer, Bettmann Archive, BSIP/UIG, Burak Karademir, Burke/Triolo Productions, Caiaimage, Cavan Images, CEF/Tim Pannell, Chris Ryan, Creatas, CSA Images, DingaLT, doble-d, d3sign, Daniel MacDonald, Darryl Leniuk, David Sacks, Deagreez, DEA/A. DAGLI ORTI, deepblue4you, Digital Vision, Dimitrios Kambouris, DreamPictures, edurivero, E+, Elva Etienne, Elizabeth Barnes, Elisabeth Schmitt, Ekaterina Romanova, erikreis , Eugenio Marongiu, EyeEm, Ezra Bailey, FilmMagic, Fly-Jet, gaspr13, Geber86, George Clerk, Geir Pettersen, Georgette Douwma, Gerhard Egger, grinvalds, Gray Mortimore/Staff, GregorBister, Hans Ferreira, hatman12, Hero Images, Hill Street Studios, Hoxton/Sam Edwards, Highwaystarz-Photography, Holger Leue, Inmagineasia, icarmen13, imageBROKER RF, iStock, iStockphoto, Jasmin Merdan, JGI/Jamie Grill, Jim Hughes, lechatnoir, Maskot, PhotoAlto/Eric Audras, Jackal Pan, JGI/Jamie Grill , Jochem D Wijnands, John Lamb, John M Lund Photography Inc, John Parra, Johner Bildbyra AB, JohnnyGreig, John Rowley, Jon Lovette, Joseph Johnson, Joshua Rainey, Judith Collins, Julian Ward, Juice Images, Katrina Wittkamp, Katsumi Murouchi, Kevin Mazur, killerb10, Kirill_Liv,

© Richmond / Santillana Global S.L. 2020

All rights reserved. No part of this book may be reproduced, stored in a retrieval system or transmitted in any form by any means, electronic, mechanical, photocopying, recording or otherwise, without the prior permission in writing of the Publisher.

Ljupco, Klaus Vedfelt, Kryssia Campos, Lawrence Manning, Lilly Dong, lisafx, Ljupco, Luciano Lozano, Luis Alvarez, Lumina Images, Maglara, mapodile, Marc Dozier, Mark Stahl, Maskot, maxkabakov, Media photos, Melvyn Longhurst, Milkos, Mikael Vaisanen, M.M Sweet, Morsa Images, Michael Dunning, Mikael Vaisanen, m-imagephotography, Moelyn Photos, Morsa Images, MStudioImages, mustafagull, mystockicons, nadia_bormotova, natrot, nd3000, Netfalls Remy Musser, Neustockimages, nicemonkey, Nick David, Nora Sahinun, Obradovic, OJO Images RF, Onoky, Owen Franken, ozgurcankaya, PATRICK LUX, pattonmania, penguiiin, PeopleImages, Peter Carlson, Pgiam, photodisc, picturegarden, Pixalfit, pixhook, poba, Presley Ann/Stringer, Prykhodov, RapidEye, Rasulovs, Ray Kachatorian, Roc Canals, REB Images, Religious Images/UIG, RG-vc, RichLegg, Robert Decelis Ltd, Roberto Machado Noa, Roc Canals, Roman Märzinger, rusm, Russ Rohde, RyanJLane, RyanKing999, Samir Hussein, Scott Olson, SDI Productions, Shaul Schwarz, shironosov, SimplyCreativePhotography, Sidekick, Simon Ritzmann, Siri Stafford, Smederevac, solarseven, SSPL/ Science Museum, South_agency, Stephen Simpson Inc, Stone Sub, Stuart Westmorland, sturti, Sylvain Grandadam/robertharding, Steven Puetzer, stock_colors, Sylvain Sonnet, Tanya Constantine, Tara Moore, Tatiana Gerus, Tegra Stone Nuess, TheCrimsonRibbon, thongseedary, Tony Garcia, Tom Werner, The Image Bank, The Washington Post, Tom Merton, Thomas Tolstrup, Thinkstock, Tomas Rodriguez, Tim Clayton – Corbis, Tim Hall, Tinpixels, Tisk, Turgay Malikli, Ty Allison, Ukususha, Uwe Krejci, valentinrussanov, VeranikaSmirnaya, View Pictures Ltd, vm, Wavebreakmedia, Westend61, Westend62, WireImage, wonry, wuttichaijangrab, Yamada Taro, Yuri_Arcurs; SHUTTERSTOCK/ A24/Moviestore, Africa Studio, AJR_ photo, Alexander Prokopenko, Allmy, Aliaksei Tarasau, Andrey_Popov, Anatoly Maslennikov, Anatoly Tiplyashin, Anna Peisl, Anttoniart, Antonio Guillem, Apple's Eyes Studio, Artur Didyk, Artur Synenko, Bakai, BoJack, baranq, bbernard, Billion Photos, Branislav Nenin, Cbenjasuwan, Constantine Pankin, Chris Ratcliffe, Color Force/Lionsgate/Kobal, Damir Khabirov, Dave Clark Digital Photo, Dean Drobot, Djomas, Elnur, flower travellin' man, Fizkes, Frantic00, Freebulclicstar, Hekla, hlphoto, Igor Marusichenko, Jonas Petrovas, Jorg Hackenmann, Julia Savchenko, Juri Pozzi, Kalamurzing, karelnoppe, Kldy, Kotin, KPG_ Payless, Krilerg saragorn, Kzenon, Ifc Prods/Detour Filmproduction/ Kobal, LoopAll, lukas_zb, LusiG, Macrovector, Marvel/Disney/Kobal, Maximumvector, Mega Pixel, Mindscape studio, modus_vivendi, Monkey Business Images, nicemonkey, OlegDoroshin, Pattanapol Soodto, pavila, Peter Komka/EPA-EFE, Phil Hill, PPstudio, PONG HANDSOME, PrinceOfLove, RexRover, Roxana Gonzalez, sebra, Serge Gorenko, Serg Zastavkin, shoot66, siamionau pavel, sirtravelalot, Smith1979, Stock-Asso, stockfour, Syda Productions, Tatiana Chekryzhova, Techa Boribalburipun, TeddyandMia, Terekhob Igor, TheRocky41, Thurman James/CSM, Universal/Kobal, Val lawless, Victor Kochetkov, Vitalinka, vovidzha, VStocker, Warner Bros/Kobal, Wavebreakmedia, Yakov Oskanov, Yevgenij_D, 9nong, Zimmytws; ZUMAPRESS/ Whitehotpix/Chris Murphy. ARCHIVO SANTILLANA

Videos: Lori Herfenist

The Publisher has made every effort to trace the owner of copyright material; however, the Publisher will correct any involuntary omission at the earliest opportunity.

Printed in Brazil by Forma Certa Gráfica Digital
Lote: 808125
Codigo: 290525573 / 2025